TAJ AL-SALTANA
CROWNING ANGUISH
MEMOIRS OF A PERSIAN PRINCESS
FROM THE HAREM TO MODERNITY
1884 — 1914

EDITED WITH INTRODUCTION AND NOTES
ABBAS AMANAT
YALE UNIVERSITY

TRANSLATION OF THE MEMOIRS
ANNA VANZAN AND AMIN NESHATI

MAGE PUBLISHERS
WASHINGTON, DC
1993

LIBRARY OF CONGRESS CATALOGING-IN-PUBLICATION DATA

TAJ AL-SALTANA
[KHATIRAT-I TAJ AL-SALTANA. ENGLISH]
TAJ AL-SALTANA. CROWNING ANGUISH: MEMOIRS OF A PERSIAN PRINCESS FROM THE
HAREM TO MODERNITY, 1884–1914; INTRODUCTION AND HISTORICAL NOTES, ABBAS
AMANAT; TRANSLATED BY ANNA VANZAN AND AMIN NESHATI.
P. CM.
INCLUDES BIBLIOGRAPHICAL REFERENCES AND INDEX.
1. TAJ AL-SALTANA, 1884-1936. 2. IRAN—PRINCES AND PRINCESSES—BIOGRAPHY. 3.
FEMINISTS—IRAN—BIOGRAPHY. I. AMANAT, ABBAS.
II. TITLE.
DS316.T33A3 1993 955.05'1'092–DC20 [B] 93-3329 CIP

ISBN 0-934211-35-3 (HARDBOUND)
ISBN 0-934211-36-1 (PAPERBOUND)
FIRST EDITION

TO ORDER BOOKS OR TO RECEIVE OUR
CATALOGUE CALL TOLL-FREE: 800-962-0922
MAGE PUBLISHERS
1032-29TH STREET, NW, WASHINGTON, DC 20007
TEL:(202) 342-1642; FAX: (202) 342-9269

CONTENTS

PREFACE

For a Western reader accustomed to the prevailing images of women in the Middle East, the memoirs of a turn-of-the-century Persian royal woman with liberal views present a refreshing alternative. Seen in the light of her own time, Taj al-Saltana's emerging feminism and her unconventional lifestyle challenged the hailed values of confined chastity and sexual segregation— values which, after a phase of secularism, have found a new lease on life in the current revival of fundamentalist Islam. Taj's *Crowning Anguish*, as the title for the English translation of her memoirs has it, gave her a chance to transcend the restricted milieu of the harem and enter an independent—albeit confusing—world of modernity, a course of emancipation with all its enlightenments and follies.

The English translation of the memoirs aptly renders that spirit of romanticism and revolt that lies at the heart of Taj's predicament, without sacrificing accuracy. The Introduction aims at illustrating the historical backdrop, while accentuating, successfully I hope, the dimensions of Taj's experience. My Historical Biographies and comments on the illustrations are meant to facilitate the reader's entry into the bygone world of Qajar Iran. The headings in the body of the memoirs serve the same purpose. It must be admitted, however (as indicated in the Note on the Text), that much remains to be discovered about the enigmas of Taj's life; for instance, we have only recently learned that she died in 1936.

I am thankful to Mohammad and Najmieh Batmanglij for their enthusiasm in publishing this work. My thanks are due as well to Anna Vanzan for her initial translation for her thesis and to Amin Neshati for skillfully revising the translation for publication. I would also like to thank Haynie Wheeler for her generous assistance.

A. A.
New Haven, Connecticut

THE CHANGING WORLD OF
TAJ AL-SALTANA

The infant girl born in 1884 to the ruler of Iran, Naser al-Din Shah Qajar, and a minor princess from the same ruling family named Turan al-Saltana had an ancestry noble enough to deserve a lofty name. The name chosen for her, however, was only a royal title: Taj al-Saltana, "crown of the monarchy," one of many generic titles coined in the title-conscious court of the late Qajar period and bestowed upon royalty and commoners alike. The "crown of the monarchy," however, turned out to be a remarkable woman in her own right, with a personality and drive that enabled her to outlive her counterparts in a waning royal house. Even though our knowledge of Taj al-Saltana is largely limited to what she cared to share with us, there are enough sincere thoughts and sentiments in her unfinished and untitled memoirs to qualify her not only as a representative of the emerging secular intelligentsia in the aftermath of the Constitutional Revolution (1906–1911), but also as an ardent feminist who reflected many of the predicaments of her culture and society in a changing age.

Belonging to a tiny, secularized upper class in a society dominated by traditional Perso-Islamic values, Taj led a rebellious lifestyle that brought her much notoriety. Still, she fares favorably in comparison with other feminists of her generation, perhaps not so much for her actions as for expressing views well advanced of her own time. Nearly ninety years later, Taj's memoirs are relevant. The realities of late-twentieth-century

11

Iran and the restrictions which Persian women have been subjected to, or have opted for, attest to the persistence or revival
of old religious values and institutions. The plight of today's
Muslim women remains strikingly and sadly comparable to
that of Taj a century ago. Yet, curiously, contemporary reaction
to the female predicaments imposed by society is still unclear.
It remains to be seen whether the sincerity of Taj's secular convictions will be matched or surpassed by women of our time.

Taj's memoirs are unusually self-revealing. Her language
and mode of expression are iconoclastic, for she not only
voices the flaws of her social class but those of her family and
herself. Even compared to the liberated upper-class Western
feminists of her time, Taj appears less inhibited. A sensitive
observer, she narrates the story of her life with the lucidity of
an intimate conversation, a style mastered by the matriarchs of
the old families. Inspired by the spirit of European romanticism, her individuality comes through effortlessly. Among the
memorialists of her time, Taj stands out for having crossed the
formidable barriers of self-censorship. In Persian prose, as in
any other formalist tradition, the authors of memoirs were,
and still are, expected to hold back the harshest and most personally revealing realities for the sake of social stature, honor,
and political expediency. Having acquired something of the
candid language of the womenfolk, the cultivated as well as
the common, Taj echoes in her narrative a refreshing divorce
from literary formalism. In spite of its many shortcomings,
her account is charged with nuances and flashes of a real life,
which makes it comparable to the memoirs of her noncon-
formist uncle, 'Abbas Mirza (III), to the secret diaries of her
father's astute confidant, E'temad al-Saltana, and to the memoirs of the shah's enlightened minister, Amin al-Dawla. She
was the only royal woman known to us who has left an account
of her life. When compared to the memoirs of her elder

brother, Zell al-Soltan, written less than a decade after her own, or the historical reminiscences of Naser al-Din Shah's grandson, Dust 'Ali Khan Mo'ayyer al-Mamalek, compiled some four decades later, Taj's candid tone becomes all the more conspicuous. The self-righteous complacency of one and the defensive nostalgia of the other stand in marked contrast to her frankness.

Written in 1914, at the disheartening close of the Constitutional Revolution (and the outbreak of the Great War), Taj's memoirs cover a thirty-year span in the life of a generation that was acutely aware of a changing world. It is as though she had chosen this culminating moment to recall her "personal history"—a tale filled with "wonder and anguish," as she put it—in order to record a cultural leap which she, symbolic of her time, made from the indulgent world of her father's harem to the puzzling, yet emotionally and intellectually challenging, world of a profane lifestyle. The driving force behind this hazardous journey to modernity was Taj's desire to embrace independence. French literature, revolutionary rhetoric, and journalism reshaped Taj's sentiments and sensibilities as distinctly as modern fashion and make-up, entertainment, music, furniture, luxury goods, and architecture reshaped her lifestyle.

In narrating her journey from the confinement of her harem mentality into what she defines as "liberated life," Taj is remarkably aware of not only her own intellectual and emotional rebirth but also the public and private lives of others around her. She takes it upon herself to demonstrate the ills of a society of privilege and intrigue: a crippled yet indulgent monarchy in its last gasp, a decaying aristocracy, abused and insecure womenfolk, a cynical officialdom, and a destitute populace so little noticed that it only flickers through Taj's account.

Hardly typical of the Persian woman of her time, Taj antic-ipated in her writings and conduct something of the emancipation movement of the Reza Shah era (1925–1941). Her memoirs are unique in consciously recording a life which she could afford to lead because she was a member of the royal house, albeit a declining one. The notable absence of Islam and its representatives in her account also points to the waning power of religion in the post-Constitutional craving for modernity; this decline was also vital in allowing Taj to break away from a conventional path.

The picture she paints is primarily of her own life cycle and the course she negotiated through diverse spheres: from the blissful days of the royal palace to an arranged childhood wedlock and a troubled married life, and further to a world of socializing and sensuality—the self-chosen liberties of a Persian *madame de salon*. Sentimental, occasionally vain and self-congratulatory, and carried away by her own liaisons, Taj nevertheless displays moral strength in the face of many agonies: an unloving and harsh mother, a benevolent but progressively childlike father, an adolescent bisexual husband, a ruinous abortion, separation, financial difficulties, the stigma of a libertine lifestyle, and the anathema of removing her facial veil.

IN THE HAREM

Even though the secret diaries and recollections of the old confidants engendered much hearsay about the royal harem (*andarun:* literally, "interior"), Taj's account is the only one so far by an insider. The European accounts of the Qajar royal harem, though informative, often tended to glamorize life in the women's quarters, lending it a certain Orientalist mystique akin to the stories of *A Thousand and One Nights*. Considering the voluptuous opulence and sensuality that surrounded the Qajar court, particularly under Fath 'Ali Shah (r. 1797–1834), it is not difficult to see why stereotypes persisted.

As a member of the shah's harem from her very birth, Taj was considered part of the collective "royal honor," the sanctum sanctorum of the Persian court, and was jealously guarded by an army of eunuchs, castrated black or white slaves in charge of the royal harem. The harem could be desecrated symbolically even by an alien's glance. There were a few unmindful residents of the capital, among them the servants of the American minister plenipotentiary in Tehran, S. G. W. Benjamin, who dared to view the cavalcade of royal women passing through the narrow streets. They were quickly and rudely made to pay the price—a savage beating from the eunuchs and guards—for not turning their backs as a sign of respect for the royal virtue. It is plausible that before her marriage at the age of thirteen Taj had never met any adult male outside the confines of the harem.

The Golestan palace in central Tehran, the principal residence of the shah and his family, was surrounded by the high walls of the Royal Citadel (Arg-e Saltanati). Like Beijing's Forbidden City, Delhi's Red Fort, the Ottoman Topkapi, Cairo's Citadel, or even Vienna's Borge, the Arg was a self-contained complex of some magnitude. Built in the eighteenth century and extensively rebuilt in the Qajar era, the Arg was situated in the center of old Tehran. The business district, the bazaar, with its labyrinth of shops, trading houses, workshops and caravanserais lay to the south, where there were also the reconstructed market square (Sabza Maydan) and the royal theater (Takiya Dawlat), built in an innovative style for the annual performance of the Shi'ite passion play, the *ta'ziya*. To the east stretched the fashionable Naseri

Avenue, with its Western-style shops carrying European
goods. Looking northward one would see the Drill Square
(Maydan-e Mashq), the barracks, and the royal tulip garden
(Lalezar), which in the 1890s had just been developed by the
shah into a new shopping and residential section. To the west
was the old Sangelaj, one of Tehran's five wards *(mahallas)*. By
the 1890s Tehran's population had increased to a little less
than 200,000—about two percent of the entire population of
the country. With several residential quarters for the shah and
his growing household—including a new bed chamber built in
the 1880s in the style of French villas, with tasteful Persian
modifications—the Golestan also housed the magnificent Hall
of Mirrors and other reception halls; the innovative Shams al-
'Emara (sun building), which was the tallest man-made structure in the capital; a small museum holding, among other
things, the legendary Persian royal treasures; and other more
mundane facilities, including a primary school for the royal
children where Taj received her early instruction.

Naser al-Din Shah's harem could not hope to match in size
that of his great-grandfather, Fath 'Ali Shah. The earlier monarch, facing an oversupply of wives and concubines, had
instituted a division of labor in the harem that allowed him to
indulge himself with as many as eighteen wives, who tended to
his bedtime needs in rotating shifts. Yet Naser al-Din's harem
was large enough to bring him more pain than pleasure. If the
estimate of seven hundred for the harem and its dependents is
accurate—this would include a total of about eighty wives
during his half-century reign—it is not hard to see the reasons
for the shah's perpetual life in the saddle. He wandered unper-
turbed like a Flying Dutchman day after day and year after
year among his eleven other palaces and summer villas and
numerous resorts, gardens, and hunting grounds around the
capital.

The walls of isolation that surrounded the harem were not as impenetrable as the stern eunuchs may have wished. Not only did the royal women take pleasure in such benign activities as discreetly watching the townspeople from the tower of Shams al-'Emara, enjoying the fireworks, and witnessing from behind the screen a whole array of people at the royal audience during celebrations and holidays, but they also accompanied the shah on some of his domestic trips, hunting excursions, and visits to the houses of courtiers and notables. The royal palaces and villas were equipped to host several households at once, and one palace complex in eastern Tehran, appropriately named "the pleasure land" ('Eshratabad), was designed by Naser al-Din to house his numerous favorites in its secluded villas. Moreover, the royal women were permitted to visit their relatives and other women of consequence in their houses—visits that could last several days. It was common for guests, often relatives, to reciprocate, together with all their servants and dependents.

Taj's description of the royal "broth making" *(ashpazan)*, where all the ministers and officials of the state were obliged to join the shah in the annual ritual of preparing the ingredients for a royal broth to be cooked in open air in a royal garden, signified another of the court's symbolic ceremonies. The preparation, one may surmise, was meant to remind the guests of their collective duty toward the monarchy as its servants, while the later partaking of the prepared food, like all other ritualistic meals, was intended to recall the shared benefits of the state for the elite. Though women only maintained a passive presence in the ceremony, they too were reaffirming the harem's functions, and thus its commitment, in the preservation of the state.

Perhaps no channel of harem communication with the outside was more effective than the servants and attendants who

The majestic appearance of the Citadel's main gate, initially erected in Fath 'Ali Shah's period, with the emblem of the two lions and the crown directly above the entrance—all that the shah's subjects could see of the royal complex. The famous Morvari (blessing) Cannon, presumably the most imposing piece of military hardware in the Qajar arsenal, augmented the image of royal might. The veranda on the upper level housed the *naqarachi*s (ancient Persian military drummers and trumpeters), who performed in conjunction with the five phases of the sun in the sky. The gate, along with its *naqarakhana* (drum tower), was trampled out of existence under Reza Shah's modernizing boots.

Panorama of Tehran by George Curzon from his 1890 visit to the capital. The minarets on the far left are those of the Naseriya Mosque complex (later known as Sepahsalar), built in the 1870s. The row of little cupolas at left in the foreground is part of the outer stretch of the Tehran bazaar, visible from the tower of Shams al-'Emara in the royal Citadel. Even after the expansion of the city in the latter part of the nineteenth century, its traditional morphology remained untouched.

The Shams al-'Emara (sun building) pavilion on the eastern flank of the Golestan Palace complex, the best example of the architectural amalgamations of the early Naseri period. Built in the mid-1860s, it was reputed to have replicated the palace of the Sasanian king Bahram V, immortalized by Nezami's lyric in his *Haft paykar*. It was the tallest building in the capital; from its towers the women of the harem could view the royal fireworks and other more mundane sights of everyday life on the street.

The magnificent audience hall of Golestan Palace in Tehran, constructed under Naser al-Din Shah in an amalgam of Persian and European styles. The pointed Persian arches here were mixed with ornate baroque latticework and huge Bohemian chandeliers and Regency chairs. The globe in the glass encasement at left is the famous creation of Naser al-Din and is made of crown jewels. The paintings on the walls represented the shah's artistic tastes cultivated during his European tours. The entire setting embraced the Naseri Zeitgeist and stood as a symbol of Qajar architectural achievement.

Two views (above and opposite) of the main royal sleeping quarters in 'Eshratabad (pleasure-land), just outside the eastern gate of the capital in the Naseri period, surrounded by individual villas inhabited by women of the harem and situated around a large pool.

'Eshratabad was among Naser al-Din's innovative royal constructions inspired by European romantic architecture.

visited to render a variety of services. Physicians, goldsmiths, clothiers, tailors, and merchants of luxury goods often served as confidants to the women. People of the lower ranks, too, found their way into the harem. Some of the most influential wives of the shah were of low birth, often peasant girls from around the capital, picked up by the shah on his never-ending excursions. In the curiously egalitarian environment of Naser al-Din's harem, the women had no qualms about receiving their poor cousins from the villages and doing their utmost to secure them pensions or posts. They often employed them as their own agents to the shah's many servants-in-attendance and other court functionaries.

The reach of the harem went beyond visits with relatives and dealings with servants and tradespeople, however. Over the years a number of women in Naser al-Din's harem, mostly his favorites but also other wives and daughters, and above all the queen mother, Malek Jahan Mahd 'Olya (d. 1873), played decisive roles in the politics of the court and the government. Mahd 'Olya's notorious intrigue which led to the execution of the reform-minded premier, Mirza Taqi Khan Amir Kabir, in 1852 has darkened her image beyond redemption. Nevertheless, her wishes to be consulted on all affairs of the state and the court, and her resentment at having her rights as queen mother ignored, were well within the bounds of Perso-Turkish political culture. A capable matriarch of some intelligence, she was a leading figure in the interim coalition that brought Naser al-Din Shah to the throne in 1848. Beyond personal frictions, the primary reason for the deterioration of her relationship with Amir Kabir was her claim to traditional privileges, which were effectively denied her by the modernizing premier. She succeeded in destroying Amir Kabir principally because she was able to mobilize the aristocracy, the court, and the competing factions within the government

A royal woman and her relatives, accompanied by their eunuchs. Beyond the facade of the eunuchs' severe vigilance, there were enduring bonds of interdependence with the royal ladies.

Indoor costume of Persian women, as yet presumably uninfluenced by the later style of white tights. The heavy use of Persian mascara *(sorma)*, the henna-tinted toes, the anklets, the braided hair *(chehel gis)*, and the jacket *(nim-tana)* were all typical of women's domestic appearance.

Anis al-Dawla and her companions, returning from a summer resort in Mazandaran, typifying the royal women's mode of travel in the Naseri period. Though fully veiled and heavily guarded by eunuchs and chaperones, the women were not entirely deprived of the outdoors. Riding on horses rather than in palanquins, they enjoyed relative freedom of physical movement.

against him. In spite of a favorable disposition towards Amir Kabir, the young and impressionable shah could not resist the pressure to dismiss him. As in other instances, Mahd 'Olya's victory demonstrated the supremacy of the harem over the bureaucracy. Small wonder that later premiers were mindful of the harem's influence.

In at least two other instances the downfall of the premiers of Naser al-Din Shah was accelerated by the actions of the harem. In 1858 the rivalry between the shah's favorite, Jayran, and his minister, Aqa Khan Nuri (who came to power after Amir Kabir with the full blessing of Mahd 'Olya), resulted in Nuri's devastating downfall. Jayran, an attractive and agile peasant girl with a passion for the outdoors and such activities as hunting, started her life in the harem as a dancing and singing concubine in Mahd 'Olya's entourage. The shah's affection for her became evident when he promoted her to the status of a permanent wife and nominated her son, albeit briefly, as the heir to the throne. Jayran's ephemeral fortunes ended with her death in 1859, but before that she had managed successfully to organize the opposition against Nuri's monopoly of power. It is debatable whether in her opposition to the premier Jayran was a willing instrument of the shah, who time and again used the harem as a pawn in his never-ending game of power.

An example of the harem's more positive influence is the career of one of the shah's favorites, Anis al-Dawla (lit., intimate companion of the sovereign), who by fulfilling the wishes of many petitioners had built up a reputation for compassion and charity. Something between a shah's favorite and a European-style queen, Anis al-Dawla, daughter of a poor miller from a village close to Tehran, was the most respected figure in the harem in Taj's time. She was safely entrusted with the directorship of the harem—a position which, after the death of

Naser al-Din, in a casual mood, shepherding some women of his harem who posed informally before the private eye of the royal camera.

the shah's mother, had become the object of some rivalry among the royal wives. Anis al-Dawla's peasant background, which she did not hide, tended to make her empathize with the ordinary people. Often at odds with her husband's incurable capriciousness and especially his intense, though nonsexual, affection for the page boys in attendance, Anis al-Dawla should be seen as the voice of moderation behind the throne. This remains true even when we consider that she colluded in a revolt against the shah's progressive premier, Hosayn Khan Moshir al-Dawla, in 1873.

Earlier that year, she had been sent home from Moscow during the royal European tour when it became apparent that her presence as a veiled woman would prove an embarrassment. Holding Moshir al-Dawla responsible for the decision that she be sent back, she seized upon the granting of the famous Reuter concession as a pretext for discrediting him. Upon the shah's return from Europe, the protesting elite, joining hands with the conservative Qajar princes and the equally conservative ulama, warned the shah of the grave consequences of outright modernization. Acceding to their demands, the shah dismissed the premier, and shortly thereafter repealed the all-embracing Reuter concession. The action of Anis al-Dawla and her allies proved to be a blessing in disguise. While it removed Moshir al-Dawla from power temporarily and slowed the pace of his reforms, it also barred the implementation of a concession that ominously sought to place Iran's communications, transportation, mining and agricultural resources, and banking in foreign hands.

The intriguing Amina Aqdas (trustee of the blessed [monarchy]), another favorite of the shah and initially a maid in his service, was also a villager, though less charitable and more self-serving than her ex-mistress and rival. The shah's acknowledged fondness for women of lower birth over women

Even though her appearance may have been embellished by the stereotypes of Orientalist paintings of the nineteenth century, Ziba Khanum as she is described by Madame Dieulafoy in 1881 was still a telling example of fashionable sensuality in the harem of the affluent. The wife of a carpet merchant in Isfahan, Ziba Khanum was previously a wife of Naser al-Din Shah, albeit a minor one. She accompanied the shah on his first European tour in 1873 but was returned from Moscow together with Anis al-Dawla when it became apparent to the shah that having tightly veiled royal women in his entourage would cause discomfort and embarrassment to himself and his royal hosts. For unknown reasons she was later divorced and dispensed with by the shah as a gift to the Isfahani merchant, possibly to pay off a monetary loan. Her revealing blouse and short skirt are part of the women's indoor outfit.

of the nobility was primarily due to the unwarranted privileges that the relatives of women of consequence expected as a
result of such unions. The shah's favoritism for his wives of
lowly background and their relatives, much criticized by the
old nobility, changed the very structure of the court and eventually the social composition of the government. The shah,
one may suppose, considered this patronage of the commoners a way not only of gratifying his wives' wishes but also
of balancing off the overbearing influence of the old nobility.
By the end of his reign the power of the high-ranking bureaucratic families, princes, and landed notables had been partially
checked by the rise of this new courtier class. The shah's
guardedness with women of high birth also stemmed from his
bitter childhood experiences when the company of servants
and other commoners in his entourage was often his only
source of moral support.

Naser al-Din Shah, the tormented soul whom Taj renders
as her father, was indeed a complex character. Taj describes
him in his early sixties, when he appeared "forlorn" and "dis-
illusioned" in his private life in spite of his public facade of
confidence. A half-century of eventful rule over a country with
massive domestic and foreign problems must have taken its
toll. By the last decade of his reign he seems to have been
losing ground to the newly emerging forces within and outside his government.

The shah's last prime minister, Mirza 'Ali Asghar Khan
Amin al-Soltan, aptly titled "confidant of the sovereign," was
raised in the royal household. A son of the shah's trusted butler
from a Georgian slave background, he had successfully capital-
ized on the sovereign's fear of independent-minded and
reformist premiers and presented himself as a benign
appendage to the throne. He monopolized the office of the
premier and turned it into a lucrative racket with shares for the

shah, himself, and other willing partners. An able negotiator and a shrewd politician, he was a valuable agent for developing friendly relations with the various factions, though it was hard to decide which party, the shah or the foreign powers (both the British and the Russians), were using the premier for advancing their objectives. In this complex game of power, however, it was clear that the Machiavellian Amin al-Soltan was an advocate of the open-door policy conducive to a European commercial presence and the sale of concessions.

During Amin al-Soltan's term, the harem, even more than before, functioned not merely as a house of pleasure but also a political powerhouse. The rivalry between the favorites of the shah and his ministers, and their natural alliances with chiefs of the army and high-ranking officials, continued, but with an obvious advantage to the premier, who was an insider. Amin al-Soltan's cultivation of the royal favorites, among them Amina Aqdas and later Khanom Bashi (whom Taj names as an accomplice with the premier in Naser al-Din's assassination), must therefore be regarded as a maneuver on the premier's part, a calculated move to fend off the hazards of premiership. His rapid rise in office from the rank of a young page boy in the palace to minister of court at the age of twenty-five, and later to the premiership, was due not only to his own abilities or to the shah's favor, but also to the support of the harem.

Taj was raised in a harem where private pleasures mingled with political concerns. The influence of the harem is detectable not solely in her political alertness but, to an extent, in her later affinity with the common people and with the downtrodden. In spite of some puzzling details in her account, we can safely assume that Taj's maternal grandfather was a Qajar prince, a son of the celebrated 'Abbas Mirza (d. 1833), Fath 'Ali Shah's senior son and heir apparent who died before his father and was Naser al-Din's grandfather (see the genealogical table). We do not know why Taj fails to give her grandfather's name.

Following the common practice, Taj's early upbringing was almost entirely entrusted to her black nanny, with minimal intervention from her mother. Taj's strong bonds with her nanny go far in explaining her liberal attitude toward blacks as well as her progressive convictions on motherhood. She is conscious of her affection for her nanny, but ambivalent, even angry, toward her mother. Years later she looked at white faces with "surprise" and, in the memory of her "beloved nanny," preferred people of dark skin. She could speak in a slave's pidgin Persian and believed that her affection for the nanny had formed "an enduring spiritual and emotional bond between me and her relatives."

The domestic slaves in Persian households were mostly East Africans brought through the island of Zanzibar (now part of Tanzania) by the slavers of Mascut, who continued to operate in the Persian Gulf even after the ban on slavery was enforced by the British in the 1850s. Raising their own families in the shelter of their masters' houses, Zanzibarian slaves, as well as the highly valued Abyssinians and Sudanese, remained in most aristocratic families even after being manumitted in old age. Black slaves, as Taj observes, abounded in her grandfather's household, for he was reportedly at one time the governor of the south-eastern provinces of Kerman and Baluchestan where there was a thriving slave trade with Mascut.

Taj's primary education in the harem, judging by her own account, was perfunctory. Her "perversity and willfulness and disobedience," as she puts it, drew her away from serious study. If her teacher had attempted to subdue her by means of "harshness or fear," her nanny would have prevented it.

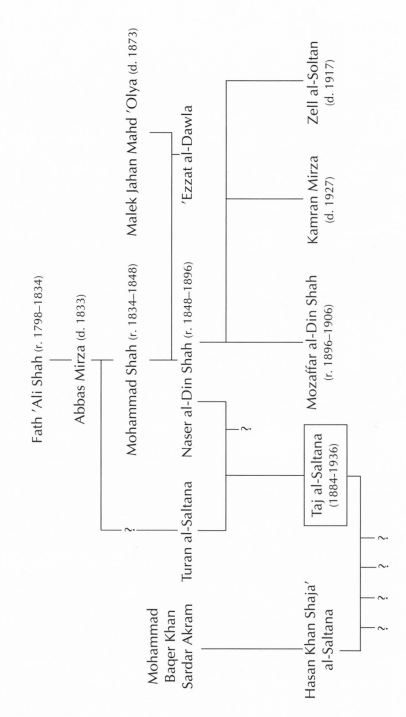

Genealogy of Taj al-Saltana

Fath 'Ali Shah (r. 1798–1834)

Abbas Mirza (d. 1833)

Mohammad Shah (r. 1834–1848)

Malek Jahan Mahd 'Olya (d. 1873)

'Ezzat al-Dawla

Naser al-Din Shah (r. 1848–1896)

Mozaffar al-Din Shah (r. 1896–1906)

Kamran Mirza (d. 1927)

Zell al-Soltan (d. 1917)

Mohammad Baqer Khan Sardar Akram

Turan al-Saltana

Taj al-Saltana (1884–1936)

Hasan Khan Shaja' al-Saltana

Interestingly enough, however, even as a princess she was not immune from discipline for playing terrible tricks on her tutor. Taj's recollections, indeed, are not much different from any pupil of her age and time, another indication of the informal nature of the Qajar court when it came to the rearing of princes and princesses. As late as the end of the nineteenth century there were no curricula or educational programs beyond the *maktab* even for the most privileged offspring of the elite. Only a shadow of the old Persian princely education system had survived, and there was little by way of modern subjects to be studied, especially for girls. Judging by what we know about the education of Taj's father and his brothers, there was limited exposure beyond traditional subjects to European languages—almost always French—or to European geography and history.

Yet, in spite of all its weaknesses, Taj's educational background was solid enough and, thanks to her nanny, liberal enough to enable her later to write a sophisticated prose expressive of complex ideas and emotions. Despite its annoying syllogisms and grammatical peculiarities—mostly the result of the bad influence of faddish, turn-of-the-century French translations—Taj's style, along with her vocabulary and even some of her knowledge of classical Persian literature, are impressive. The alteration of word order in Taj's style, odd as it may sound, should be seen as part of a greater effort to broaden the boundaries of Persian prose so as to accommodate a more personal and intimate narrative than was customary in the formalized Persian of the time. In this respect she is more innovative and articulate than the women of her time and even of later generations. Most women of the nobility, judging by their many spelling and grammatical errors, could hardly claim a sufficient command of Persian, though like Taj, they were quite expressive and uninhibited.

Taj's memoirs should be seen as a turning point in Qajar courtly literature. Her grandmother, Mahd 'Olya, though a talented letter-writer who maintained a woman poet laureate in her entourage, never produced an autobiographical account. Nor, at least so far as we know, did any of Naser al-Din's wives or other daughters. The absence of such accounts—if indeed this is the case—should not be seen as a sign of literary disinterest. Two of Taj's sisters, Fakhr al-Saltana and Eftekhar al-Saltana, were known for their artistic and literary accomplishments. Another of Taj's sisters, Fakhr al-Dawla (pride of the state), was responsible for recording the popular adventure romance, *Amir Arsalan Rumi*, and similar works in simple Persian. These stories, narrated by the court storyteller, Naqib al-Mamalek, at the shah's bedside and written down by Fakhr, must have been popular pastime reading for the women of the harem and perhaps exercised some influence on Taj's simple prose. The romance of *Amir Arsalan* may also have served as a popular "mirrors for princes" for the Qajar royals. Naser al-Din Shah himself must have been thrilled with the adventures of the fictional Ottoman (Rumi) prince in the lands of Europe (Farangestan). Amir Arsalan's amorous affair with the daughter of the king of Europe, the never-ending mischiefs of the evil moon-minister against the righteous wisdom of the sun-minister, and the hazards the hero met on the way before reaching his blond beloved, were no doubt influential in the way Europe was perceived in the imagination of the shah, his household, and his people. Translations of popular European novels, as Taj points out, provided other sources of leisure reading.

It is likely that Taj had, at an early age, read her father's simple and expressive prose. His numerous travelogues of domestic and European tours were available in print as early as 1871. These works, though often dry and far less imaginative than the *Amir Arsalan* romance in their approach, were something of a novelty with their plain personal language—a prose which anticipated the popular writings of the Constitutional period. The contents of the travelogues provided further food for the hungry minds of the royal women who were only permitted vicarious travel through the shah's trips. In fact, apart from a trip to Europe by one of the shah's wives in full cover to seek medical treatment, they were never allowed to venture on a foreign tour with their royal spouse. Thus, Naser al-Din's descriptions of palaces and royal gardens, zoos and aquariums, railroad and fire engines, balls and receptions, European royalty and dignitaries, operas and music halls, food, dress, and entertainments were the closest they could come to the experiences of their husband and his male entourage.

Naser al-Din also compiled *Montakhab al-Soltan*, a personal anthology of two celebrated Persian classical poets, Sa'di and Hafez, which was lithographed in 1872. Produced by the celebrated calligrapher, Kalhor, this collection reflected the shah's literary taste and complemented his own pedestrian poetry and his patronage of uninspiring neo-classicist poets at his court. The royal library, originally consisting of a few thousand volumes and enlarged under Naser al-Din Shah, contained in addition to classical Persian literature a collection of European travelogues, geographical and historical works, books on current affairs, novels, and Western works about Iran in Persian translation. Commissioned by the shah for his personal use, these manuscripts were accessible to the women of the harem, though it is not known whether Taj ever used her father's library.

The complexity of harem mentality was remarkable. The crudest of superstitions and intrigues lived side by side, at times in a single mind, with literary and artistic refinements.

Athletic and physical activities, and illicit pleasures of the flesh, were not entirely foreign to the harem. The shah's legendary favorite, and presumably his only true love, Jayran Forugh al-Saltana (light of the throne), was renowned for her hunting and horse-riding skills. Though physical activity was generally discouraged as undignified, and a dull and solemn composure preferred, the memory of Jayran lived longer in the shah's mind than any of his other favorites. Reportedly Naser al-Din first became attracted to Anis al-Dawla because as an ex-maid to Jayran she reminded him of his late beloved. Much later, he justified his old-age passion for another young favorite, as Taj observes, because of her physical resemblance to Jayran.

Yet, with few exceptions, the standards of female attractiveness in Naser al-Din's harem are puzzling to contemporary tastes. The pictures of the often badly dressed ladies, huddled together in front of their husband's camera, hardly support the stereotype of the harem beauty portrayed in Orientalist novels and paintings or idealized in the Persian lyrics. As an amateur photographer, Naser al-Din had a knack for capturing his wives in dull poses, as though he was settling his many grudges with them. A combination of starched miniskirts and white tights, apparently a bizarre mixture of the Persian *shelita* and the Parisian ballerinas' tutu, blouses revealing of large breasts, heavy make-up on flabby cheeks, and artificially bridged eyebrows, blackened with silver nitrate, completed the appearance of a Naseri woman. Taj's vanity—she uses every occasion to praise her own charm—must have been innocuously aroused in later years when she compared herself with many of her harem cohorts. Yet, while in the harem, her appearance was not drastically different from the others.

As in other sectors of society, so too in the harem the boundary between childhood and adulthood was blurred. Children, girls and boys, were seen and treated as mini-adults and some primitive sexual awakening at a young age, as in Taj's case, was expected if not actually encouraged.

The childishly romanticized amours between Taj and the shah's enfant terrible, Gholam 'Ali 'Aziz al-Soltan (favorite of the king), better known by his coquettish nickname, Malijak (Kurdish for little sparrow; more vulgarly pronounced Manije, as Taj recorded it), are a case in point. A feeble-looking, spoiled page boy with trachomatous eyes, a stutter, and a foul mouth, Malijak was brought up in the shah's private quarters under his watchful eyes. Royal care could not have nurtured a more un-princely person. Many were the palace guards who became victims of his trigger-happy habits, many the public audiences disrupted by his childish demands. Even in his early teens Malijak was notoriously unhygienic. During the shah's 1889 European tour, when Malijak accompanied His Majesty all the way to Buckingham Palace, he was so infested with lice that, in order to encourage him to wash, the shah ordered his entire private entourage to visit the bath-house and the barber shop. Malijak was considered by state officials and the nobility an appalling embarrassment to the dignity of the king and his court. Yet the shah reserved his purest sentiments, to the point of total infatuation, for this son of a Kurdish village boy. His father, a younger brother of Amina Aqdas and an earlier favorite page boy of the shah, was married off to a lowly concubine in the harem in order to breed a son that, from his very birth, was to become the object of the shah's unconditional attention. By allowing, even encouraging, Malijak's crudest obscenities, to the point of offending his courtiers, Naser al-Din may have intended to deflate the overblown ego of his officialdom. The real reasons for his affectionate self-mockery, however, ran deeper. It was as though the shah found a grudging satisfaction in rewarding Malijak's banal indulgences and misbehavior, perhaps reenacting his own unhappy childhood when as a sickly and insecure boy he was denied fatherly love and often perceived as a political nuisance.

By the time Taj was nine years of age, Malijak was the only non-relative male that could still roam about the harem at will and flirt with the shah's younger daughters. Theoretically a grown-up, Malijak, who was then fourteen, was married to Akhtar al-Saltana, a sister of Taj's who was roughly the same age. Perhaps, among other reasons, the marriage was intended to make Malijak's access to the forbidden quarters legally admissible. The royal marriage present for Malijak, ironically, was part of the confiscated residence of the late premier, Mirza Hosayn Khan Moshir al-Dawla, the celebrated reformist of the Naseri period. Later, during the Constitutional Revolution, Malijak saw the same residence become the seat of the parliament (Majles), while he languished in dire destitution. Even his new title, Sardar Mohtaram (respected army chief), which he acquired in the court of Ahmad Shah, proved as ineffectual as it was improper. The union with Akhtar did not prevent the young Malijak from sending illicit love messages to Taj and other women in the harem.

Taj's barely acknowledged liaison with Malijak is a blow to the viability of another stereotype about the harem's strict sexual faithfulness. Rumors and circumstantial evidence only weaken such an image: the promiscuous relationships of Mahd 'Olya, lesbian affairs among the royal women, lovers escaping through the roofs of the harem, and royal concubines surprised in the basement with adolescent page boys or half-castrated but still sexually active eunuchs. Yet, as long as petty scandals did not turn into a common practice or into a public embarrassment, the shah was willing to overlook the royal women's occasional liberties in the hope that his rejuvenated appetite for child concubines, an example of which Taj witnessed, could be indulged without serious objection by his senior wives.

The whole environment of the late Naseri inner court, the private quarters *(khalwat)*, and the harem *(andarun)* was comically puerile. The shah's bizarre succumbing to Malijak's most foolish and reckless amusements, and occasional participation in them, as appear in the secret memoirs of his outraged royal chronicler and confidant, E'temad al-Saltana, no doubt was the chief reason. The grotesque game of switching off the electric light and allowing the women to release their anger and frustrations at each other in the dark, as described by Taj, was another of the shah's childish, yet crudely clever, games with obvious sexual undertones. In such surroundings of juvenile sensuality Malijak's adolescent passes at Taj furnished the young princess with her earliest awareness of adult femininity.

Marriage was a different business altogether. Taj's account of the circumstances leading to her wedlock demonstrates the basic function and value of unmarried females in the high society of her time and, most of all, in the court. As a commodity produced in the harem to be bartered for wealth or loyalty, the female royal offsprings were in high demand. They were often disposed of to appropriate bidders at the earliest occasion. Though the basic right of refusing the suitor was not entirely lost—and examples of resistance to arranged marriages were not rare, as in Taj's case—the advantages of political or economic unions were often so great that they outweighed other considerations. Taj was as much a pawn in the possession of the harem as her future husband was the slave of his father's political ambitions.

Gholam 'Ali 'Aziz al-Soltan (Malijak) in his finery, after he eventually outgrew his infamous lack of hygiene in childhood. His medal-bespeckled chest, outsized decorative sword, and other accoutrements bespoke his royal patron's unwavering devotion.

Remarkably, it was Anis al-Dawla, the recognized head of the harem, and not the shah, who finally arranged the union—an indication of the critical control the harem exercised over its most crucial resources. Her effort to marry off Taj to Hasan, the young son of Mohammad Baqer Khan Sardar Akram, the head of the royal guards and a descendent of an old military family, may have run counter to the shah's own wishes. If Taj's slightly confused account can be relied upon, she would have been married off to the shah's beloved Malijak had it not been for the utter contempt with which he was viewed by Anis al-Dawla as well as by her ally, Taj's mother. The shah's willingness to comply with their wishes indicates the power of the harem to check the influence of Malijak's party, while the sovereign's decision to delay the actual marriage until Taj reached the age of twenty reflected his liberal attitude. Under Islamic law a marriage contract (*'aqd*) can be drawn up years before the marriage is actually consummated, while the bride still resides with her parents. The fact that Taj's future husband was approximately her age, rather than a man many years her senior—even by as many as fifty years—confirms the shah's changing values. Some four decades earlier he had married off his fifteen-year-old sister, 'Ezzat al-Dawla, to the celebrated Amir Kabir, then in his mid-fifties.

Taj admits candidly that marriage to Hasan was primarily a means of liberating herself from the suffocating world of the harem, an option sought by many young women of her status. Her expectations of married life, however, which she later came to regret, were naive at best. Her knowledge of her future husband was virtually nonexistent, even when at the age of thirteen she finally moved to his house. Ironically, the assassination of Naser al-Din Shah and the subsequent crisis in the court and the harem fulfilled Taj's wishes and gave her a taste of the few delights and many agonies of married life.

The assassination of Naser al-Din Shah on 1 May 1896, on the eve of his golden jubilee (according to the lunar Islamic calendar), was an exceptionally momentous event in the life of all the women of the harem. The dramatic yet bizarre picture that is skillfully painted by Taj of her first hearing of the news and the ensuing chaos in the harem shows the dependence of the entire political system, the court and the government, upon the shah's existence. For the shah's subjects, his few friends and his many foes, the assassination set in motion a new dynamic in the state and the society that only a decade later culminated in the Constitutional Revolution.

In the end it was the sequel to the assassination that proved to be the most crucial for Taj. The accession of Mozaffar al-Din Shah (r. 1896–1906) marked the beginning of a new phase, one which brought with it more anxiety than comfort to Taj and the other women of Naser al-Din's harem. Hard pressed for space and money, Mozaffar al-Din and the hungry entourage that came with him from Tabriz, the provincial capital, in search of fame and fortune were anxious to promptly dispose of his father's widows and young orphans. Taj's account describes the major overhaul in the court. The childless and pension-less wives were unceremoniously evicted from the harem while widows with younger children, such as Taj's mother, were housed in a separate residence. Such actions were not uncommon for a new ruler, though Mozaffar al-Din's behavior evinced an element of personal animosity. Given all his misgivings toward his father during forty years of rancorous and often humiliating relations, such an attitude was to be expected. Yet, to Mozaffar al-Din's credit, Taj was sent off to her husband's house with all the customary wedding festivities and with a large pension.

THE UNHAPPY UNION

Taj's marriage to Hasan, later Shaja' al-Saltana (valor of the kingdom), was another sign of transitory times. Their union started as a traditional bond between extended families and resulted in complex problems typical of modern families. Taj's father-in-law, Sardar Akram, came from an old military family with a record of service going back to the late-Safavid period. With the arrival of a new entourage at the outset of Mozaffar al-Din's reign, Sardar Akram had even more reason to solidify his link with the court through marriage while allying himself with Amin al-Soltan, who, dismissed temporarily in 1896, was reinstated in 1898 for another five years. As it turned out, Sardar Akram was a prominent figure in the Mozaffari court establishment and a devout monarchist.

Taj's husband, then a thirteen-year-old juvenile, was no more than "a child whose words and concerns were limited to childish games." Taj's recollections of the first days of their married life, comical as they appear, hint at a deeper problem. On their first night together they quarreled over a game of cards. While he withdrew to a corner of the room, sulking, Taj, increasingly enchanted with her physical beauty, admired herself in the mirror. With wounded vanity she began wondering why her husband did not "worship" her. Hasan obviously was more interested in a game of "king and minister," which Taj found utterly insulting to her royal house. Even more frustrating for Taj, Hasan's sexual awareness came through flirting with black slaves in the household and possibly even an illicit relationship with his "morally corrupt" black nanny. It was probably her unrequited sexual wishes that prompted Taj to insist on her charm and attraction. "My beauty shone like a diamond," she writes when referring to Hasan's "wild behavior and mocking shows of affection." In retrospect Taj also confesses her own arrogance, immaturity, and emotional distress at the time of her marriage, and attributes them to her pampered upbringing. Whatever the reason, it became increasingly plain to Taj that her marriage was a mismatch.

If Hasan was not prepared to adore Taj, others were. Under Mozaffar al-Din Shah the Persian high society of the time was beginning to taste the pleasure of amorous liaisons with greater liberty. Taj's account of her own experiences is daring testimony to the permissiveness of the time when the ethics of Naseri puritanism began to fade in the face of a rushed modernity. Her courage even to record her affairs reflected the changing values in the post-Constitutional period. Indeed, she has provided us with a rare glance at the private life of the elite in the Persian court, who, conscious of their self-esteem, hardly ever wrote about private matters such as their spouses or their family lives—let alone their illicit affairs and sexual orientations.

As innocently as she portrays them, the sentimental confessions of the young and charming envoy of Mo'azzam al-Saltana to Taj were a novelty; far more flagrant was the flirting of the affluent youth, including Hasan, with Russian circus girls. Such relative laxity, no doubt, was patterned out of the Mozaffari court. In the less respectful language of the street the new shah was known as "sister Mozaffar" *(abji Mozaffar)* for his derelict standards, of which Taj gives vivid examples. News of the royal court's nocturnal scandals traveled as rapidly as hired prostitutes, of both sexes, frequented the houses of Tehran's nobility. Regardless of all the moralizing, Taj's account of her own "crush" on Mo'azzam al-Saltana's friend is a courageous example of self-expression that could only be attempted by a privileged woman of her stature. Fatherless, deprived of her beloved nanny, and emotionally at odds with her mother who continued to demand obedience, Taj felt helpless. She was caught between a cynical father-in-law, who began to regret the depreciating value of an ex-shah's daughter, and a libertine of a husband, who quickly learned to squander his father's wealth first on girls, later on boys, but always on horses and (oddly enough) on mules. She therefore felt that she was entitled to reciprocate Hasan's neglect and infidelity by responding favorably to her growing number of admirers.

Though there were temporary reconciliations in Taj's otherwise ruptured marriage, they were not substantial enough to preserve it. In the absence of any meaningful marital life, what seems to have kept this odd couple together, other than the dictates of their families, was their settling into a mutual independence—one which, short of divorce, appeared to be the only working alternative. In spite of her sharp criticism of Hasan's indulgent and carefree lifestyle, complete with all the available vices in the market, Taj reserves some sympathy for his seemingly maladjusted adolescence, though even that sounds farcical. It was her "poor husband" who, trying to escape the pain of losing Katy, the Russian circus girl, rode around their courtyard in heat or in cold in a little chariot pulled by a miserable red goat.

So far as Taj's version of events reveals, such sympathy brought her victimization more than it did freedom. Her platonic infatuations, even if they never materialized in affairs with other men, could hardly match her husband's bisexual sorties. "Had I cherished any real love in my heart for my husband," writes Taj, describing her husband's love affair with a young man among her own relatives, "I would most assuredly have suffered terribly; but I only harbored conjugal respect and affection for him, so I was not particularly concerned with what he did, and left him to himself." Taj's liberal tolerance sounds strikingly modern, finding precedents for extra-marital affairs among eighteenth-century French aristocracy—as portrayed by Dumas and Laclos—rather than in the male-dominated values of the equally libertine Qajar aristocracy.

Having children proved to be a temporary consolation to Taj's otherwise dim days. They occupied every moment of her life, she is proud to tell us, when it is obvious there was little else. But here, too, the emotional and physical blows were serious. Not only had she lost an infant son, a norm for her time, but she had also resorted to a dangerous abortion at the hands of a *doctor,* a European-educated physician, which had long-lasting effects on her body and mind. Her husband's venereal disease, presumably gonorrhea, prompted Taj to take "poisonous medication" so as to remove the chances of miscarriage or defective birth. The growing promiscuity among the upper classes, often with native and European prostitutes, spread venereal diseases, which soon reached alarming levels. It is possible that Taj confused gonorrhea *(suzak* or *ateshak)* with the more dangerous syphilis *(kuft)*—which first came from Europe to Iran in the seventeenth century via the Ottoman Empire—for it is the latter that was likely to have affected her unborn child. The diagnosis of hysteria, then a fashionable neurotic disorder in Europe, was apparently due to the belief that the illness was caused by a disturbance of the uterus. Hasan's venereal disease, yet another blemish in the catalog of his vices, was shared by many men of his generation. After the Revolution, as early as 1909, remedies for venereal diseases were among the most conspicuous advertisements in the press. Hasan's fascination with things Western, from gadgets to women, was no less uncommon—but only for those who could afford them. A decade after Naser al-Din Shah's policy of cultural quarantine came to an end, and on the eve of the Constitutional Revolution, it is interesting to note that European entertainments, particularly the circus, were among "vices" whose removal was demanded by the protesting ulama.

But if the substance of Taj's increasingly disjointed emotional life was lonesomeness, rejection, and frustration, her vehicle for expressing these agonies was the language of Western sensibilities, which had just begun to appear in the cultural ethos of the Persian intelligentsia. Even before the turn of the century, the romanticism of popular European novels, their familiar intrigues, sensuality, dramatic pitfalls, and hard-to-acquire redemption, was to fascinate a small but influential readership. Available in books and journals in Persian translation or home-brewed imitations, such romances had captured Taj's imagination and shaped her idiom, even when she was still in her father's harem. More strikingly, she seemed to behave, almost consciously, after the model of heroines in French romantic novels—a Madame Bovary, perhaps, who though different from Flaubert's heroine in social standing, nevertheless was as daring and as tragic as the French romantic character. Certainly, like Madame Bovary, Taj's love of luxury and her weakness for expensive clothes brought her near to bankruptcy, and likewise into trouble with a silk merchant. The glamour of Parisian fashion, expensive jewelry, horses, and carriages, and other accessories of an extravagant lifestyle were as irresistible to Taj as they were to many of the Europeanized nobility of her time.

Taj's financial problems were indeed typical of many members of her class after the Constitutional Revolution. Throughout Mozaffar al-Din Shah's era, Taj's father-in-law, an ally of Amin al-Soltan and the minister of war, had managed to accumulate a substantial fortune by giving himself and his son enormous salaries and appointing the young and unqualified Hasan to positions of huge but unaccounted income *(madakhil)*. As commander-in-chief of the army (Amir Nezam), a post once occupied by celebrated men like Mirza Taqi Khan Amir Kabir, Sardar Akram appointed his fifteen-year-old son the commander of the Azarbaijan army, the most prestigious force in the country. This was not uncharacteristic of the military establishment, to say nothing of the entire Qajar government. In the military, like other organs of the government, monopolies were created by appointing relatives and clients to sensitive posts. Even as late as the turn of the twentieth century, there was a tendency to secure institutional continuity by allowing hereditary succession even if the inheritor was very young. This practice was open to great abuse, especially when it was further compounded by the shah's or the premier's personal favors, or, more commonly, by bribery and gift-taking.

The appointment of ten-year-old generals and adolescent commanders, such as Hasan, looking miserably inadequate in their oversized military uniforms, was the subject of much underhanded criticism and ridicule by domestic and foreign observers.Hasan, born to unearned privileges into a military family, presumably had not even cultivated the skills necessary for swindling and corrupt deals, let alone those for military command. To Taj's disappointment, the only one of his family's military proclivities he inherited was an insatiable love of horses—another expensive habit of the young nobility of his time. Though Taj looks down on her husband's other interests in animal husbandry and farm life, these were probably the only redeeming activities that Hasan could discover in military life. There was little chance of making a career in the barely functional army of the late-Qajar period. Moreover, young gentlemen of Hasan's generation enjoyed far too much luxury in hunting, socializing, drinking, music, and European travel to prefer rugged military field maneuvers—provided, of course, that their hereditary pensions remained untouched.

Though she never admits it, there is enough evidence in Taj's account to suggest that she clung to her husband in part out of financial dependence. By 1900 her royal pension had been appropriated by her father-in-law, probably to pay off her incurred debts. Taj recalls with nostalgia the days when her husband's lucrative post as the chief of the royal guards, formerly held by his father, earned them the annual salary of thirty thousand *tuman*s (six thousand pounds sterling at 1899 rates), ten times Taj's own pension. This was a hefty salary for a normal family, though not enough to pay for such expenses as Taj's 2,800-*tuman* (£560) purchase of silk clothing in two years (or three), or for other personal effects imported at exorbitant prices. She recalls their wasteful lifestyle:

> We two youngsters spent all we had, always imagining that life would continue in the same fashion. We had never tasted the hardship of poverty. Having always been surrounded with wealth and respect, we could not conceive of the springs of our riches and dignity ever running dry, or the river of gold and eternal happiness ceasing to flow. We had not reckoned that a rock untimely loosened, or a tangle of underbrush carelessly tossed in the water, could impede the flow and afflict us with a deathly thirst.

The Constitutional Revolution was indeed that loosened rock and the common people who joined it the tangle of underbrush of Iran.

But even before the Revolution abolished the hereditary pensions of the old nobility and revoked their land assignments, some of the members of the elite had begun to feel the financial pressure generated by the lukewarm reforms of the Mozaffari era. By the turn of the twentieth century, borrowing

Tehran crowd gathered for 'Ashura (mourning ceremony commemorating Imam Hosayn's martyrdom) in Sabza Maydan square on the entrance to the Tehran Bazaar and across from the royal citadel (Arg). Such swarming multitudes prompted Taj to liken the people to the "tangle of underbrush" that propelled the "rock untimely loosened" of the Constitutional Revolution (1906–1911) and exposed the Qajar nobility to "a deathly thirst."

from foreign banks, particularly the Russian Mortgage Bank, had become a devastating habit of the elite who had lost their traditional sources of income to inflation, reform in the bureaucracy, and sheer indulgence. They looked to the Persian government as their model, with its heavy borrowing from foreign states and financiers. The government's declining revenues and its rising expenditures, mostly due to the growth of the administration, the overburdening of state pensions, Mozaffar al-Din's wasteful European tours and his court's growing expenses, had brought the state to the verge of bankruptcy. The parasitical officialdom and princely class that relied on the government for the greater portion of their incomes were thus obliged to mortgage their unpaid salaries and pensions, and later their estates, their houses, and their belongings. Ravaged by the fallen value of Persian currency, they bartered away their affluence when the impoverished Persian state was no longer capable of sustaining them. As Taj seems to indicate, her husband, too, pawned off pieces of their fortune perhaps to spend lavishly on his new lover, a male dancer called Tayhu.

Dust 'Ali Khan Mo'ayyer al-Mamalek, a descendant of an old and powerful family of state officials and a grandson of Naser al-Din Shah, who kept a diary throughout the Constitutional period, renders a telling self-portrait of this despairing nobility. When in 1912 their hopes for restoration of a royalist regime under Mohammad 'Ali Shah were dashed, the more affluent sought refuge in European capitals and fashionable resorts in search of women, casinos, and mineral baths. The less affluent resorted to frequenting the valleys and gorges of Alborz around Tehran in search of game, thus completing the ecological disaster that began with zealous over-hunting, or else to chasing the coquettish women now more visible on fashionable Lalezar Avenue, in the public gardens of

The facade of the headquarters of the Imperial Bank of Persia, decorated on Mozaffar al-Din Shah's birthday. The ornate exterior masked the bank's menacing functions from the nobility. The Persian flag hanging from the mast is a prototype of the later standardized national flag.

northern Tehran, at the horse races, and at the private parties thrown by the revolutionary nouveaux riches.

Despite her financial troubles, Taj was determined to preserve her independence, even at the cost of selling her jewelry. Even before Taj was abandoned by her husband sometime before 1906, she was well known enough in Tehran's artistic circles to be desired by, among others, the then upstart poet, singer, and composer, 'Aref Qazvini, who soon became the celebrated bard of the Revolution. In one of the few independent accounts of Taj that we have, 'Aref narrated to the editor of his *divan* how, arriving at her house without invitation for the first time, he managed to impress the attractive though plump lady by reciting a few passages of his poetry. But for his superb musical talent, 'Aref might have been pulverized under the shovels of Taj's gardeners for his insolence.

In his account the amorous poet records his enchantment with the unveiled princess who lived on her own in a garden villa in an exclusive suburb of the capital. Nor does he deny Taj's liberal, even permissive, conduct toward her male guests, her intimate parties for the sons of the nobility, her taste for liquor, music, and even lovers, all in blatant defiance of the prevailing values of her society. 'Aref's account corroborates Taj's description of her troubled marriage, her husband's debauchery, and her lavish lifestyle. Mozaffar al-Din Shah, Aref tells us, was furious with Taj for her wantonness, leading to rancor between them—a rancor that is reflected in Taj's disparaging portrayal of her royal brother. 'Aref's rapport with Taj seems to have continued over the years. Four years later, in 1910, he composed a song *(tasnif)* in her honor in the Afshari mode which he performed in private concerts:

> You, Taj, are a crown *(taj)* worthy of kings' heads;
> Your intoxicating eyes turned a whole world volatile...
> At your doorstep there is a public melee.
> How could you ever recognize 'Aref?

The poet 'Aref of Qazvin, in a semi-traditional outfit, complete with cloak and turban, and in a modern pose then in vogue among the literati. The photograph dates roughly to the time when he first met Taj.

'Aref's weakness for women of high society brought him not
only to Taj's doorstep but also to her sister's, Eftekhar al-
Saltana (pride of the kingdom), another daughter of Naser al-
Din Shah, acclaimed for her artistic appreciation, her physical
appeal, and her intelligence. 'Aref's passionate love for
Eftekhar, who was married to the poet's best friend, Nezam al-
Soltan, is celebrated in another famous song by the poet.
Although caught in a love triangle, Nezam al-Soltan, who
himself was at one time a companion of Taj, was unabashed by
an affair between 'Aref and his royal wife. Like the homosexual affairs of Taj's husband and her own romances, the
prevalence of liaisons such as these indicates a far more liberal
society in the first decade of the twentieth century than
stereotypes would have us believe. The prevailing ethics of the
modernized elite were more in tune with the Persian lyrical
tradition of wine, music, and passion than with the stern piety
of the ulama and the ferocious honor-shame chastity they represented—an aspect of life largely absent from Taj's cultural
refashioning. At least for the educated elite of the time, traditional religion and its code of prohibitions were discarded.

NEW HORIZONS

Taj's declining affluence and her greater access to the outside
world during and after the Constitutional Revolution coin-
cided with her intellectual awakening and the emergence of a
conscious feminism. Helpless and socially deprived as a
woman—despite being a princess of some consequence—she
began to see how the misfortunes of her life were perpetuated
by a patriarchal ethos that was honored by society and sanc-
tioned by normative religion. Taj's objections to this ethos
were not based merely on a sheer sense of despair. The mix of
the old and the new is not absent in Taj's sociopolitical critique;

nor can she hide the conflict in her mind between old loyalties and modern convictions. Though she observes a meaningful silence about the political developments of the Revolution, of which she was an economic victim, she does not hesitate to voice her criticism of the old regime and call for reforms, above all the emancipation of women. Such intellectual orientation was largely the outcome of the Revolution, though it had its roots in a decade of cultural change during the 1900s.

Taj's self-proclaimed independence, even before the Revolution, of family and husband permitted her to augment her life of luxury and entertainment with the cultural experiences of study, music, French, painting, and above all socializing. It goes without saying that only her privileged position as the sister of the reigning monarch enabled her to venture into activities almost entirely denied to the average woman of her time. Educated women of her generation were adept at literature, music, and fine arts in the privacy of their homes but few, if any, had emerged from the harem to engage publicly in social life, at least not since the Babi heroine Qorrat al-'Ayn half a century earlier, and then under a very different set of circumstances. However, the matriarchal residue of the bygone Qajar nomadism was not altogether dead. Like many matriarchs of the royal family, Taj, too, displayed a spirit of assertiveness and independence; but unlike them (or at least unlike the stereotype that comes to mind) she managed to modernize somewhat this spirit of grandmotherly domineeringness into a championing of women's emancipation.

Taj's intellectual blooming had begun perhaps around 1904, even before her unnamed relative, possibly a socialist, persuaded her to take up French lessons with him. During these sessions he not only expressed his "fervid, intense affection" for his student but also managed to convert her, at least temporarily, into a naturalist. It seems that Taj's "great love of learning" was not unrelated to her emotional distress, particularly in the aftermath of her abortion. Though she does not elaborate on the circumstances of her three suicide attempts, they were, no doubt, symptoms of her inner crisis. Her adopting the European mode of dress, abandoning regular prayer and other devotional acts, and above all unveiling herself in public—not to mention her uninhibited socializing—were enough to confirm her husband's suspicions of unfaithfulness. But more distressing for Taj, these changes seem to have stirred in her a crisis of faith, a sense of guilt, as she began to move away from an innocent "God-fearing" world of damnation and "torments of hell" to a world of rational causality and secular tenets.

Learning about the real causes of thunder and lightning in contrast to her earlier superstitious beliefs, to which she refers almost deliberately as a sign of her intellectual enlightenment, is symbolic of the way modern knowledge, transmitted by popular scientific writing of authors such as Talebov altered the religious outlook of the men and women of Taj's generation. With a change in outlook also came a change in lifestyle. The experience of adopting Western dress—in a culture in which attire denoted one's personality and status—and subsequently entering the secular domain of uniformity was not unique to Taj. Among the younger mullahs, merchants, and bureaucrats all those who in the post-Constitutional period traded their cloaks for coats and their turbans for fezzes (and later the rimmed French hat of the early Reza Shah era) went through some crisis of identity and faith.

Even among those who stubbornly clung to their traditional outfits there were many who surreptitiously carried beneath their cloaks translations of Western books on geography and simplified sciences, political polemics, and newspapers. They, too, were tormented by questions of faith.

But if the traditional man practiced the time-honored art of dissimulation, indicating his half-hearted adherence to modernity, the Western-minded intellectual had no qualms about displaying his anti-traditional convictions and his command of European knowledge and languages. On the eve of the Revolution, European-educated Persians and their counterparts, graduates of Tehran's Royal Polytechnic (Dar al-Fonun) and the School of Politics (Madrasa-ye Siyasi), were advocating a mixture of constitutionalism and romantic patriotism to remedy the evils of despotic rule, withstand aggression from imperial powers against Iran, and foster overall economic and educational reconstruction by combating material backwardness and religious superstition. This three-pronged message came to represent the core of revolutionary ideology during the Constitutional era.

The rapid growth of publishing before and during the Revolution made available to the small but conspicuous readership an array of new material which was as crucial to the emergence of modern sensibilities as it was to the rise of political consciousness. Taj's knowledge of the West was in part based on such literature: translations of popular romances, European histories and geographies, newspaper articles on international affairs, and possibly even Christian polemical literature. Traces of "enjoyable romances" are visible throughout her account. Not only does she liken the past behavior of her drawing teacher to "the famous Don Quixote," but, more interestingly, wishes that she was herself "a competent writer like Victor Hugo or Monsieur Rousseau" to make her memoirs "sweet and delightful." "Alas," she adds, "I can write but simply and poorly." No doubt she was acquainted with Rousseau's *Confessions*, which she used as a model for her intensely personal account—one, like Rousseau's, that depicted a tormented life of anguish and revolt against the existing social order. Like Rousseau she, too, tried to be daring and conceal nothing to her own discredit. Her interest in Hugo reveals something beyond fashionable praise for the eloquence of his *Les Misérables.* Hugo was a monarchist turned republican who opposed Napoleon III's dictatorship. In Hugo's romantic activism Taj could have seen a justifying model for her criticism of the Qajar monarchy.

The fact that by 1914 neither Rousseau nor Hugo was translated into Persian would lead us to believe that Taj must have read them in French (or at least read about them), probably with the help of her French tutor and intellectual mentor. A few years earlier she had not known enough French to read her husband's intercepted love letters from his French mistress; we should conclude, therefore, that during the decade before writing her memoirs Taj acquired enough proficiency in French to read literature and other subjects. By 1903 the Alliance Française not only had established the first French school in Tehran but had set up a library of 8,000 volumes in the French embassy that was accessible to the Tehran intelligentsia. By 1908 French had become part of the curriculum in all modern Iranian schools, and cheap editions of French classics (mostly published by Armand Colin) had a small but avid readership in Iran. Persian translations from the late nineteenth century included a number of Alexandre Dumas' (père) well-known historical novels, rendered into Persian by the Qajar prince Mohammad Taher Mirza Eskandari. Judging by Taj's references to eighteenth-century French history, it is likely that she had studied *Les Trois Mousquetaires* and *Comte de Monte Cristo,* among other works. After the return of a new wave of Persian students from abroad, more translations from French, English, Russian, Turkish and Arabic were available and included works in history, current affairs, social criticism, and literature.

Under her mentor's direction Taj also read some European history and social thought, though her knowledge of those subjects remained scanty and superficial. She praised Spartan mothers for providing the chief impetus for the courage and sacrifice of that city's warriors. Though quite incongruent, her comparison of Amin al-Soltan to the Roman emperor, Caligula, indicates a familiarity with Roman history which is further confirmed by references to Julius Caesar, Brutus and Mark Antony. Though Gibbon's *Decline and Fall* was in part translated as early as the third decade of the nineteenth century, it was never published, leaving us to surmise that Taj read some French account of Marcus Aurelius's *Meditations*, or perhaps the Persian translation by 'Abd al-Rahim Talebov, published in 1894. Taj knew enough of modern European history not only to cite Bismarck's remark about education, "We prevailed over France thanks to our school teachers," but to mention a complementary view which gave primary credit for the success of education to mothers.

Sharply critical of the old political order and speaking as a member of the nobility, Taj stands out as being more progressive than the radical critics of her time. Her appraisal of the Qajar monarchy, and particularly Mozaffar al-Din, draws a sarcastic comparison between Peter the Great's lofty goals while visiting Europe and Mozaffar al-Din Shah's frivolous preoccupations during his European tours. Voltaire's *Histoire de l'empire de Russie sous Pierre le Grand*, one of the earliest historical works translated into Persian, was first published in 1847. She remembered enough of her reading of French history some years later to liken the hooked nose of Solayman, Taj's much scrutinized drawing teacher, to that of the French princely family of de Condé, the cadet branch of the house of Bourbon. It is worth noting that Louis Joseph de Bourbon, Prince de Condé (III), enjoyed a dubious position in French history for being the organizer of the emigré "army of Condé" that fought against the French revolutionary forces. Tantalizing as it may sound, drawing a comparison between Prince de Condé and Solayman, be it based on the shape of their noses, is not entirely absurd. Whereas Prince de Condé of French Revolution fame tried unsuccessfully to defend his royal house against the revolutionaries, the pensive Solayman of the Qajar house, Taj's paternal cousin (possibly a grandson of Naser al-Din's celebrated sister 'Ezzat al-Dawla from her fourth marriage), like many princes of her house, found solace from the ravages of the Revolution in art and mysticism.

Like most of her contemporaries Taj was an admirer of the West. What affected her life were not the high politics of rival imperialists but her own surroundings, family, class, and gender. And it is to these matters that she invariably returns. Beyond her fascination with the West's material glamour—fashion, furniture, and even the motorcar, which made its first appearance in Iran as early as 1903 when Mozaffar al-Din brought one from Europe—she was also taken by its high culture.

The playing of Persian music on the piano was one example of integrating Western and traditional culture. Ever since the director of Naser al-Din's royal ensemble, Sorur al-Molk, discovered that by imitating the *santur* (Persian dulcimer) technique he could play Persian traditional music on the piano, this Western instrument enjoyed some popularity among high society, especially the women. By the turn of the century the piano had become a fixture in affluent households, and techniques of playing it had improved by the time of the Revolution. Adapting Persian classical modes for the piano was symbolic of a desire to reconcile Persian high culture with the culture of the West, a mixed blessing that engendered a few tasteful innovations but many awkward fads as well. Taj's interest in Persian music gradually shifted from the piano to the *tar*, the Persian six-string lute, also popular among women who performed it in private. It was as though she discovered a greater authenticity and technical range in an instrument that stood at the center of Persian musical efflorescence during the Constitutional Revolution. Her age was blessed with the artistic innovations of some of the greatest names in Persian music. Familiarity with European music, notation as well as composition, allowed such masters as Darvish Khan to introduce new musical forms responsive to the needs of the time, thus contributing further to a rich musical tradition that had already achieved much under Naser al-Din Shah.

Similarly, the tasteful and measured adoption of European realism in painting in the Naseri period, from Sani' al-Molk to Kamal al-Molk and his school, also greatly helped free the Persian painting of the Constitutional period from the confines of the court and religion and enabled it to emerge as a reflection of the ordinary people, though it never achieved the attention and popularity of Persian music. Established by Kamal al-Molk, arguably the greatest Persian painter of the nineteenth century, the School of Fine Arts produced a fine group of Persian painters whose work bore an affinity to Millet's realism but who, like their teacher, were fascinated by Rembrandt's technical mastery.

By the first decade of the twentieth century Europe was no longer a forbidden domain to the elite. The hazy frontier from which only diplomats, soldiers, missionaries, and choice luxury goods used to come had now become accessible for study, pleasure and political refuge. Contrary to Naser al-Din's era when, fearing liberal dissent, the shah had long maintained a ban on European travel except for diplomatic missions, the age of Mozaffar al-Din began to quench the thirst for travel. Often through the Caspian route to the Caucasus and therefrom through the Russian railroad to Europe or via Istanbul by the Oriental Express, not only Russia and Europe but occasionally the United States and Japan were now being visited by Persian travelers who proudly kept journals of their most mundane activities. Even the arid accounts of Mozaffar al-Din's travels, mercilessly mocked by Taj for their banality, were a source for the Persian readers back home who craved details. These accounts, as well as what appeared in the press, were nevertheless informative enough to broaden the ordinary readers' horizons beyond the old geographical boundaries and confronted their often intact ethnocentric world-views with tangible realities, both sweet and bitter.

Though she cherished a desperate longing to go to Europe, Taj had to content herself with such secondary sources as well as all the "descriptions of the world's beautiful cities" which she had read about in "European novels." Even by 1914, the number of Persian women who visited the West was very small. If the Islamic restriction on travel to the land of the infidels was lax for men—and, indeed, often ignored altogether—such laxity did not extend to women, and certainly not to unaccompanied women. No doubt, visits to European resorts, mineral baths, luxury hotels, casinos, and night clubs in France, Austria, and Switzerland, then in vogue among the affluent Persian elite who found Tehran's revolutionary atmosphere suffocating, added to Taj's yearning. Her sister, Eftekhar al-Saltana, was among the first to visit Europe in 1911.

The reading of French, which revolutionized Taj's intellectual life, and the explosion of information in the press of the Constitutional period were sufficient to fill the gaps in what she knew about the West through such accounts as her

Mozaffar al-Din Shah in his automobile, perhaps the first brought to Iran around the turn of the century. This was one of the more useful items that accompanied the bulk of frivolous luxuries imported by the monarch.

Both among low-ranking professional female musicians at the turn of the century (top) and women of status in the 1930s (right), the *tar* (six-string Persian lute) was the most popular musical instrument—a testimony to women's fondness for music depicted in many illustrations of the Qajar era.

Whether emphasizing a woman's entertaining role in the household, or as a means of self-expression or escapism—as in the case of Taj—the Persian musical tradition thrived behind the walls of the women's quarters in conjunction with musical development in the outside world.

father's and her brother's travelogues. She was up-to-date enough to know, for example, about Robert Peary's 1909 North Pole exploration and the new aviation and maritime advances in Europe and the United States, and even John D. Rockefeller's thirty-year "amassing" of dollars, as she puts it. Indeed capitalism was not the only ideology she associated with the West. She felt confident enough to discern that Jamal al-Din Afghani's political thought was "neither theological nor ideological *(maslaki)*," but rather "against all religions and ideologies." Compared with socialism, which she considered as the most "uninhibited and broad-ranging" ideology of her time, Afghani's thought, she believed, would amount to anarchism. It was "opposed to all bonds of temporal authority." Taj's impression of Afghani, no doubt, was rooted not in his advocacy of Pan-Islamism or in his pious addresses to the high-ranking Shi'ite ulama during the Régie protest, but rather in his role as mentor to Naser al-Din Shah's assassin. It is hard to believe that Taj, however well-read, was aware of the exchange of letters in 1883 between Afghani and the French philosopher, Ernest Renan, where Afghani's unorthodox defense of Islam may have lent itself, in the eye of a rigorous reader, to such an opinion.

Taj's equivocal opinion of Afghani did not soften her criticism of the Persian *ancien régime*, however. Sympathizing with her father for being condemned to rule, she nevertheless notices the pitfalls in the way of arbitrary rule without falling victim to the political rhetoric of the Constitutional period. The monarchs, she writes,

> are foremost in misery among the people of the world. From early childhood they hear and see nothing but lies, hypocrisy, and deviousness. Every person who bows to them does so out of fear or necessity. Anyone who shows them affection is after money or jewelry. Every service performed for them is motivated by the hope of prestige or preferment.

The solitude of the throne is well evident from the above passage, yet Taj does not shy away from censuring her father's shortcomings. She wishes that instead of writing about Naser al-Din's bizarre attachment to his famous cat, Babri Khan, about which a sarcastic passage appears in her memoirs, she could have written of her father's care for his subjects, of his educational and other great undertakings. Like Malijak who appeared some years later, Babri was one of the few psychological obsessions of Naser al-Din's private life.

In discussing her father's obsessions Taj goes so far as to caricaturize the ruler. She barely recognizes, for instance, the domestic and diplomatic challenges Naser al-Din was up against. Witnessing the final years of his reign from the angle of the harem, where personal weaknesses were magnified, she does not credit him for preserving a degree of stability, precarious though it was, while resisting neighboring powers. In the late nineteenth century Iran had to face not only the old dilemmas of maintaining the internal balance between the central government and the peripheral sources of power, but also the diplomatic and commercial rivalries between her two imperial neighbors: the expanding Russian empire dominating the north, from the Caucasus to Central Asia; and the less menacing, but more demanding, British Empire in the south, dominating the Indian subcontinent, most of Afghanistan, and the Persian Gulf. In spite of repeated setbacks and indefensible follies, Naser al-Din was by and large successful in striking a balance in both the domestic and the foreign arenas. The tribal khans, the religious establishment and other urban notables, the princes and the bureaucratic factions were persuaded, or coerced, to heed the authority of the sovereign in an unspoken consensus. He achieved a relative equilibrium in foreign policy, at the same time, by pitting the powers against each other. Nevertheless, having little access to financial and military resources, he could not preserve this equilibrium without a price. Throughout his reign the shah resisted an autonomous ministerial office distinct from the throne, though such resistance might result in removing his high-ranking statesmen (sometimes at the cost of life as well as political office).

Moreover Taj holds her father responsible for destroying the old Persian aristocracy, a fact which the nobility of the Constitutional period tended to exaggerate as the root cause of the Revolution. She adds astutely, "He must have read the history of the French Revolution several times." By this enigmatic reference Taj no doubt had in mind Louis XIV, the ruler often held responsible for the weakening of the French aristocracy. To "ensure the independence of his throne," Naser al-Din, too, utilized "great tactics" (*politikat-e 'azim*) to weaken the entrenched nobility and replace it with "base, ignorant men." Given Naser al-Din's keen interest in European history and the biographies of his European counterparts, it is likely that he was inspired by the deeds of the French monarch, as well as by those of Tsar Peter the Great and Frederick the Great of Prussia. By 1904 there was even a published Persian translation of Voltaire's *Siècle de Louis XIV*, which may have served as Taj's source.

Having the model of a French benevolent dictator in mind, Taj is charitable to her father's memory when she suggests that on the occasion of his jubilee he intended to "emancipate" his subjects, establish a "firm constitutional basis," and even put Amin al-Soltan on trial in the "national parliament" and execute him for his misdeeds. By virtue of his lifelong struggle for absolute power, what he called "independent monarchy" (*saltanat-e mostaqella*), it is possible to conceive that Amin al-Soltan, sooner or later, might have faced the danger of being dismissed by Naser al-Din Shah. But it is highly unlikely that such an event would have come about through the granting of a constitution and convening of a parliament under Naser al-Din Shah. All the historical evidence—suppression of liberal reformist dissent, numerous instances of royal sabotage of any effort to convene even a semi-independent governmental consultative council, the shah's life-long suspicion of liberal Western ideas—points to the opposite.

Ever since the 1880s Naser al-Din's political outlook and conduct had become decidedly autocratic, well beyond the traditional Persian concept of a just ruler. Like his neighboring monarchs, Sultan 'Abd al-Hamid II of the Ottoman Empire (r. 1876–1909) and Tsar Alexander III of Russia (r. 1881–1894), Naser al-Din nurtured paranoic fears of subversion and revolutionary conspiracy among his subjects. If any evidence was needed, the widespread urban riots during the Régie protest of 1891–92 were sufficient to make him more suspicious of all liberal-modernist trends, their advocates, and their supposed foreign backers. The growing audience among the Persian intelligentsia for the criticism voiced by religio-political activists such as Jamal al-Din Afghani, then living in Istanbul, and Mirza Malkom Khan (d. 1910), the exiled veteran diplomat and editor of the journal *Qanun* (constitution) in London, justified such fears.

During the Régie protest a widespread popular movement headed by an informal coalition of merchants, political activists of various shades, and high-ranking ulama threatened to bring the Qajar regime to its knees. After some resistance the shah was forced to repeal the highly unpopular concession recently awarded to the British Régie company granting it a monopoly to purchase, sell, and export tobacco throughout Iran. Tobacco was a commodity of great importance to the Persian economy of the time and an item of universal usage among the populace. The indigenous merchant community, who along with tobacco producers and retailers engaged in the export of tobacco, considered the foreign concession a serious threat to their traditional economic independence. The support of the ulama, the old allies of the bazaar, proved to be crucial, for it transformed the economic dispute into a widespread popular protest. At the same time, the harem was not entirely insensitive to the political events that were in progress beyond its thick walls. During the Régie protest, which Taj mentions in passing, the royal women fully complied with the ban that was placed on the use of tobacco by the celebrated Shi'ite leader, Mirza Hasan Shirazi. This great sacrifice—for nearly all women of high class were water pipe addicts—was noticed by the shah with grave misgiving. Anis al-Dawla told the shah that she had enforced the ban in the harem on the same religious grounds that legitimized her marriage to the shah.

In the years that followed the Régie protest the shah, whose authority was seriously challenged by so popular a movement, resorted further to a police apparatus which under his favorite son, Kamran Mirza, had became more efficient and therefore more oppressive. Taj's efforts to put all the blame on the shoulders of her brother's henchmen notwithstanding, Mirza Reza Kermani, the shah's assassin, was actually a victim of Kamran Mirza's military police. Sharpening the edge of popular discontent was the random persecution of political dissidents, many of them of Babi persuasion. They were sympathizers with a messianic religion that had survived decades of pressure to represent one of the few avenues of dissent against the political and religious authorities. Likewise, the images of the libertine Qajar court—corrupt and crafty ministers amassing private fortunes, foreign concessionaires robbing the nation of its resources—though sometimes exaggerated beyond proportion, reduced the old

Shirin Khanom posing proudly with her water-pipe *(qalyan)*, characterizing women's fondness for smoking, which made tobacco a critical commodity in the Persian market. The wife of Aqa Sayyid Mohammad Hosayn of Isfahan, Shirin had a dignified yet glamorous demeanor that denoted a certain refinement in the *andarun*s of the high-ranking ulama. The lace gloves must have been a recent European addition to her colorful ensemble.

prominence of kings as the defenders of the faith and protectors of the land in the eyes of the public. Such images no doubt helped undermine the more positive aspects of Naser al-Din's rule: his able, if not always effective, conduct of foreign policy, and his remarkable command of intricate details of his administration, a command which frequently obscured in his view the urgency of addressing the broader and more essential questions. His political perspective remained fundamentally conservative while his patience with advocates of justice, the constitution, and political reforms grew shorter.

Taj's assessment of her father's political conduct reflects something of an inner struggle. Though she is critical of his government as a whole, her loyalty to his memory remains largely intact. Not surprisingly, she holds Amin al-Soltan, the arch villain in her eyes, responsible for every evil. The conspiratorial motives that she attributes to the premier in the shah's assassination is one of many speculative scenarios that were then in vogue. Placing Amin al-Soltan at the center of the conspiracy, however, raises more questions about the motives and circumstances of the assassination than it answers, particularly as Taj imputes acquiescence, even collusion, to Khanom Bashi, the shah's favorite and, as Taj puts it, "the real king of Persia" at the time.

Apparently relying on Anis al-Dawla's recollections, Taj alludes mostly to circumstantial evidence which may have been colored by Anis's misgivings and her grudge against Amin al-Soltan. In Taj's view the secret war between the premier and Kamran Mirza; Amin al-Soltan's rapport with Khanom Bashi and his efforts to use Khanom Bashi to counterbalance his rivals and outwit the shah; the assassin's possible contact with the premier to deliver a message from his spiritual master and political instigator, Jamal al-Din

Afghani; and even the rumors regarding the shah's imminent assassination on the eve of his jubilee are evidence of Amin al-Soltan's involvement. Whatever the accuracy of these claims, Taj traces the chief motive for the conspiracy to the highly unlikely wishes of the shah to rid himself of Amin al-Soltan and create a constitutional regime. Although in the past Naser al-Din abruptly dismissed and destroyed his ministers or, on the other hand, occasionally allowed brief periods of administrative liberalization, it is very unlikely that he wished to tolerate a constitutional regime. Even more remote was the possibility that Amin al-Soltan would initiate, or even condone, an assassination against his master, even if he was afraid for his own security.

Taj does well not to exaggerate in her speculations, given that her evidence is barely supported by any other credible source. Writing in the aftermath of the Constitutional Revolution, Taj's portrayal of Amin al-Soltan as the sole agent of deceit and corruption was no doubt influenced by the ex-premier's battered image during the Revolution, when, reappearing in a liberal guise, he tried to make a political comeback in 1907—a fatal attempt that ended with his assassination in front of the Majles at the hand of a revolutionary terrorist. Still, one should not dismiss Taj's sympathetic depiction of Naser al-Din as sheer fantasy. Even allowing for posthumous embellishments, the self-assessment she has attributed to the shah on the eve of his assassination has an element of truth. Naser al-Din, indeed, viewed his rule with a certain degree of self-righteous complacency, even as he viewed his end with a curious touch of fatalism.

In Taj's idealization of her father's liberal proclivities we can see a post-revolutionary nostalgia for Naser al-Din's period and personality, which is best symbolized by his posthumous title, the Martyr Shah *(shah-e shahid)*. The overall state of disorder and social upheaval that followed on the heels of the Revolution, aggravated soon after by the outbreak of World War I, the occupation of Iranian provinces, and the threat of partitioning of the country, enhanced the age of Naser al-Din in the minds of many nobles and commoners as an era of stability and relative affluence. In the early years of Mozaffar al-Din Shah's reign this image was skillfully promoted by Amin al-Soltan, who even commissioned theatrical eulogies to Naser al-Din Shah to be performed as a prelude to the Shi'ite passion play *(ta'ziya).* By stressing continuity in the Qajar monarchy, Amin al-Soltan took aim at political radicals, while continuing to consolidate his premiership in the face of his many rivals. Taj is thus correct in her portrayal of Amin al-Soltan as the mover and shaker of Qajar politics. From the late 1880s to the early 1900s he enjoyed as much success in making himself indispensable to Naser al-Din and Mozaffar al-Din in their dealings with foreign powers as he did in convincing the foreign powers of his political wisdom and skill.

Taj is not as charitable toward her brother, Mozaffar al-Din Shah. He was the monarch who granted what came to be known as the Constitutional Decree of 1906, albeit from a position of weakness and shortly before his death from a lingering illness. She holds him responsible for the weakening of the monarchy and for allowing the inept and corrupt officialdom to dominate the government. "The more ridiculous the man, the more warmly he was received," Taj recalls; "the more contemptible, the more attention he got." Unquestionably, Taj fully shared her father's view of Mozaffar al-Din as being "unworthy of the crown." The remarkable depiction of her first encounter with the new shah shortly after Naser al-Din's assassination and the noticeable changes in the court illustrates Taj's powers of observation. The scene of the shah, dressed in ordinary clothes, sitting unassumingly on a chair in

Mirza 'Ali Asghar Khan Amin al-Soltan, Atabak-e A'zam (Grand Atabak), posing for the camera during his European tour in early 1907. In his mid-forties, the Qajar politician seemed to have his eyes set on the office of the premiership, this time under a Constitutional regime. His sagacious appearance and his European outfit, however, belie his claims that this kingpin of the Qajar court was ever converted to liberal politics. His confident demeanor reflects the court politics of a bygone age rather than those of the Constitutional Majles.

the open air with his inner household gathered around him, "utterly unmindful of royal protocol," watching a performance by a band of vulgar female musicians, was a terrible shock to Taj's sensitive mind. With literary flourish she compares her brother's clumsy banality to her late father's grandeur. This curious scene was further imprinted in Taj's mind by the memory of the candle, held by a careless maid above the shah's shoulder, that dripped hot wax on his sleeve and therefrom onto Taj's hand. Mozaffar al-Din's comment, meanwhile, that his father was a mighty king but "his affairs were in disarray," seemed particularly ironic. The call to dinner, in the most vulgar language, turned the grotesque into the ridiculous.

Yet Taj barely appreciates the opportunities created in Mozaffar-al Din's era in education, the press, and contact with the outside world as opposed to her father's repressive reign when liberal trends, indigenous or not, were liable to severe persecution. She overlooks the fact that had it not been for Mozaffar al-Din's leniency, the early course of the Constitutional Revolution would have been much bloodier; such, indeed, proved to be the case under his successor, Mohammad 'Ali Shah. Taj's criticism of Mozaffar al-Din's lax rule reflects the nobility's complaint against their impoverishment and the weakening of their social status in the face of public resentment. She does not, however, condemn altogether the ensuing Revolution.

Predictably, Taj's feelings toward the Constitutional Revolution remained mixed. While she resented the loss of her privileges, she could not, rationally and emotionally, ignore the root causes of the Revolution or dismiss its objectives. Poverty and discontent had reached such a stage during her father's reign, Taj observed, that the "thunderous clamor of

Exhausted and in poor health, Mozaffar al-Din Shah in this 1902 portrait stands in marked contrast to his father's often fastidious appearance. With his drooping mustache, unbuttoned frock coat, and listless eyes, Mozaffar al-Din does not inspire awe. One can well picture the wax dripping on his sleeve, as Taj reports in her acerbic depiction of her brother. The sword-wielding lions holding the Kayanid crown on the shah's sheepskin fez and standing above the inscription of his name represent the only emblems of majesty in his demeanor.

the multitudes" was about to shake the pillars of the monarchy. She laments more for her fatherland than for her father since she, too, as the daughter of the shah, was a victim of a system that turned her and other women of the harem into instruments in the hands of the ruling elite, legitimizing their tyrannical excesses. "We unfortunate ones were tools in their hands," she recalled, "weapons that nature ultimately turned against ourselves." Taj knew that her relatives—the pronoun "we" in her collective consciousness—would condemn her openness and her criticism of Qajar rule, a fact that, incidentally, indicated her wishes to publicize her memoirs. She was even daring enough to cite 'Abbas Mirza, the patriarch of her royal house, in his letter (c. 1833) to Mohammad Khan Amir Nezam Zangena in which he decried the Qajars' inherent opportunism and abuse of loyalty. This charge was reiterated in 'Abbas Mirza's other correspondence, constituting his political testimony, toward the end of his short life. Taj feels that although she belongs to the Qajar family, it is her conscience and her "Persianness" *(Iraniyat)* that should guide her in rendering an uninhibited history of her family. "O my homeland! Is it possible to overlook thy rights out of fear for one man? No, never! Thy love has been etched in my heart as indelibly as the blemishes of thy enemies and destroyers on this page." Such an eruption of patriotic sentiment is true to the spirit of the Constitutional Revolution, which moved a princess like Taj away from a pure, and often arrogant, family "us" to a new plane of national identity and loyalty. A few members of her family and class—including the dependent bureaucrats and the court elite—shared Taj's newly acquired nationalistic "us," among them the future premier, Mohammad Mosaddeq, and the leader of the Social Democratic Party, Solayman Mirza Eskandari. The majority of the Qajars, however, preferred to cling to their rapidly fading aristocratic glory through land ownership or social prestige, only to be overshadowed by the new middle class that emerged during the Pahlavi era.

It is an injustice to the aims of the Revolution of 1906–1911 if we label it as merely "constitutional." As the example of Taj demonstrates, the Constitutional Revolution was a widespread movement of protest, broad enough to inspire not only the educated folk but commoners as well against the political system that for long had resisted even limited popular participation. Like other modern revolutions, the Persian Constitutional movement not only objected to the absence of civil and judicial institutions, but also to the endemic material backwardness, religious conservatism, and economic difficulties that by the early part of the twentieth century had reached a new point of crisis. Though at its center lay a critique of arbitrary rule for which it sought, sometimes naively, the panacea of "constitutionalism," the Revolution was also shaped by the other great ideals of modern times: patriotism and individual liberty.

Championed by indigenous activists, many of them of Babi background, and by Western-style intellectuals, the Constitutional Revolution was led by an alliance of enlightened clergy who were lionized by the lower ranks, merchants who were supported by the guilds of the bazaar, and some younger members of the nobility who were inspired by the ideals of European constitutionalism. The Revolution's broad base thus collided with the privileges of the monarchy, the conservative ulama, the nobility, and above all the encroaching imperial powers. Of lasting consequences, the Revolution brought Iran onto the threshold of modernity while allowing her to carry along a large bundle of her old beliefs, institutions, and social divisions. Though like any other revolution it brought to the political stage a new class of actors, mostly from the emerging bourgeoisie, and though it made possible greater political participation by ordinary people, it did not eradicate the old institutions entirely. While it helped weaken the old order's twin pillars—the Qajar monarchy and the Shi'ite clerical establishment—it did not remove the nobility. By 1909 the Qajar monarchy and its immediate dependents were all but ruined and the conservative religious establishment was severely degraded, losing its popular base and its prestige. Yet at least in part the landed nobility and bureaucratic elite managed to keep a safe enough distance from the *ancien régime* to allow them to survive and even thrive in the post-Revolutionary days.

By 1908 the newly elected National Consultative Assembly *(majles-e shura-ye melli)* was able to draw up a constitution which, in spite of its weaknesses, restricted the shah's arbitrary rule perhaps for the first time in Persian history. It gave legislative power to the Majles, enshrined a division of power among the legislature, the executive, and the judiciary, and held the government responsible to the Majles. The Majles and the constitutionalism it represented were thus held in popular esteem as the embodiment of national assertiveness against foreign domination, despotism, and economic backwardness.

But not everyone was in favor of the Constitutionalists. Mohammad 'Ali Shah, who came to the throne in 1907, was as deeply resentful of the Majles and the Constitution as he was suspicious of the legislature's radical support among secret and semi-secret societies. He viewed the Majles and the Constitutionalists as personal enemies of his royal family and Qajar heritage. With the blessing and backing of tsarist Russia, the shah launched the coup of July, 1908, bombarded the Majles building, executed some of its most ardent advocates, and suspended the Constitution. The ensuing civil war, which was triggered by the royalists' attempts to extinguish traces of Constitutionalism in the provinces, ended in July 1909 in victory for the Revolution and the forced abdication of Mohammad 'Ali Shah, who was succeeded by his minor son, Ahmad Shah. Hence, the convening of the Second Majles was a turning point. The term "revolution" *(enqelab)* came to denote, for the first time, not only the fall of "despotism" and its reactionary Shi'ite ally, but also the victory of secular values and institutions of the modern world over the time-honored traditions of the Islamic past. But this was only a partial triumph for the Revolution. In the years leading to World War I the interventions of the imperial powers increasingly preoccupied the Constitutionalists and forced them to compromise against their best judgment in what amounted to a further weakening of the central authority and another phase of instability and chaos in the country.

Taj was writing in an environment where even the staunchest supporters of the Revolution were frustrated by its outcome and began to scrutinize the causes of its setbacks and failures.

In spite of his bleak record, Taj is silent about Mohammad 'Ali Shah, the villain of the Constitutional Revolution who stood for the absolutist regime that she repeatedly condemns in her pages. In part this was probably because, even by 1914, Mohammad 'Ali's fate had not been settled. Two years after his forced abdication in 1911, he had made an unsuccessful bid to regain the throne, wreaking much havoc and causing trouble for the Constitutionalist regime. Meanwhile his brother, Salar al-Dawla, embarked on another counter-revolutionary campaign in northwestern Iran. Upon the Constitutionalists' marching into Tehran in 1909, the house of Taj's staunchly royalist husband, Shaja' al-Saltana, was bombarded and his belongings looted. Presumably in the employ of Mohammad 'Ali Shah, he escaped to Russia to join the deposed shah's anti-revolutionary army. This separation may well have dealt the final blow to Taj's already shattered marriage. Though we know little about the circumstances of their divorce, it is conceivable that the Revolution added an ideological dimension to their parting of ways. Taj may have thought, as many among her cohorts did, that the chances of a counter-revolution succeeding were not yet altogether lost— an eventuality that she might even have hoped for. The newly enthroned monarch Ahmad Shah was still a minor and the Constitutionalist government in total disarray, while tsarist Russia, now in alliance with Britain for the first time since the Napoleonic wars, lost no opportunity to undermine the Revolution and moved to occupy the northern provinces of Iran.

Unlike some members of the nobility, however, Taj was realistic not to entertain any conspiratorial views of the Revolution. She was optimistic, even romantically sanguine, about the possibility of a change for the better. Her proposed economic program, which she defines as "public conservatism," reflected something of this optimism. She advocated public investment in trade and manufacturing to meet domestic needs, mining and oil exploration for export, agricultural development, road and transport expansion, and irrigation and forestry. She even proposed a model for land distribution, believing that in Iran, as in California, arid land should be given for free to people for cultivation.

Taj's agenda for economic independence reflects the debates in Constitutionalist circles of the time. These debates resonated later in such economic surveys as Mohammad 'Ali Jamalzadeh's *Ganj-e Shaygan* (The Kingly Treasure), published in 1916 as part of the debate on the approach to economic development by the expatriate Persian journal *Kaveh*, which was published during the War years in Berlin. The economic reforms of the early Reza Shah era and after were deeply influenced by such debates. Even as early as the

Mohammad 'Ali Shah Qajar in 1907, on the occasion of his coronation. The young shah's frozen facade hints at his difficulty in sustaining the implements of his royal authority: an overweight Kayanid crown and a disproportionately large ceremonial sword. His precariousness of balance is further accentuated by his position at the edge of a stool instead of on the Peacock Throne. His fierce demeanor betrays a nature little friendly to constitutionalism.

Second Majles (1909–1911), the radical wing of the Constitutionalist camp had begun to recognize the importance of the
economy and economic independence for building an effective government free from domestic tyranny and imperial
intervention.

In this regard, Taj's reference to oil exploration is
particularly remarkable and should be seen as one of the
earliest expressions of concern over British control of the
nascent oil industry in southwestern Iran less than a decade
after its inception. "I would seize the rights to the Bakhtiyari
oil fields [in Khuzestan] which generate tremendous annual
profits," Taj declares, "not leave them to the British." In 1908
the British-owned, Anglo-Persian Oil Company (the first in
the Middle East and ancestor to the present British
Petroleum) had acquired for a trifle the rights to exploration
and export of petroleum in southwestern Iran from an
Australian explorer and engineer who was first granted a
concession by the Persian government in 1901. By 1909 the
newly formed APOC considered the Persian oil resources
promising enough to invest seriously. By 1915 Persian oil, the
first to be struck in the Middle East, became the principal
source of fuel for the Royal Navy and soon thereafter for the
growing motorcar market. The pathetic royalty paid to the
Persian government must have raised in the mind of Taj and
her like-minded compatriots, who witnessed the growing
British presence in the south, the same questions that in the
early 1940s and 50s troubled many Persian nationalists. It is
worth noting that Mohammad Mosaddeq, the Iranian premier
and leader of the movement for oil nationalization, belonged
to the same generation as Taj. Born in 1882, he was a member
of the Qajar nobility, aspired to the same reformist goals of
the Revolution as did Taj, and like her witnessed its undoing
which eventually led to the collapse of the Qajar throne and

the rise of Reza Shah in 1925. Unlike the ailing royalty of the late Qajar period, however, Mosaddeq and statesmen of his bureaucratic background were saved from the revolutionary storm primarily because of their administrative skills, their European education, their political versatility, and their undisturbed affluence.

Taj was not an advocate of economic or cultural isolationism. This was in contrast to some conservatives in her generation, particularly among the ulama, who having lost to modernists began to nurse a grudging rejection of Western modernity. Nor did she resort to dismal conspiratorial theories to explain away the political ills of her time and the failure of the attempted remedies. On the other hand, the absence of references to the European imperial presence in Taj's memoirs (except for the aforementioned reference to oil exploration) at a time when their intrusions were most conspicuous is noteworthy. It is true that by 1914 the ramifications of the secret Anglo-Russian pact of 1907, which determined the "zone of influence" for each power in southern and northern Iran, were not yet widely known to the Persian public. Its ominous implications became fully apparent after the treaty of 1915 and in the course of the War when Iran was virtually occupied by Russian and Turkish forces in the north and the northwest, and by a proxy British force in the south. Yet even from 1911 diplomatic intervention by the British and flagrant military occupation by the Russians were too apparent to be missed by any Persian patriot.

Taj must have witnessed not only the early British support for the Constitutionalists but the Russian opposition to them. By 1908 it was the Persian "Cossack" regiments which, under their Russian command and with the support of the tsar, brought about Mohammad 'Ali Shah's coup, bombarded the

Majles, and supported the royalists during the "Minor Tyranny." In 1909, wary of the Tabriz Constitutional resistance, the Russian forces crossed the border and marched into the city on the pretext of protecting their citizens and proteges. Soon after, in 1911, the joint Anglo-Russian ultimatum demanding that Iran expel Morgan Shuster, the celebrated American financial consultant to the Constitutional government, led to the closure of the second Majles and suspension of the constitution for the second time. In Tabriz scores of Constitutionalists were executed by the Russian occupying forces and their domestic allies, while the deposed Mohammad 'Ali Shah, supported by Russia, made a sortie through the Russian territory deep into eastern Iran. These events perpetuated political instability in the center as successions of short-lived governments wrangled with the parliament. The ill effects of the Great War and the near partitioning of Iran by occupying forces were further exacerbated by famine and epidemics, popular uprisings, and secessionist movements. The rise of Reza Khan to power in the coup of February, 1921 proved to be the end of this turbulent phase. It was cautiously welcomed even by some ardent supporters of the Revolution. The defunct Qajar aristocracy, though by no means representative of the entire nobility, soon detected in Reza Khan a terminator of what had remained of the Qajar monarchy. When he declared himself Reza Shah in 1925, the old royalty was all but dissipated.

REGENERATED HOPES

Of all the issues of the Constitutional Revolution, however, the one which absorbed Taj the most was women's emancipation, an issue which rapidly emerged as a social concern in the following decades. In the course of the Revolution, as in other instances of urban revolt in the past, women represented an important force of dissent, often appearing in the front line of demonstrations. Whether it was the intensity of their economic destitution which brought them out of their houses to participate in the bread riots and protest the rising prices, or whether the relative security of their *chadors* afforded them a shield against the assaults of government troops, in essence they were the most obvious candidates to protest deprivation and social oppression.

Though the Constitution denied suffrage to women, and their political demands met great resistance both inside and outside the Majles, there was a conspicuous women's presence in revolutionary demonstrations from the start. Morgan Shuster witnessed in 1911 what he called "the frequent manifestations of the influence and high purpose of the Muhammadan woman." The women's response to the rumors that the Majles would yield to Russian threats "performed the crowning act of the noble and patriotic part which thousands of their sex had been playing since Persia's *risorgimento* began." Since 1907, Shuster went on to say, Persian women had become "almost at a bound the most progressive, not to say radical, in the world."

> The women did much to keep the spirit of liberty alive. Having themselves suffered from a double form of oppression, political and social, they were the more eager to foment the great Nationalist movement for the adoption of constitutional forms of government and the inculcation of the Western political, social, commercial and ethical codes. Equally strange is the fact that this yearning by the people received the support of large numbers of the Islamic priests, a class which stood to lose much of its traditional influence and privilege by the contemplated changes.

Shuster's positive view of Persian women is backed by several accounts of their protests against royalist designs and foreign interventions, the same interventions that ended in the Anglo-Russian ultimatum of December 1911, the forced departure of Shuster, and the suspension of the Majles. The American banker and supporter of the Constitutional Revolution had seen three hundred women "with the flush of undying determination in their cheeks, clad in their plain black robes with the white nets of their veils dropped over their faces. Many held pistols under their skirts or in the folds of their sleeves. Straight to the Majlis they went, and, gathered there, demanded of the president that he admit them all. What the grave deputies of the Land of the Lion and the Sun may have thought at this strange visitation is not recorded." Shuster adds that in the president's reception hall the women "confronted him and, lest he and his colleagues should doubt their meaning, these cloistered Persian mothers, wives and daughters exhibited threateningly their revolvers, tore aside their veils, and confessed their decisions to kill their own husbands and sons, and leave behind their own dead bodies if the deputies wavered in their duty to uphold the liberty and dignity of the Persian people and nation."

With such a spirit of activism and political presence the women of the post-Constitutional era were potentially in a good position to benefit from individual freedoms and improvements in social standing, especially when the conservative ulama, the natural allies of the royalist regime, were forced into isolation. In contrast to the recent Islamic revolution when the victory of the clergy and their lay allies has proven to be a great loss for Persian women, and contrary to some recent champions of "Islamic feminism" in the West who are apologists for even the most discriminatory treatment of women, the Constitutional period did not shy away from the West and its image of the liberated woman.

Taj had no compunctions about advocating the liberal values of American, British, and French women who struggled for their political, social, and legal rights. Even more remarkable, Taj wished to travel to Europe, meet these "freedom-seeking ladies" *(khanomha-ye hoquq-talab)*, and ask them to "cast a look at the continent of Asia" and see the plight of the women there. Her dramatic portrayal of women behind elevated walls and guarded gates, bound, battered, starved, ailing, and depressed, was hardly an exaggeration. In spite of her privileged position and her affluence she viewed herself as one of these "ill-starred" women whose choices were symbolically limited to the mournful black veil in which they were buried alive, and the white shroud in which they were buried dead. With a touch of romantic melancholy Taj opts for the latter. In the seclusion of her home she aspires to the shroud as though it were "an eagerly-awaited lover"; only in it was there a ray of hope for salvation from her dark, ghastly days.

Taj thus saw herself as a genuine voice for women's social grievances and in the years following the writing of her memoirs remained an advocate for women's rights. She was one of the founding members of the Society for the Emancipation of Women (Anjoman-e Horriyat-e Nesvan), established in the late 1910s. Other women of the nobility, including Taj's sister, Eftekhar al-Saltana, were among the members. One of the earliest associations for women in Iran, it evolved from the revolutionary societies of the Constitutional period and was an heir to the diffused emancipation trends during the Revolution. European and American women's charity organizations also served as models for the Anjoman whose aims were not unlike those Taj delineated in her memoirs or those that appeared in the progressive literature and press of the post-Constitutional era.

The membership of Mary Jordan, the wife of the celebrated American Presbyterian missionary Samuel Jordan, in the Society is particularly noteworthy. During their long residence in Iran between 1898 and 1941, the Jordans played a notable part in the emergence of a modern elite by introducing elements of American education into the Persian environment. The American College established in 1876 in Tehran as a grade school for boys, and later under Samuel Jordan as the Alborz junior college (and from 1928 as a liberal arts college), stood as a testimony to the dedication of American Presbyterians to education. The Jordans were also conspicuous in the social arena, a fact vouched for by their acquaintance with Persian intellectuals and educators.

Mary Jordan's acquaintance with Persian feminists may have started as early as the 1910s when, in the aftermath of the Constitutional victory, the debate on women's rights was promoted, among others, by the American missionaries. She believed that advancement in the condition of women could only be achieved if men were alerted to its necessity. As a teacher of English in the all-male American College, she instructed her students to write: "No country rises higher than the level of the women of that country"—a truism that would have been pedestrian had it not been uttered in an environment permeated with a patriarchal ethos. Taj's remarks about American feminists hint at something of Mary Jordan's preaching.

Clara Rice, the wife of the British consul in Isfahan and an observer of the women's awakening during the Constitutional period, noted that women's political societies in various cities were under the umbrella of a central organization. She also noted that the women's newspapers *Shokufa* (Blossom) and *Zaban-e zanan* (The Tongue of the Women), both published in the late 1910s, were interested in suffragettes. "An interesting feature of these papers," she wrote, "was the way in which scraps of news concerning women in politics in England and elsewhere were got hold of, translated and inserted [in the papers]. Lady Astor excited great interest."

Taj's vision of emancipated women was inherently tied to her reformist views, particularly on education and economy. In her view, both at home and in school, progress depended on women's ability to improve their lot, advance their education, and arrive at greater social awareness. Her expressed regrets for not having brought up her four children within a sound family environment lend a realistic touch to what might have otherwise been a platitude. She draws not only on her own childhood memories but on "morals of history" to highlight her own awareness. Though she does not offer a blueprint beyond what she wrote to Bakianov in 1908, it is evident that she had thought about emancipation beyond its rhetoric, and in realistic terms. Women's segregation, symbolized by a facial and a mental veil, she argues, lies at the very heart of socioeconomic backwardness for the urban poor as well as for the affluent classes. She correctly identifies veiling as an urban phenomenon whose abolition would release a massive potential work force. Reducing the economic pressure on the male breadwinners, in turn, would contribute to the economic prosperity of the family and the society.

Discussing the correlation between Iran's lack of material progress and women's subjection to facial veiling, Taj describes the hypothetical case of an affluent woman and her husband, which is unmistakably modeled after a realistic understanding of her own troubled economic life. The husband of the imaginary woman in Taj's example is a minister from the class of notables (*a'yan*) and earns a salary of three hundred *tuman*s per month and a revenue of seven hundred from his estate. For a decent harem for his wife, Taj argues, this man has to maintain a lavish household with servants, butlers, and other attendants. She not only needs a chambermaid, a page boy, a servant, and a nanny, but also hired female singers and musicians. Like Taj this typical affluent wife spends money on luxuries. The European moiré dresses that she wears and the parties she frequently throws are but a few of her expenditures. The husband, like Taj's, has married his wife because she is "the daughter of such and such military commander or shah" and carries a large dowry. Since he does not love his wife, he has to spend even more money to escape his unhappy marriage. He needs a mistress, a garden in the suburbs, expensive liquor, a confidant, and a private attendant. Lonesome and bored, the wife, too, resorts to numerous female companions who advise her to commission costly charms (provided by Jewish physicians, as Taj says) to rekindle her husband's extinguished love. In frustration she breaks the chinaware and the furniture whenever her husband is late coming home. When the expenses add up, the husband's income is not enough for the upkeep of the unhappy family. Thus the man, a *saltana*, a *dawla*, or a *molk* (suffixes for titles given to the nobility) will be encouraged to embezzle, extort, sell out his country, and receive bribes, collecting bundles of cash in the middle of the night, as Taj graphically describes, only to end up utterly disgraced, inwardly besmirched, and outwardly desperate.

Taj attributes all these wasteful misfortunes to the evils of arranged but loveless unions dominated by concerns other than the wishes of the marrying couple. In the account penned in 1908, six years before the writing of her memoirs, the fate of the imaginary couple demonstrates Taj's effort to objectify beyond any sentimentality her own plight as an example of the women of her class. She sees a clear link between her own misfortunes and those of her country, a tangible connection that came to prominence at the height of the revolutionary civil war, the era of "Minor Tyranny" (1908–1909), that witnessed Constitutionalists fighting against the royalist forces and the nobility of which Taj was herself a member. The ascendancy of the revolutionaries over the royalists seemed to reaffirm her personal emancipation from the old social order.

Taj's advocacy of women participating in the work force was the realistic echo of her age. The growth of urbanization in Iran in the early twentieth century, as in the rest of the Middle East, made such a proposition pronounceable—if not yet tenable—for the first time. Equally drastic, and innately related to the women's handicap, was Taj's belief that removal of the veil, education, and freedom of marital choice would undermine the precepts and habits of a male-dominated culture, which she condemns as "the Persian character" (*akhlaq-e Irani*). No doubt, the popular stigmatization of "the Persian character" rampant in the literature of the period prompted Taj to blame the Persians for being ignorant, inconsistent, and shallow; such portrayals were typical of the self-loathing of the intelligentsia in the aftermath of the Revolution. The forlorn spirit in the poetry of 'Aref, and later 'Eshqi, was one aspect of this sense of failure. Admiration for Morier's *Hajji Baba*, which was first published in Persian translation in 1886 but became more accessible around 1905, was another. A cynicism familiar to all revolutionary downturns began to prevail, especially when the new elite that came on the scene after the Revolution proved to be ineffective at restoring peace and prosperity.

Taj's emphasis on reforming social morality, in contrast to the prevalent fixation with the law (*qanun*), nevertheless reflects her concern with the cultural dimensions of change.

She is careful not to attack the ulama and what they represented (at least in the available incomplete version of her
memoirs) perhaps for fear that there would be reprisals if her
memoirs were published. Yet her modernist views on veiling,
education, and marriage made little secret of where she stood
on religion. Such bold views were not expressed in a void.
After the 1909 victory of the Constitutionalists, the ulama,
whether supporters or opponents of the Revolution, began to
lose their political relevance and with it their social status.
Whereas the execution of Shaykh Fazlollah Nuri, the chief
ally of the royalists among the clergy, symbolized a growing
anti-clerical tendency, the assassination of the celebrated
leader of the Constitutional movement, Sayyed 'Abdollah
Behbahani, signaled the ulama's political insolvency. A conspicuous rise in secular modernism after 1909, first in
education and public behavior, then in legislation and the
judiciary, pushed most of the ulama back to the privacy of
their seminaries where they grudgingly witnessed the disman-
tling of their constituency under Reza Shah.

Taj's call for women's rights thus anticipated a decade of
women's activism that began in earnest in the 1910s and
culminated in the 1920s. Like most other early reforms under
Reza Shah women's emancipation in the 1930s, too, became a
non-political endeavor left over from the Constitutional
period. That it was implemented by the state at least partly
deprived it of its earlier sociocultural vigor. When Taj was
writing her memoirs, the press of the time, including some
women's journals, began to advocate with diminishing
hesitancy women's education, legal rights, and even unveiling,
a call echoed in the romanticism of poets such as 'Aref, Iraj
and 'Eshqi. However, the perception of sensuality that was
associated with the image of the unveiled or even thinly-veiled

woman did not subside, particularly since freedom in the post-Constitutional period allowed for greater sexual indulgence.

Taj's perceived religious affiliation may reflect something of this popular image. As she tells us, her mother accused her of being a Babi when she heard Taj's atheistic pronouncements. Whatever her religious sentiments, by the time she was writing her memoirs, Taj seems to have been experiencing a crisis of faith. With some trepidation she had parted with the folk religion of her mother and nanny and opted for her mentor's irreligiosity. But her new convictions did not bring her spiritual satisfaction. "I suffered a loss for having knowledge," she declares with nostalgia for her old beliefs. "Lacking fear of anything and freed from any particular beliefs," she was transported to a hedonistic plane of living where "there was nothing in life I considered bad."

The remorse in the closing passages of Taj's memoirs, however, is a reaction to the excesses of her earlier carefree lifestyle. She felt that she had turned "simple and stupid," because her belief in a life of pleasure had allowed others to use her for advancement, money, or gratification. A "fallen" woman in search of redemption, Taj's personal crisis and her political convictions ultimately converged in a sense of womanhood. Shaped by daunting memories of the harem, her broken marriage, and her precarious independence, she passionately recounts her awareness in a romantic idealism reflective of her age. The tormented maiden of the royal harem who was innocently traded off to embark on a disastrous marriage was subsequently driven into a fallen life of sensuality and extravagance, only to be saved by the wisdom of social concern and gender affinity. Taj's image of her own life, complete with all the pastoral and poetic nuances, seems to be a living testimony to such a romantic drama.

It was as though in her own simple way she drew on the romantic themes of vice and virtue, agony and hope, repentance and destiny, to express her condition. The inspiration for such drama was not boorishly borrowed from Baudelaire or Byron, nor were her social sensibilities derived from *Émile* or *Les Misérables*. There was something genuine in her words which echoed her personal experience and her culture's indigenous ethos. On her journey to Tabriz, when Taj passed through the villages along the way, she saw unveiled peasant women working side by side with the men. The "honor and pride" that she detected in their simple pastoral lives, parity in wealth, choice in marriage, joint labor, care, intimacy, sincerity and happiness were no doubt idealizations, in a truly romantic fashion, of the reality of a harsh and insecure life. But she detected an advantage in the rural life over the urban, since it cast off the veil and all its social values, a moral conclusion that well justified her idealism.

In another instance, escaping the harrowing ravages of a cholera epidemic around 1904, she stayed with her family in the pilgrimage town of Qom. There, in the town cemetery, she repeatedly witnessed macabre scenes of death and burial which she describes graphically. The encounter with death, another focus of romanticism, invoked in Taj an emotional ordeal. "Seeing the corpses—the way all of us would end up—was a great lesson for me," Taj recalled, "and held in check my youthful pride, my vivacity and self-centeredness." Here, too, the morbid scenes remind Taj of the romantic image of being "tied to the strings of fate." But they also remind her of the moving poem by the celebrated thirteenth-century Persian poet and moralist, Sa'di, which she cites in full. The eternal battle of human greed and rebellion against compassion and a good name—an enduring theme in Persian literature—was drawn upon by Taj to highlight her own agony, her past mistakes, her remorse, and her regenerated hopes.

> The world has turned much, and more will it turn—
> The wise man sets not his heart upon it.
> You, strong of hand, put forth your power now
> Before you are forever rendered helpless.

Commitment to change the lot of her fellow womenfolk, and her compatriots at large, sums up Taj's attitude toward life. Inspired by revolutionary ideals, she moved away from the opulence and vanity of a privileged life to feel affinity with ordinary people, but she did not become remote enough to deny her own identity. A unique product of late-Qajar society, Taj was able to absorb much of modernity without losing sight of her cultural past. Even at the turn of the twentieth century the bond with her literary and cultural heritage was remarkably strong. The West, no doubt, had challenged some of those values and nullified others altogether; but the sense of Taj's "Persianness" still remained largely intact. Defying the stereotypes of the Qajar era as an age of "decline," Taj's endeavor scores high marks in demonstrating the intellectual refinement of her generation as well as displaying in earnest its agonizing failures and renewed hopes.

That Taj's death in 1936 occurred in obscurity testifies to her unhappy end. Both Sayf Azad, who as the editor of *Divan-e 'Aref-e Qazvini* wrote a short biography of Taj, and Badr al-Moluk Bamdad, who wrote about Taj in her account of women's emancipation in Iran, emphasized Taj's agony, illness, financial hardship, and forced separation from her daughters. Bedridden and "suffering intense and almost unbearable pain" from an untold disease, she died, as Bamdad observed with a touch of sanctimony, "thanking God and trusting that this penance for

her sins in the lower world would save her in the world above."
Sayf Azad is no less sanctimonious: "After going through days of
darkness and misery she inclined toward virtue and
righteousness. She was remorseful and in pain about her past
and cursed those base persons who misguided her to a wrong
path."

Even those who cared to write about Taj's fate sought in her
a repentant sinner—a potent image particularly when the subject was a woman. It is as though in her agonized end they
were trying to find reassurance for the ways of goodness, for
subdued virtue, and for the futility of rebellion.

CROWNING ANGUISH

"The blessed portrait of Princess Taj al-Saltana at the age of fifteen, rendered by the most humble Mirza Abol-Hasan Khan, the chief royal painter" (1899), depicting something of the solitary world of Taj al-Saltana early in her marriage. Despite Taj's cheerless countenance, framed by an austere scarf, and her stiff pose in a starched skirt, this early portrayal of a woman as the subject of a painting owed something to the portraits of European ladies in their drawing rooms. The harmony between literary interests and feminine delicacy—symbolized by one hand clumsily resting on a set of books and another clutching a handkerchief—seems to spring rather from Taj's imagination than the artist's mediocre craftsmanship. There is a distinct difference between the forlorn Taj of this painting and the liberated Taj of the post-Constitutional period. The artist (not to be mistaken with his celebrated namesake Abol-Hasan Sani' al-Molk) was active at the turn of the twentieth century.

It was Thursday evening, the last day of Rabi' I, 7 Aquarius 1332 [27 February 1914]. The afternoon was dark and overcast, gloomy as my reveries. Sitting in a half-lit room, I was busily occupied in painting. Outside it was snowing heavily, and no sound was heard except the whiffling of the wind. A despondent silence and stagnation, heightened by the dim red glow radiating from the heater, enveloped me.

I was utterly oblivious to the melancholic youth who sat behind in an armchair, watching with an indulgent eye my clumsy and haphazard brush strokes on the young woman's face that I was painting. From time to time he heaved a doleful sigh. Finally he said, "You work too hard and tax your brain too much. It would be well for you to rest a little. The light, too, isn't very good, and it's rather difficult to paint right now."

Startled by his totally unexpected voice—for I had thought I was alone—I twitched involuntarily and cried, "Ah, Solayman, were you here all this time?"

With a peculiar laugh he said, "Your agitated and chaotic state of mind makes you forget everyone present, including yourself. You are so frequently lost in thought that it causes me concern. When you feel a pensive mood coming on, it would be better if you occupied yourself with enlivening conversation, or walked outside to admire nature, or read some historical book."

With a bitter smile on my lips I let out a cry impulsively and said, "O my dear teacher and cousin! My past and present life excites both wonder and anguish, and you expect me to be interested in another's tale? Isn't the review of one's personal history the best undertaking in the world?"

Shrugging his shoulders, he said, "Ah, but I don't consider the ups and downs of individual experience as history. If your life story is truly as strange and remarkable as you say, why don't you tell it to me so that I may profit from it?"

I answered, "The story of my life is so weighty and replete with difficult situations that I couldn't finish recounting it even if I spent every hour of an entire year. Besides, it alternates so rapidly between sorrow and laughter that it's bound to perplex the listener."

With an inquiring look he said, "Well, well, surely you must be joking?" But then, quickly seeing the seriousness on my face, he forgot his facetious mood and said thoughtfully, "Madam, would you please tell me your story?"

"No," I said.

With the utmost earnestness he began pleading to hear my story. The more I refused, the further he importuned. Finally I said, "I don't have the strength to relate it to you verbally, but I do promise to write it all down." Fully gratified, he thanked me. And here I think it appropriate to describe briefly this teacher of mine and introduce him properly before I proceed to tell my story.

This young man was born on 11 Moharram 1307 [8 September 1889] and educated at the elementary school. In the year 1324 [1906], at age seventeen, he had joined the circles of poverty and mysticism. For two or three years he had observed an exacting asceticism, following the mystics and poets. Then he had enrolled in the School of Political Science.

Tiring quickly of this school, he dropped out to join the School of Fine Arts. He has been a painter for two years.

The many changes in this young man's life provide us with clues to his character—erratic of nature and with no firm purpose. As it turns out, at the age of eighteen or nineteen he had conceived a fanciful love for someone and adopted the mannerisms of the famous Don Quixote. Finally united with his illusory love, the frenzied lover had found his beloved unfaithful. After having caused him much pain, she went away at last, leaving this dear "artist" teacher of mine afflicted with the agony of separation.

But enough said about his character. Now I must say something about his appearance. He has an honest, agreeable face with large dark eyes expressive of a pensive temperament. His cheeks are sunken, his skin almost sallow, and his nose like an eagle's beak. Looking at him I am reminded of one of the histories of France in which I had read about Prince de Condé's family, whose noses were always compared to eagles' beaks. He is very gentle and calm—humble and affable toward his inferiors, and amiably disposed toward his fellow mystics. Such are my teacher's appearance and demeanor.

Now I begin the story of my life, thereby earning this strange young man's eternal gratitude. At the same time, in reviewing my past, I record both my sufferings and my good fortune and happiness.

BIRTH AND CHILDHOOD

I was born towards the end of 1301 [1884] in the royal palace. My mother belonged to the royal family, being a first cousin of my father's. When I was born, she was very young, very beautiful, and very virtuous. Profoundly given to piety and devotion, she spent all her hours praying to God, reading the scripture and reciting from it.

But this was not enough: being a good princess does not necessarily translate into being a good mother. She lacked the qualities required of motherhood. Heaven forbid if it seems that I am disavowing my mother, for whom I hold a devout reverence! No, she was not to blame. But I must reproach the traditions and ethos of a nation that barred the way toward happiness to all women and held them, wretched and unenlightened, in a world of utmost ignorance. All moral defects or evils in this country have originated and spread from the absence of education for women.

At the same time, a careful and intelligent appraisal shows us that every invention, every revolutionary discovery, and every item of commercial, political and military knowledge has originated from mothers. All those that have contributed to the world's history were raised by educated mothers and by fathers who encouraged reform, whereupon they became leaders in industry and invention, and true servants of world civilization. Similarly, great warriors, true liberators, and genuine freedom-lovers have been brought into the world and raised by capable mothers.

The people of Sparta, for example, though themselves savage and uncouth, trained their children in the art of warfare so well that they were able to preserve their independence for years and to destroy Athens, the capital of Greece. To cite an instance: on returning from battle a son said to his mother, "My sword is too short." She calmly replied, "My dear, take one step further!"

Another example: when Rome first won her independence, the Gauls attacked the Romans in a massive battle. After a while matters ended in a truce, but the Gauls demanded

A frontal view of Golestan Palace in Tehran during Taj's early childhood. The neoclassical facade, complete with baroque stuccowork and chandeliers, exhibits the European influence on the Naseri court.

hostages as a surety. Among these was a girl who was interrogated on certain "political" matters. For fear of jeopardizing Rome's independence by her answers, she bit her tongue in half and spat it out into the ruler's face. Then she jumped into the river and, with some difficulty, swam across to join her people.

Yes, it is a good mother who imparts character training; it is a knowledgeable mother who brings up illustrious children. But then again we have the mothers of today, who have plagued us with a misery and ignorance that has shattered our independence and consigned us to the depths of perdition. They have completely extinguished, from early childhood, our spirit of patriotism and our serious determination for honorable reform. Nothing have they taught us except eating, sleeping, and the despicable practice of self-gratification.

> There is a difference between him who holds his darling in
> his arms and him who sits by the door with watchful eye.
> (Sa'di)

Yes, one must know the difference between true knowledge imparted to the child and what emanates from him as a youth—behavior that he exhibits ostentatiously in imitation of people around him, having learned foolish notions and an undignified demeanor. However intelligent man may be, he can never put aside what he has learned as a child. If he tries to fit in with the crowd, he exhibits a mere facade, not his true self.

It is the mother, then, that first opens the door to happiness for her children. Unfortunately, this pathway to well-being was closed to me, and it is here that the great misfortunes of my subsequent life found their source.

A wet nurse from the middle ranks of society and two nannies, one of them a negress, were engaged for me. The nanny specifically had to be a negress, since honor and grandeur at that time were measured by ownership of creatures whom God has made no differently from others, except for the color of their skin—a distinction that in all honesty does not exist at the divine threshold. These poor people were kept in captivity and abject submission, made the instruments of their owners' greatness, and called "bond servants." They were bought and sold like so much cattle. Since my mother and I lived in the royal palace, where she was a distinguished resident of the harem, and since her father had been honored for several years with the governorships of Kerman and Baluchestan, we had many negresses and bond servants in our quarters. A female cradle-rocker, a valet, a chamberlain, and a washer-woman were also assigned to me, all from the same race.

These unhappy people have always been looked down upon and treated no differently from brutes. Their masters have relegated them to the abyss of ignorance and rendered them incapable of distinguishing "a" from "b," let alone observing the rules and protocols of civilized life. Yet theirs was the task of educating me and bringing me up. The chief eunuch, too, was of the same people, his task being to order everyone to bow in homage to the suckling baby that I was. If by chance someone was remiss in observing this duty, the chief eunuch was instructed to beat him with a cane. Such were the people under whose care and direction I was to be nurtured. Poor me! Reared by these odd tutors, I was supposed to acquire a good character.

In view of the dictates of royal protocol and requirements of space, my residence was separate and located at some dis-tance from my mother's. Twice a day, after permission had been granted, I was taken into the presence of my respected mother for an hour or so and then escorted back. Growing up by degrees, I soon began to walk. I remember nothing of my infancy. But I was an intelligent child, and I have retained vivid recollections of life after the age of five. When I was old enough to know and understand, for instance, I bore a great love for my wet nurse and nannies—above all, my black nanny. Here I find it necessary to describe this woman's physical appearance so that the reader may be acquainted with her, since she was so diligent in the refinement of my character and my upbringing.

About forty or forty-five years of age, of average height, this woman had a very dark face with large eyes. She was generally reticent, but on the few occasions that she did speak her speech was crude and harsh. This dear nanny of mine, having also brought up my mother, had risen to the rank of "Matron Nanny." Wielding a good deal of authority, she had complete control over the food and drink supplies and the cellar, and enjoyed numerous privileges. She was very affectionate to me and very formal and serious with others. I had grown so accustomed to her presence that, despite her fearsome looks and dreadful physique, if she was parted from me for a day, I cried the entire time and nothing could console me. I never left her side, and there was no remedy for being apart from her. Thus it is that, to this day, in memory of my beloved nanny, I am averse to fair-skinned people while having a special regard for tawnier faces.

The love between Matron Nanny and me had grown so deep that I shied away from my dearly-revered mother completely. If she tried to hold me in her arms and kiss me, I screamed and ran at once to the refuge of my nanny's arms. Her pockets and her dark, veined hands were a constant source of curiosity, and she always had something to give me, such as a piece of my favorite confection. I was keen to speak in her accent and follow her mannerisms and habits. Even today, after all these years, when I come across some relation of my beloved nanny's, I am overcome with joy and can talk to him very clearly and fluently in his dialect. This affection for my black nanny has forged an enduring spiritual and emotional bond between me and her relations.

My teacher! Do not be surprised if I tell you all about my childhood behavior and character. I promised you a complete biography; therefore I am obliged to omit no detail and write down everything. How I wish I could have felt the same tenderness for my venerable mother that I did for my nanny, a tenderness I am trying to describe here! Then I could tell you about her, rather than about an unimportant black woman. But alas, wrong-headed thinking and artificiality conspired with pomposity and unnecessary pandering to turn the childhood sweetness of maternal love into a bitter taste in my mouth, and kept me away from my worshipful mother's arms. I can do nothing but set down the truth as it is for you.

An enduring concern which always causes me regret is the issue of breast-feeding. Why should a mother not breast-feed her children and nurture them in her tender, loving bosom? Why must she drive them away and abandon them to a stranger's arms? Hiring a wet nurse for the child leads to its repugnance and aversion toward the mother, just as the child appears unimportant and unworthy of consideration in the mother's eyes. The simplicity of affection is thus distorted into an improper ceremoniousness. So it was that I, poor thing, found myself excluded from the glow of my mother's love and treated with the strictest formality. This is an important consideration for the refinement of children's characters and their future.

Take me, for example. I have four children, all of whom are fully grown. Although I made every effort to educate all four, each has his own character. When I ponder the issue, I see that their characters are replicas of their wet nurses'; they certainly do not take after me in any way, and I find that their wet nurses live on in them. Had I breast-fed and raised them myself, had that natural affection been coupled with maternal love, I never would have abandoned them during their childhood; nor would I have separated from their father, albeit I suffered a thousand torments and was afflicted and miserable every hour of my life.

If we consider the point, a mother's first duty is to put aside self-indulgence and not separate herself from her children, thereby avoiding the ruination of both the family and the child's life. She should not prefer superficial grandeur to natural, spiritual things, and not wreck the lives of her children and herself. "Naught but what is in the jug shall ooze from it."

Every mother's first responsibility is the edification of her children. The very salvation of the world lies in character. Toward the close of the nineteenth century, there was a celebrated French scholar who had a keen understanding of the social sciences and whose writings were considered authoritative by men of learning: Monsieur Jules Simon.

At a time when orators wearied listeners with their thundering speeches in the French Parliament; when the pens of skillful writers and newspaper editors clashed like razor-edged spears; when the French nation observed this controversy like a patient perplexed by having to choose among different medicines and treatments—at this time Jules Simon was busily compiling his book of true reforms.

What was the reason for all this excitement, this bubbling of ideas? In a word, the search for genuine reform. One group believed in revising the laws of the State. Another considered it necessary to separate the religious establishment from secular authority. Some spoke of the necessity of promoting agriculture, while others pointed to the need for increasing the education budget and revamping the system from within. A group of experts, at whose forefront was the famous Jules Ferry, theorized that the prosperity and welfare of France depended on the expansion of her colonies.

In the midst of this clash of opinions what was Jules Simon saying and writing? Here is a summary from his incomparable book:

> Every patriotic reformer who seeks to eliminate existing defects in order to raise his society to the level of perfection must know that the sacred words "Freedom," "Brotherhood," "Equality," "Justice" and all the desirable influences they exercise will be beneficial and fruitful only when their foundation is solidly laid. Suppose we formulated a law that embraces every aspect of freedom for one of the peoples of the world; that we firmly incorporated liberty, in sum and substance, in every phase of their lives; that we circumscribed the authority of rulers with deputies at home and rivals abroad—what result would all this bring forth? Happiness and prosperity—provided the individual members of this nation recognized the needs of the age and were not slack in implementing the means of progress. Walking the path of selflessness, they would be guided by knowledge and action in their progress toward their goal. We can benefit from freedom, brotherhood, equality, and justice only when we inculcate nobility in our character. The experience of history, the sayings of philosophers and learned men, the fundamental principles underlying every religious code and creed teach us that nobility of character is the breath of life to the body of man, the source of spiritual strength to the people of the world, and the sure pillar of reform.

> The roots of noble conduct, which can be likened to a young tree, grow in two places. What are these two spots

where humanity takes root? At school and at home. Yes, the roots of great character and superior virtues, such as sincerity and honesty, courage and patriotism, effort and enterprise, grow in these two places. Through the watchful care of the loving gardener in the home and the vigilant teacher in the school, deficiencies of character will be transformed into perfection. Who is the gentle gardener in the home? The mother. And what is her responsibility towards her children? The imparting of education, information, knowledge. Ethical and social reform must take precedence over political reform. To do otherwise would be like neglecting to strengthen the foundation of the house while embellishing the ceilings and walls.

Obviously, education at home begins before school. In fact, the former is the basis for progress in the latter. And this is one of the special gifts and favors God has bestowed upon women. Hence, a nation's social betterment, the nourishment of its germ of happiness, the flow of its "sweet and refreshing waters of life," and its admission into the caravan of contemporary civilization are contingent on the betterment of the status and education of its women, who, in turn, will impart education to their children. Not only will their children thus find happiness and bliss, but a tremendous service will also have been rendered to the world of civilization.

My teacher! Do not weary of the fact that I often digress into historical narrative, for I do so involuntarily. It disheartens and grieves me to think that my fellows—that is, the women of Persia—are ignorant of their rights and make no effort to fulfill their obligations as human beings. Completely deficient in character and unsuited for any task, they crawl into the corners of their homes and spend every hour of their lives indulging wicked habits. Excluded from the community of civilization, they roam the valley of confusion and ignorance.

For instance, now that the path to progress has been opened somewhat to women, and families can afford to send their daughters to school and thereby brighten their futures with the light of learning and accomplishment, most of them still say: "We consider it an abomination for our daughter to go to school!" Even in this day and age, they bring up these poor girls in the abyss of doom and ruin, ignoring the fact that these girls will become mothers and their children will be trained under their care.

My dear teacher! These are the families which often, or perhaps always, consider knowledge shameful and take pride in their lack of it. But do not lose patience! Here I will resume the story of my life.

First of all, I must describe my appearance and character as a child. I was exceptionally intelligent and clever; it seemed God had spread open the wings of his bounty over me. I had beautiful brown hair, long and naturally curly. My complexion was rosy, my eyes dark, and my eyelashes long. The picture was completed by a well-proportioned nose, small mouth and lips, and white teeth that gave a wonderful glow to my ruby lips. In the royal palace, which was the gathering spot for the choicest of lovely women, there was no face prettier or lovelier than mine. Truly, I was a beautiful, adorable child. My play and prattle, likewise, was all sweet and engaging. Among my father's wives and other occupants of the royal palace I enjoyed a special regard which was almost a source of trouble and annoyance. No sooner did I step outside, eager to go about my play, than I was accosted at every moment by the ladies passing to and fro. Their kisses and caresses resulted in delay and cost me precious play time. Soon I began to sense when I was about to be trapped. Making my escape, I ran as fast as I could and flung myself into my nanny's arms. If one of the women gave chase and finally succeeded in taking a kiss, I wiped my face in resentment, and with my large, dark eyes cast a reproachful look at her.

I had five or six playmates—all passably bright girls, though they belonged to the middle ranks of society. While they were all older than me in age, none was as intelligent. Often when we were at play, sewing or playing with something else, they would do something wrong and infuriate me. Beating them with my little white hands, I would resume playing with myself after having punished them.

Here I will give you a brief physical description of these playmates, my playroom, and the toys with which I diverted myself during my childhood. These girls were all deprived of education and manners. Their talk was very simple and slang-ridden. A couple of them were pretty to look at. One was fair-skinned with blond hair and blue eyes, always sad and thoughtful, gentle and meek, but also mischievous and inquisitive. She spent most of her time singing and making music. The other girl was darker, with a thick head of black hair and large eyes that were slightly askew. She was a frivolous chatterbox, a fairly good dancer, and an extraordinary buffoon. She invented a new joke or some nonsensical trick at every moment, and laughed with such raucousness that my nanny often lost her temper and swore at her. The other girls were not much different. Each had her individual character, but none was suitable company for a young girl. In fact, it was necessary to eschew such companions.

Every kind of toy was plentifully available to me, but I had an uncommon enthusiasm for music. I would have had no complaints if playing the piano and the organ had constituted my only play. Almost the entire day was thus spent in play. In the evenings I usually visited His Imperial Majesty, my enthroned and revered father. He always said something in my praise before caressing me lovingly. Then he gave me a present of some sort. Pulling a gold coin out of his pocket, for instance, he would often say, "This girl is very pretty, like one of Fath 'Ali Shah's princesses!"

I held my father in such awe that whenever I glanced at him I burst into tears, and regardless of all his efforts to mollify me I would not be consoled. Having never laid eyes on any man other than my father, I found him extraordinary and formidable. As for the money that I received from him, I would bring it with great alacrity to my beloved nanny and offer it to her tenderly. She would kiss me and promise to buy me another toy.

Now I must tell you something about the setup of my father's harem and the behavior of its inhabitants. No doubt you will laugh at me as you read this section. You consider me an educated woman, not a scholar in all areas of learning, and therefore will find it odd that here I must be the engineer. But my dear teacher! Surely you realize that your pupil is better informed than you give her credit for.

The royal palace was situated in the middle of the town, bounded by walls and called "The Citadel." Inside, there was a large, extensive courtyard, laid out in the style of a hundred years ago. On all sides of this building—north, south, east, and west—rooms had been built along the perimeter, one connected to another, two floors high. At the center of the courtyard stood a three-story structure, hemmed in by a blue fence. Truly, the landscape appeared like a beautiful European hat trimmed according to the fashion of the time. This building, to which only my father had access, was known as "the sleeping quarters." The care of the building had been entrusted to Agha Nuri, chief eunuch and assistant to the harem custodian. He also held all the keys to the royal quarters and the harem doors, both within and without.

It behooves me here to describe this chief eunuch to you. About forty years of age, he was sallow-complexioned, ugly and repulsive, and had a strident voice. When he announced the *qoroq*, especially, his voice could be heard from a great distance. He wore a white sash around his perpetually dirty blue frock from which hung an enormous bunch of keys, and he carried a sturdy cane in his hands. Exceptionally cruel and fearless, he treated everyone with a cold reserve. He had special charge of the entrance to the *andarun* and jealously watched all the comings and goings. No one entered or left the seraglio without his permission. Even His Majesty the Sultan's wives, after obtaining their husband's leave, needed to be dismissed by Agha Nuri Khan. If he saw fit, he could deny them permission. The thirty or forty eunuchs who served in the harem had all been committed to his charge by the harem custodian. He took his job very seriously and was far more attentive and exacting than his master. The care of all the ladies had been entrusted to him.

Illiterate in Persian, all he had learned was the Koran, so that he could recite from it aloud when he was not busy. I know nothing of his lineage, except that he came from peasant stock. As a child he was brought into the seraglio and trained by my father, growing up in the royal household. From a young age he had cultivated the soul of cruelty and despotism as his second nature, and this rigidity and harshness had raised him to higher positions and given him the authority to command. To cite one instance, if someone was in the throes of death and needed a doctor, and Agha Nuri happened to be in the bath, the patient had to die without the benefit of a doctor's visit. It was unthinkable for a man to enter the harem

The inner quarters (*andarun*) of Golestan Palace around the time of Taj's childhood. The residential apartments surrounding the central courtyard were inhabited by women of the harem and their domestic suites. They were built during the renovations of the 1860s and later demolished partially to make way for another, more elaborate royal chambre in 1886 (see p. 197). This courtyard may have been what Taj reminisces about in her memoirs.

unless accompanied by Agha Nuri. Such, in short, was the guardian and second-in-command of the harem and the surrounding residences.

The adjoining apartments were distributed amongst all the ladies related to the sovereign. Some of the interior courtyards had outer sections which also contained residences. His Imperial Majesty, my father, had about eighty wives and concubines, each of whom had about ten or twenty maidservants and domestics. The number of women in the harem thus reached some five or six hundred. Moreover, every day the wives, concubines, or domestics received numerous relatives and visitors, so that there was a constant flood of about eight or nine hundred women in the harem. In addition, each lady had a residence, a stipend, and the requirements—maidservants, menservants, and all the household necessities—to live outside the harem. Seldom did two ladies share the same house; the exception was when new wives, chosen from villages in the vicinity, were committed to the care of other ladies to be educated in etiquette. Later, they were given houses of their own.

Among all these ladies only seven or eight had children, the rest remaining childless. The royal concubines were housed in another courtyard under the control of an overseer. The concubines were Turkomans or Kurds who had been captured in the Turkoman battles, all of them beautiful. Aside from being concubines, they were also temporary wives. The overseer was a Turkoman woman called Aqol Baga Khanum. Competent, distinguished, well-educated, and benevolent, she was a capable manager of the concubines. She managed both their expenses and their stipends. Each of them received a certain sum of money from the government for additional expenditures.

Amina Aqdas, too, managed her own separate operation and controlled a small royal treasury. Through the good offices of her nephew, she enjoyed a special closeness to the royal person. This respected personage was a Kurd from a tribe of peasants and nomads in Garrus. Previously she had served Jayran, who had enjoyed His Majesty the Sultan's particular regard and affection. When Jayran died, she had become governess to Babri Khan the cat. After the death and disappearance of the cat, her nephew, who had been its playmate, gained greater access to His Majesty the Sultan. Little by little, thanks to her nephew, this slave woman climbed up to the highest ranks.

I feel compelled now to describe this beloved cat who had been the cause of the advancement of Amina Aqdas's family. Viewed through the lens of impartiality, this omnipotent Sultan whom we consider the most well-favored man of his time was, in fact, exceptionally unfortunate, for he had succumbed to a weakness for women, accumulating a large number of them in his harem. Owing to the petty jealousies with which womankind has been endowed by heaven, a sultan as mighty as this dared not display his love to his wives or children. So overcome was he by his passions and carnal desires, and so absorbed in his worldly delights, that he had even forgotten his regal privileges. Since every human being needs a confidant or a friend who will be uppermost in his affections, this powerful yet overpowered sovereign, out of regard for his wives, had directed all his love to this animal, even preferring it to the rest of his family. I have seen pictures of the cat in all the royal apartments: a bristly calico with beautiful, dainty eyes. This cat was decked with all manner of fine, expensive trimmings and fed with sumptuous foods. Waited on like a human, it had servants and paid attendants, the aforementioned Amina Aqdas being its nanny.

O my dear teacher! My eyes have welled up with tears out of pity for the miseries of kings. For myself, too, I am overcome by sorrow. What people consider the means of happiness—kingship, glory, wealth, comfort, ambition—I look upon with disgust. There is no bliss to be found among men. If there were, it must be sought in sterling qualities of the soul, in asceticism and total seclusion. Here one of Arthur Brennerman's thoughts comes to mind. He writes:

> What is happiness? How can one obtain it and what is the best way of preserving it? Man has been pondering this question since the dawn of creation. Many are the labors he has expended and many the ideas he has considered in an attempt to understand it. But up to now he has been unable to find the correct answer. Before the temple of man was dressed with the cloak of life and the human species came into existence, animals had had the same debate, according to their nature. Even Satan, when fulfilling his obligations of servitude in the heavens, was vexed by the same thought. Undoubtedly, Adam posed the same question to Eve. It is a question that has been asked from time immemorial.

> People of all races and groups meditate on it. It will form the subject of conversations for millions of years to come. For example, we construe happiness to lie in a man's tying a red cravat around his neck and fastening a brilliant diamond pin to it. Avron, who dedicated thirty years of his life to experimenting and examining the nature of insects, considered himself to be happy. Rockefeller has been amassing dollars for thirty years, believing this to be the key to happiness. Children imagine themselves happy with crying and screaming, old men with silence and peace.

> One man goes to explore the North Pole and exposes himself to numerous perils, confronting death a thousand times; but he is content with his plight. Another goes to a well-established inn, seats himself at the table, and delights his taste buds with various delicacies, thinking, "The meaning of happiness is this, and the blissful one is such as I."

Mark Antony found happiness in love, Brutus in glory, Julius Caesar in power; the first was disgraced, the second despised, the third repudiated. All three fell victim to murder. The Roman emperor Marcus Aurelius has said, "Happiness lies not in intellectual debates, nor in wealth and fame, nor in gluttony and sensual pleasures. Where, then, is it found? In performing actions which call for intelligence. I now know that ultimate happiness can change according to the differing conditions of time and place, and that it is impossible to describe it within the clear boundaries of precise definition. One must say, therefore, that an intelligent person finds happiness in performing deeds which benefit humankind."

How much better it would have been if, for instance, my imperial father had devoted himself to the cause of humanity, to the betterment of his nation and of education and the arts, rather than to an animal? Had he not been so uxorious and so corrupted with carnal pleasures, and instead spent every hour of his life in governance and advancement of agriculture, how much better off we would be today! And rather than being compelled to describe his cat to you in this history, how much more grand it would be if I wrote of his kindness to his subjects, of his quest for learning, of the principal royal accomplishments! And if I could inscribe him as fortunate rather than miserable, how glad my heart would be at this hour! Alas, my dear teacher! In that day and age everyone wallowed in ignorance, deprived even of the breath of humanity. So tainted were they by baseness and evil that the damage they have wrought cannot be remedied for centuries to come.

At any rate, I have no recourse but to resume a tale which, despite being about a cat, should occasion no wonderment. As this cat reached the apex of its happiness and glory, the women found their husband constantly occupied with the poor creature. Growing jealous and resentful, they took recourse to means that are particularly the domain of women. With the large sums of money at their command, they paid someone to seize the cat and hurl it to its doom in a deep well, thereby robbing my poor imperial father of the one joy he had in life.

I find it appropriate to set down an admonition to you: the jealous one is never free from hardship. Owing to this vice, he is in a state of confused bondage throughout his life. I want to tell you a story that I just remembered having read in a novel about two friends.

Two girls went to Russia for a visit. They had been friends and schoolmates from early childhood, and actually bore some kinship to each other. Both were wealthy and pretty. Stopping in one of the charming towns in Russia, they spent their days in excursions and sight-seeing, their nights at the theater and the ballet. These two girls were so close and united as to be almost one soul in two bodies. As it chanced, one of the girls fell in love with a noble youth, and he reciprocated her affection. They decided to get married. The other girl, the bosom friend, found herself engulfed in an ocean of jealousy, sinking to the depths of despair and sorrow. It was planned for the couple to return to her home town where they would solemnize their union. During the return trip, the jealous girl saw that matters were at an end and her friend had been wooed and won. She plotted to poison the youth, and succeeded in her plan. His sudden death aroused the suspicion of the townspeople, whereupon the two girls were arrested. After she confessed to her guilt, the poor jealous girl was condemned by the law to life imprisonment.

Now be fair! Are envy and jealousy worthy of man—him who is the noblest of creation, him who is endowed with all the divine qualities? No, it cannot be! Another point should not be forgotten: the jealous one will never attain his goal.

At any rate, after the disappearance of the cat, His Majesty the sovereign took the harshest measures, but to no avail. The cat was dead and gone, its return from the realm of the spirits quite impossible. Therefore, the child companion and play-mate of the cat now became the object of royal attention, took the cat's place, and was given the title "Manija" (Malijak). The same courtesies and privileges enjoyed by the cat were bestowed, twofold, on this child.

Let me now write something of the parentage and appear-ance of this person, whose path crossed mine numerous times in my life. Know him well, and keep in mind his fine character and noble virtues.

This child seemed almost blind; that is to say, he suffered so much pain in his eyes that they were chronically red and ugly. Despite his finery and his closeness to the royal person, he was excessively dirty. He was sallow-complexioned, unpleasant to look at, and uncommonly short. In its attempt to silence the complaints of this darling child, Nature had also rendered him mute and unintelligible. He was illiterate and bereft of any learning, not even having heard the words "edu-cation" and "civilization." Some twenty or thirty boys from the middle ranks of society were his playmates, or to use a loftier term, "page boys." Day and night he was occupied in mischief, running all over the courtyard and pestering the ladies and guests. No one had the authority to question his behavior or call him to account. He pelted the ladies with dirt and stones, rather than with flowers, in the summer and with snowballs in the winter. He was not averse to any manner of wild, uncouth behavior and had a mean streak in him, even to the point of attempting murder. One day, for instance, he fired a gun at a eunuch named 'Abdollah and wounded him in the leg for fun; the unfortunate man still carries that souvenir of the boy's childhood and walks with a limp. The child's father had been a shepherd in Garrus. Such is the character, appearance, and parentage of this person whom we will meet several times in the course of this narrative.

Every year, from the first month in spring His Majesty my father would set off on his trips, spending the better part of spring, summer, and autumn traveling. He was especially attached to hunting and horse riding. His first stop would be Sorkhe Hesar for *ashpazan* (broth-making), one of the favorite recreations of the ladies. Although you surely know all about it, I will describe it here again for you.

A tent, twenty meters by twenty meters, was set up along one of the long avenues of the orchard. On two sides of the tent they would lay out trays with every kind of food, and all the dignitaries, nobles, and ministers had to work on the cleaning and preparation. After the food had been cleaned, my father would pour it into the pot with his own hands. The others would follow suit with the rest of the food and get busy with the cooking. While the food was being prepared, musicians would play their instruments and dancers would dance. After the show, the ladies would walk about to view the gardens. When they returned, the cooks would serve the meal. The food was exceptionally delicious, such that one could never get enough. After *ashpazan*, he would go to Saltanatabad or Niyavaran, and then on to Posht-e Kuh.

Another pastime of my father's was horse racing, which took place every New Year's eve. Some of the activities which had at first been recreational later became part of the royal routine, and their occurrence became obligatory. Among them were the tournaments of the valiants. Every year the

An eastern view of the palace of Saltanatabad, one of a handful of royal mansions frequented by Naser al-Din Shah during his endless daily excursions on the slopes of the Alborz mountains around the capital.

sovereign would ascend the marble throne, watching from the threshold as the sportsmen wrestled. This show was not without interest; in fact, it was quite amusing.

Throughout the day, the ladies had recourse to such pastimes. It is impossible for man to conjure up in the realm of his imagination a sweeter, easier life. In the course of the year they were not visited by any grief, difficulty, pain or bitterness. I am sure that if someone had asked one of them, "What is suffering?" she would have gaped in amazement at the questioner, unable to answer the question, incapable even of understanding it. Thus it was that when the sun of their fortunes set, and they were expelled from the palace after the assassination of the king, most of them died in a very short time and little remained of them.

This child I have been describing entered the scene before I was born. What I write here was narrated to me by my nanny at times when she wanted to put me to sleep. When I was a little older, and somewhat more understanding, this child had grown and was between ten and twelve years of age.

Before I go on with my story, it is necessary also to give you a picture of the character and habits of the ladies.

These ladies often banded together in friendship two or three at a time. They spent most of the day entertaining and playing *laskana*. (*Laskana* consists of playing with colorful and ludicrous masks cut out of cardboard.) Talking and laughing together, they would pass the day until it was time for dinner. All of them were religious and dutifully observed the prayers and the fast. Each tried to outdo the others in dressing up, primping and trying to appear extraordinary so as to attract the attention of the Shah. Every evening, without fail, they would spend two or three hours on their colorful clothes and toilette, turn themselves into goddesses, and appear in His

Young harem woman in white tights and short skirt—a Persian woman's typical indoor outfit in Taj's time.

Majesty's presence. He found no distinction in any of them, however; except for one who was the beloved of his heart and who enjoyed his special regard. This was a young woman, about twenty years of age, tall, dark-haired and ivory-complexioned. Her eyes were incomparably beautiful and languid, her eyelashes turned up and long. She was amiable and pleasant. With all the affection the Sultan poured out on her, she was humble and kind, very simple and unaffected. Her father was a gardener wholly devoid of the ways of civilization.

It is important for us to take recognition of this woman. After the assassination of His Majesty, certain malevolent individuals and others who were jealous of her but could not display their hostility earlier, found ways of slandering and casting aspersions on her. But I know her to be untainted by this crime. Even if she had no affection for my father, she would have valued her personal privileges and not have consented to his murder and her own downfall.

I wish I were a competent writer like Victor Hugo or Monsieur Rousseau and could write this history in sweet and delightful language. Alas, I can write but simply and poorly.

Such was His Majesty the Sultan's seraglio. Now that we know everyone well and are acquainted with their characters, let us go back to our story.

EDUCATION IN THE HAREM

When I was seven, I was put in school by order of His Majesty and given a teacher, a private tutor, and a eunuch. I must acquaint you here with this dear teacher of my childhood years. He was a man of about thirty, with a massive beard and black eyes and eyebrows that seemed to run into each other. A native of Gilan, he was passably educated. He was the son of a judge and considered the judgeship a hereditary bequest. Upon the death of his father, however, his uncle took over the judgeship, and this man took shelter in the Grand Vizier's house. In order to be rid of this refugee, the Grand Vizier had him appointed as my teacher.

My tutor was a dear maternal relative: my grandmother's uncle. This beloved uncle was a khan. On days when audiences were granted, he would don his military helmet, hold a gold-tipped feather in his hand and present himself at court. After the audiences, he would sit at home with nothing to do. The dear man was between forty and fifty years old—very dignified, well-respected, cautious and honest. He wore a very long beard.

I was taken to school and received the honorific robes amid celebrations. But I was very downcast to be deprived of the freedom of play and separated from my beautiful toys, my darling dolls. On most days I was out of sorts with my teacher and tutor, and no palliative could induce me to study. Short on alternatives, they beat my female playmates in order to discipline them, but such beating had no effect on me. I was very stubborn and headstrong, obeyed no one, and did as I pleased. I paid no attention to the reprimands and admonitions of adults, considering myself fully invested with intelligence and absolute authority. This was because from the time when I first became conscious of the world, I had seen nothing but submission, reverence, and humility displayed toward me. I was given everything that I asked for, so I could not bear unkind treatment and was easily offended.

My teacher had no choice but to forgo teaching. He became, instead, a storyteller, narrating tales all day long. Few were his attempts to teach me anything. Nevertheless, I overlooked no opportunity to harass him, constantly hoping that he would fall ill or die so that I could regain my freedom for a few days and resume my mischievous play. As it happened, however, this man was young and of a sound constitution, and never fell ill. One Friday I told my page boy playmates, "If you do something to make our teacher ill and confined to bed for a few days, I'll give you a large share of my toys." They agreed and decided on a plan to plague him. On Saturday, when we went to school, one of the page boys, named 'Abbas Khan, placed a large quantity of gunpowder under the teacher's seat and extended the fuse to the door of the room. When we were dismissed for lunch, he lit the fuse. The poor teacher, totally oblivious to all that was happening, sat back on his cushion, and suddenly the gunpowder went off. With all his clothes going up in smoke, the poor teacher was completely burned from his waist down.

We were dismissed for the afternoon and freed from our lessons for about a week. Later it was discovered that this prank had been at my behest. Some four blows of the cane on my hands ensured that I never again committed an incivility against my teacher. Having never been beaten before, I was laid up in bed for a week or so by the blows of that cane.

I spent every holiday playing, completely carefree, and made no effort whatsoever to prepare myself for the lessons the teacher was going to teach. One year passed in this manner. In fact, most of my education consisted in what I have described. If we look at the situation objectively, though, the teacher really knew barely more than he taught us; all he wanted to do was earn a living and make ends meet. Ah misery, that I was unfortunate enough never to have a good, understanding teacher and thus remain deprived of progress in life. Today I see clearly that an illiterate human is baser than inanimate matter. "It is knowledge man must embody in himself, for even matter has life in its mass."

Making progress means drawing closer to truth and happiness. Just as it lies beyond man's ability to encompass the realities of all things, so is it tremendously difficult to attain total happiness—so much so that man even denies its existence. Yet, despite all this, man is empowered to some measure to recognize truth and find happiness. The law of creation has deprived us of understanding the meaning of many things; but to this involuntary deprivation we have added a deprivation by choice. What we can understand, we refuse to comprehend. That measure of comfort and happiness which it is possible for us to have, we give up. And why? Because we lack that guide whose name is knowledge.

Despite his weak frame, man subdues by his overwhelming hand not only powerful beasts of prey, but the forces of nature as well. He transforms dry land into sea and sea into dry land. He passes over the roaring waves of the ocean and through formidable tunnels in towering mountains. He traverses the length and breadth of the earth—enormous though it is— with the powerful forces of electricity and steam. He comprehends the essence of the matter on the earth's surface and the dimensions and movement of celestial spheres. Unraveling the secrets of the marvels of creation, he knows how to provide the means of prosperity for his kind. What is the source of this extraordinary power that encompasses happiness and ensures union? Undoubtedly, it is knowledge. Power, wealth, lofty ideas, good character, progress of all kinds—these are all the products of knowledge. Thus, we can theorize that progress ensues from knowledge.

But alas, a thousand times alas, that through history women have found the door of knowledge closed in their face and discovered no guide or teacher. For this very reason, my education was severely limited, ultimately nonexistent, and my eternal loss came to be my companion and mate. On his return from Paris, Bismarck remarked that he was taking all his conspicuous victories away with him. He told all those present, "We prevailed over France thanks to school teachers."

A scholar who has taken exception to these words says that the influence of teachers in educating children and shaping their personalities is unquestionable, but that Bismarck has neglected to mention the moral force represented by the influence of mothers. The child profits from the teacher's guidance only when its education at home has been well managed. If a child's conduct begins to degenerate, if he is overcome by improper manners that etch themselves into the tablet of his character, what can the teacher do with him then?

I have been wrongly disparaging my teacher here. Suppose they had appointed Plato or Aristotle instead of my teacher from Gilan. What could either of them have done with my perversity and willfulness and disobedience? Had they tried to tame me through harshness or fear, my nanny would not have stood for it and would have stopped them.

Spending a year in school in this manner, I reached the age of eight, whereupon I began to hear my nannies and my aunt frequently talk about my wedding—about how I would take a husband and how they would receive clothes and sweets. Such talk gave me immense pleasure, for I thought of unbridled freedom and a house of my own. Often, instead of stories, the talk centered on the wedding and instructions for my future life. I listened with rapt attention, recording everything in memory. So greatly had they diminished my future husband in my estimation and hoisted me over him as superior, that in the realm of fancy I had dreamt up a score of tortures and torments for him and considered it a game and a diversion for myself. Then, unfortunately, what I had feared came to pass.

A gathering of Persian women in the *andarun*, engaged in letter writing and conversation, as appears in this photograph from the turn of the century—a scene typical of Taj's harem life. The importance of literacy, as highlighted by the prominence of the women in the center, reflects the state of educational deprivation in the *andaruns* of the Qajar nobility.

The previous year my mother had given birth to a son. This boy was very delicate and beautiful, with curly black hair. My mother loved him very much. Since I was petulant with her and bestowed all my affection on my nanny, my mother bore no special love for me. Furthermore, owing to the strange predictions and particular aspirations of the time, the boy received preferential treatment. This was supposed to be a subtle form of preference, not an obvious one. But I was so intelligent and alert that they could not hide anything from me. Sensing this partiality on my mother's part, I felt slighted and became more withdrawn from her. Sometimes I felt so unhappy that I considered myself the most unfortunate human being. From that time I began to develop a great hardness of heart, setting off on my journey through life with a condition akin to lunacy. This situation had also caused me to withdraw somewhat from my beloved nanny and aunt, and I was moping constantly.

I could not recognize jealousy because I did not know what it was, nor had I heard the word. Each time my mother kissed my brother or caressed him, my heart fluttered and my forehead broke out in a cold sweat. So I had vowed to myself that I would never love anyone and would treat everyone badly. In fact, even today the idea remains with me, and I often find myself unnecessarily and unconsciously causing my friends pain. But when I think about it, I see that it was uncalled for and there was no hostility intended, aside from the obstinacy and hostility that had entered my heart as a child. So it is that one must acquire everything in childhood and learn the things required of a civilized human being.

At this time, numerous suitors for me were coming and going. My father would not give his consent, saying, "She is only a child; she cannot have a husband!" However, with a view to my mother's antipathy, he had not revealed his true plan.

COURTSHIP AND BETROTHAL

One morning when I was in his presence and a number of ladies were standing nearby, several eunuchs came in carrying trays on their heads. When the covers were lifted from the trays, a large quantity of expensive toys and splendid precious jewelry presented itself to view. Everyone wondered what this was and for whom it was intended. After a lengthy silence my father said, "'Aziz [al-Soltan, Malijak]! These are yours. Give them to any girl you want." The boy had been advised earlier to choose me as his betrothed. However, one of my half-sisters, who was about two years older than I, had also been made a candidate for marriage to 'Aziz. Her mother, having cajoled and threatened the boy's nanny, had won her over to her side and had made the servant promise that 'Aziz would choose her daughter. The boy had acquiesced in the plan.

As soon as my father had spoken, the boy picked up a ring and put it on my sister's finger, saying, "S-s-s-sir, I ch-ch-ch-choose th-th-this girl as my b-b-b-betrothed!" My father embraced him and said, "My dear 'Aziz! Your betrothed is this other girl, and it is my wish that you have her."

The boy stuttered again, "V-v-v-very well!"

My mother who was present shouted, "Oh, I would sooner poison my daughter and end her life than consent to such a son-in-law. Isn't it a pity to give my darling, sweet girl to this child whose parentage is well known and whose appearance is so repulsive?"

It needs no telling what effect these harsh words about 'Aziz had on my father. He raised his voice like a roar of thunder and bellowed, "What did you say? Do you wish to die? Is it in *your* power to choose for my daughter?"

Pandemonium broke loose. With great difficulty they took my mother out of his sight, while I stood rooted to the spot.

Nevertheless, as I write to you now, I recall that I wished my mother had not interfered and I had, in fact, been given to him in marriage. Not that I understood what a husband was or knew the meaning of love. All I knew was that if I were married I would leave home and no longer see my mother coddling my brother. Besides, there were some exquisite dolls in the trays which I could not bear to lose. I longed for someone to give them to me at once so that I could run to my playroom and smash and tear them apart.

My mother's objections had emboldened the boy and he said, "I w-w-want the same g-g-girl. I d-d-d-don't want this g-g-g-girl!"

Everyone congratulated him. It was almost a formal engagement, and the dolls and jewelry were taken to my sister's house. I came home angry and unhappy. As soon as I walked in my mother called me and said, "Why are you here? What did you come back for? Go back to your father. Or if you want to remain in my house don't go to your father any more!"

I went crying to my room. Throwing myself on the bed, I wept bitterly. Later I dozed off, overcome by sleep. In a dream I saw an expanse of meadow in which numerous people of all kinds were walking about. Laden with jewels and extravagant clothes, I was also taking in the sights. Gradually the people began to descend on me, snatching away my ornaments and jewels and leaving me naked. Like a helpless dove trapped in the claws of falcons, I was at the mercy of these people who were pulling off my feathers one by one.

I woke up terrified and started to cry again. My nanny entered the room and found me in that state. Deeply moved, she held me in her arms, kissed me and asked why I was crying. I told her about the day's events, my mother's anger, and the dream. She let out a moan and said, "In order to be happy in life, it's not enough for one to enjoy a high position or belong to royalty or be as pretty as you are. Many other things are necessary for well-being which I will teach you if I live long enough." With great difficulty she calmed me down and engaged me in play. Soon I had forgotten the episode entirely. The interpretation of the dream and the meaning of my nanny's words came to me several years later. In due time I will tell you what they are.

Soon after, the chief custodian in Khorasan sent for a bride, and it fell to my unfortunate lot. My father and mother had almost come to the point of agreement, and it was not long before I was to be married off and sent to Khorasan. When I learned of this, I began to cry and refused to be separated from my kindred, my father and mother, and begged not to be given to this suitor. My wish was granted and the suitor went away rejected. Shortly after this, one of my father's wives who was a princess and related to the royal family sought me for her nephew. At the time, the family had few worldly posses-sions and did not hold any important offices. So my mother refused the offer.

Many were the suitors who would thus appear in the morning, only to disappear by evening. Finally, one day someone came from the house of Anis al-Dawla, one of my father's wives, and summoned me on her behalf.

I must describe this venerable lady to you briefly. She was of peasant stock from the district of 'Emama. During one of my father's visits to that area, he had seen her in the desert and asked her a few questions. The girl had answered his ques-tions sweetly and engagingly, and had won his heart. Bringing her back with him to his harem, my father had entrusted her to the same Jayran whom I mentioned earlier. When Jayran died, her house and furniture were given to this girl, who also inherited Jayran's mantle of respect and devotion. So intelligent and upstanding was she that, despite being homely, she held the first rank in character and respectability. At the time of our story she was about thirty. Of medium stature, she was very simple, gentle and dignified. Her tan face was ordinary, even ugly, but quite commanding. All the wives of foreign ambassadors were received at her house where they were admitted into His Majesty's presence on festive and formal occasions. This great, well-respected lady had no children. She bore a special love for me and treated me like her own child. All the influential and noble families and all the wives of ministers and other functionaries were also received at her house. Most petitions were submitted through her because when she presented them to the sovereign they were accepted.

This spiritual mother of mine had chosen a fiancé for me from a noble, aristocratic family and on this day had called me to her house so that I could be seen. After we had made our entrances and gone through the formalities, she seated me by her side, as usual, and kissed me. She spoke about various things and asked me about the games I liked to play. I replied in sweet, measured tones, giving clever answers to her questions. Occasionally making childish gestures, I gave added emphasis to my words. Soon I realized that a large, stately woman was sitting in the room, listening carefully to my childish prattle and smiling. Little by little, I became friendly with her and we began to talk. Meanwhile, an eight-year-old boy, very light-skinned and fat but also very sweet and appealing, entered the room in military uniform and headpiece and, going directly to the lady, planted himself between her knees. Looking at him, I felt terrified and stood up impulsively. All their entreaties that I stay were to no avail. Deeply scared and sad at the same time, I left the room. My earlier

Dressed more in European than Persian fashion, Anis al-Dawla captures the harem's wishes to share with the shah the perquisites of monarchy. The tiara, the embroidered band bearing her title in Roman characters, and the initials on her cuffs represent attempts to emulate European royalty. Anis al-Dawla's stature in the Naseri court as a benevolent protector of the weak was not incongruent with her modern image.

cheerfulness and sense of joy vanished completely, giving way to dejection. Returning home, I went to my mother. In response to her numerous questions I could only sigh. Finally, she left me to myself and asked my nanny for an explanation. My nanny said, "It seems this lady has approached Anis al-Dawla regarding a bride for her son. Among the girls, she has chosen this one."

My dear teacher! Even at this hour, when almost twenty-two years separate us from that day and age, I cannot control the nervous trembling that I feel as I write this. Perforce I must lay down my pen for an hour or so and heave wrenching but unavailing sighs. Truly, what greater misfortune could one suffer than to have to take a husband in childhood, at the age of eight? Especially if it was not her heart and mind that had chosen him but rather the wishes of her mother and elders, who nurtured empty and illusive hopes. It seems to me that in my lifetime I have lived under a cloud of misfortune and vexation, all of it beginning from that ill-fated day. A point which I have mentioned before bears repetition: throughout my life, believing in intimations of the heart, I have had premonitions of everything that was to happen to me. That day I began to feel an incredible oppressiveness and heartache that has been with me since; I have always been sorrow-stricken and depressed. I had a sense then that this marriage would be followed by profound misery. The thought of that lady and her son produced in me a headache, a quivering of the nerves, and a knot in the heart that reduced me to tears.

Two or three days passed, but I continued to feel dejected. Nothing could take away my unhappiness—not my mother's kindness, or my nanny's caresses, or excursions and amuse-ments and games. I could not even smile. Finally, my delicate constitution could not endure this agony any longer. I fell ill and was confined to bed with what the ladies referred to as chicken pox. My smooth, pretty face was spangled with red pockmarks.

As I lay sick and almost unconscious with a high fever, my mother was negotiating the terms of the marriage. Since it was Anis al-Dawla who was asking for my hand on behalf of the bridegroom's mother, my father also gave his consent, albeit with reluctance. He did stipulate, however, that while we could celebrate the engagement right away, the nuptials would have to wait until I was at least twenty. Satisfied with this arrangement, both parties quickly made plans for an engagement ceremony and began work on the preparations.

I recovered slowly from my illness and felt somewhat better. To welcome me back, my playmates talked of nothing but the wedding. Unlike the previous times, however, when I had listened eagerly and with pleasure to such talk, now I could only listen in dumb sadness, answering with a sigh. What had happened to reduce me to such grief? What had turned me away from play, from running about and enjoying myself? I asked myself this question a thousand times, but found no answer. Day by day I became thinner and my eyes became more spiritless, losing their luster.

The arrangements for the betrothal, to be celebrated with a lavish spread of confections, were concluded and the ceremony began; the day that I had dreaded with hopelessness had arrived. While the members of my family were busy enjoying themselves and having a grand time—and, indeed, for a child of eight such music and singing and celebration and noise can be enormously entertaining—I was dumbfounded, turning this way and that like a drunkard. Wholly insensible to what I felt, people construed my behavior as bashfulness and embarrassment, and, satisfied with this explanation, they left me to myself. The true reason for my suffering, however, was unknown to all, myself included.

All the noble and aristocratic families, all the prominent princesses had received invitations from Anis al-Dawla. It was a phenomenal spectacle. Every part of that large courtyard rippled with colors and patterns and arrays, and the sparkle from the diamonds was blinding.

I was taken to a secluded courtyard for my toilette. One of my father's wives was a competent bride stylist, aptly named Delbar Khanum (Lady Coquette). Every bride that she dressed up was honored by the sovereign with an expensive piece of gold cloth. I distinctly remember feeling that I was about to die under the weight of the gold cloth and the jewelry and constantly cursing that unpropitious day. All the little girls who were my age were gathered in this courtyard. A small band of musicians and dancers had been picked and brought here to perform. There was music everywhere, and the throngs of people had raised a tremendous hubbub. Almost a thousand platters of confections and fruit and several gold trays filled with colorful jewelry had been prepared for this celebration. An enormous company of officials, administrators, and aristocrats was led around the courtyard to the accompaniment of music and finally brought to our house. The group had to move very slowly and deliberately so that they could scrutinize all the gifts the guests had brought and, considering what had been given to the bride, estimate her value.

Ay me! Like a captive slave with all her outward accoutrements I was sold off to a husband whom I had not had a chance to observe and to whose character I was not accustomed. This lifelong mate of mine I had accepted in theory, nurturing in my imagination merely the idea of husband and

An all-female wedding party held for an absentee bridegroom. The two mullahs on the right, representing the spouses in the wedding ceremony and accompanied by the male members of the two families, stand clearly outside the women's circle. The barely distinguishable bride, veiled and surrounded by relatives and women of the household, is sitting in front of the wedding *sofra* (with its symbolic sugar cones and ornamented dishes) and looking at the mirror for a good omen. She, however, is by no means the focus of attention. The two dancers, one of whom carries a large tambourine, are more central and are accompanied by two other dancers on the far left who are presumably performing a single-skirted dance. The black nanny attending children is one of two represented in the painting. The popular Persian painting of the Qajar period accurately depicted nuptial scenes not much different from Taj's royal wedding.

wholly oblivious of a husband's sweeping prerogatives. Yet, I must be married off to the tune of a thousand platters of sweets and fruit, five or six trays of gold and silver and pearls and jewels, and several sealed envelopes containing cash!

Ah misery! Of mankind's great misfortunes one is this, that one must take a wife or husband according to the wishes of one's parents. This bizarre custom does not stand to reason and is contrary to law. Here the Europeans are right—but then they surpass us in all areas of learning and progress. It is a source of regret to me that we should be so ignorant as to be incapable of distinguishing between right and wrong. If we lack something, why can we not learn it from others at least? Man must always strive with determination to provide for his future, for the past has slipped through his fingers and at present he is a moribund patient whose life is ebbing every moment. Flawless and perfect natures, when subjected to worthless companionship for a length of time, become vulnerable. Man must always choose his eternal companion well, and get to know her thoroughly before making his choice, so that he does not ruin his life and fall prey to temptation.

To make a long story short, they took inventory of all the contents of the trays and locked up the valuables. After lunch, which was accompanied by tremendous noise and hoopla, I was taken to the conclave. I remember clearly my pink silk brocade dress, covered with gold lace and other patterns. It resembled the costume of dancers who performed at the theater: a short camisole which puffed up with the aid of a device attached to springs. To this was added a thin lacework veil fully covered with silver embroidery. Around my head was tied what they called a "Qajari-style" headpiece, consisting of cloth and cotton; two long artificial ears, inlaid with gems and covered with glossy gold coins, protruded from my head.

The all-male feast held in the reception hall of Golestan palace (later demolished by Naser al-Din Shah to make room for a more elaborate hall) was typical of banquets held on such occasions as Taj's wedding. In this painting by Mahmud Khan Saba, one of the most creative artists of the Qajar period active in the 1870s and early 1880s, the cream of the nobility and ranking officialdom are portrayed staring in the direction of the viewer. The guests' solemn and attentive pose accentuates the shah's invisible presence at the head of the hall. Oblivious to the dancers and musicians at the other end, the decorous guests seem obliged because of the royal presence to ignore the trays of Persian candies and crystal goblets of rosewater drink laid before them. In Saba's observant eye only the low-ranking attendants of the inner court who are clustered at the doorway seem to be enjoying the entertainment. The contrast between the guests' traditional outfit and the Bohemian chandeliers, the opaline vases and the mantelpiece clocks, all tokens of a taste for European luxury goods, alludes to the transitory opulence of the Qajar court.

I looked quite ludicrous. When I was given a mirror to take a look at myself I was shocked. A face so naturally pretty had been painted with rouge and ceruse and been transformed completely from its likeness. My eyebrows had been reduced by half, the hairs painstakingly and painfully removed with a tweezers. Using mascara, they had shaped them into perfectly smooth arcs. So thick was the coat of paint on my face that all the natural contrasts of my complexion had disappeared. In addition, they had applied a thick layer of rouge to my lips. I was quite a sight.

A thousand braziers were lit for burning incense and wild rue. Two people were to lead me by the arm and I had to shut my eyes and follow them, pretending to be blind. Such was the custom. If the bride opened her eyes, then she was immodest and uncivilized.

They led me, as I was, first to my father. After I had kissed his feet, he showered me with much kindness and praise. Then I was taken to the feast and seated on a golden chair, and gold and silver coins were tossed over my head with cheers and bravos. It was quite comical that my feet were half a meter off the floor. I was so little they had to carry me upstairs. The day and all the tumult that was raised to mark the beginning of my wretchedness came to an end, and I was released from the yoke of suffering.

On this day a strange thing happened that caused me much grief. 'Aziz al-Soltan, my erstwhile fiancé, became jealous, regretted his earlier choice, and kicked up a big fuss. First he had a brief discussion with my father asking him to switch the brides, and was turned down. In despair he started to disrupt the meeting, flinging so many snowballs and ice pellets at honored guests and passersby that they began to protest vociferously and made a row. The boy felt that he was in love with me. It is remarkable that, despite his ugliness, his love had gradually begun to attract me; as a result, he was raising a commotion. I was not at fault here; however many virtues a child has, he still mimics his parents' behavior. The love my father bore this boy was not a condemnable childish affection. And although I had grown up harsh and cold, yet sometimes I acted in an impulsive and mercurial way, which I regretted almost immediately. I was not so dull-witted as to deny my faults. Here my greatest shortcoming was that I understood what I was doing and did it deliberately. That is why when I think about it, I see that I am somewhat out of my mind, and I marvel not a little at myself. It seems as though this experience created a second self within me which I still possess. Not only in childhood, but even today—when I have a reputation for being sensible and ethical and civilized—this shortcoming remains with me. And, dear teacher, you yourself have witnessed this endearing slackness in me; yet why you have refrained from criticizing me for it, I do not know. What I do know is how I came by this flaw, which I will now explain to you.

The root of the problem is that in childhood I was pampered and raised to be spoiled. If, for example, I broke a valuable Chinese vase I would be told, "It's a shame. This was a very precious vase. But since you felt like breaking it, you did well!" Or, "You set fire to this thing. What a pity! But because you wanted to do it, it doesn't matter!" And so on. This was nothing but hypocrisy and sycophancy, and it further compounded my testiness and vengefulness with the added ingredient of egotism. Kings and rulers, leaders and great men often murder, pillage, torture, imprison, tyrannize, or commit sinful acts. This is not because they do not know what they do. Oh no! They are fully cognizant of their deeds, but they act out of habit. Like woebegone me, they were deprived of the true educators—knowledge and humanity. So most of them ended up murdered or overthrown, having bedecked history with mementos of their savage and bloody deeds, and leaving a foul name to posterity. Likewise, I lost every chance of happiness and everything that nature had provided for me in the highest degree. Believe me, had I been murdered or brought down in life it would have been sweeter to my taste.

I cannot call myself unfortunate. Fortune is a figment of the imagination born and bred in superstitious minds, not unlike the suds children make with soap that momentarily turn into bubbles. What I can say about myself is that I was not raised well, though I was quite educable. That is why today I feel ashamed, and find myself demeaned and disconsolate. I began my life in sorrow, and in sorrow will I bring my days to an end.

Yes, sorrow and pain are inevitable in life. Humanity has always been caught in raging storms. Life is not pleasure, it is endurance. The good and evil in life are transitory, and one must put up with every difficulty in its time. Man must never become conceited or allow pride and arrogance to guide his life. Likewise, in times of adversity, he must allow no one to hear his complaints.

Days and nights passed. The residents of the palace spent their time in pleasure and enjoyment. I, on the other hand, was perpetually downcast, feeling threatened by an external menace. A year went by during which nothing new happened worth writing about. The time passed as if by routine.

Amina Aqdas, who had gone blind in both eyes during the last couple of years, died at the end of the year. All her furniture and possessions, which amounted to considerable value, were given to my sister. The same year my sister's wedding preparations began. All this while, I was besieged by strange

In one of his last photographs from 1896 Naser al-Din Shah accompanied by his favorite, 'Aziz al-Soltan (Malijak), to his right, in a typical visit to royal gardens surrounding the capital. Even in moments of leisure and relaxation, smoking a water pipe, the shah was attended by an obsequious crowd of court retainers. Standing at the shah's side, Malijak, the youngest of the attendants, clearly enjoyed a special degree of intimacy with the monarch, whose gaze into the camera projects an aura of protectiveness for his favorite page boy.

looks and odd sighs emanating from this boy who was approaching adolescence. My mother had strictly forbidden me from speaking to him, but since I was required to appear before His Majesty every afternoon and remain until six or seven, there was no way to prevent eye contact.

I had grown considerably, both in physique and in beauty. Like a lovely garden arrayed with all manner of flowers, a fresh blossom would unfold every day and be added to the beauties of my face. My mother was very important and great of status. In the matter of spending money on fine, expensive clothes—whether for herself, me, or my brother—she did not stint. Every day she dressed me in new clothes and had me done up. My father had ordered that I be dressed in the European way, preferably in pink and white. So they procured cloth of exceptional quality all the time and sewed me new dresses, which they embroidered with floral patterns. Not only had my beauty caused much anguish to this poor youth, but now I found myself surrounded by a multitude of sighers, trapped like a helpless sparrow in this bonfire of woe. My mother perceived this great turbulence clearly, and every day devised a new way to be severe and restrictive with me. Little by little, she took away my play, my freedom, my outdoor activities, and kept me confined at home, though she could not bar me from my father's presence. All these infatuated devotees could do at that time was to be content with a view of me from afar. As for me, habitually depressed and unhappy, I was almost weary of life. This melancholia had imparted to me an extraordinary charm and dignity which only enhanced my beauty and lent greater luster to my complexion.

My sister's wedding took place that year. Before this wedding, my prospective mother-in-law died and took to the grave her desire to see her only son married. This caused me great sadness and regret, for that venerable lady's death compounded my misfortune and further darkened my future. A few months later, my future father-in-law took one of the daughters of the Grand Vizier to wife. After his marriage, he petitioned my father to allow me to be married, too; or if permission was withheld, it could wait until he was so inclined.

Permission for my wedding was granted, and they began to celebrate. The preparations were done beautifully and exquisitely, but the numbers were smaller than at the betrothal ceremony. I relapsed into a state of frenzy bordering on insanity, constantly fearful of some external threat. I found myself sinking deep into a whirlpool with no means of escape. I wept and pleaded a great deal, entreating that my wedding be delayed. But the force of my father's wrath subdued me, and, using threats, he compelled me to submit.

The day that I had dreaded arrived, and the wedding ceremony began. They placed me at the head of a prayer rug, in the presence of my Heavenly Father—the one truly worshipped—like a sacrifice offered up to ancient deities. I wore a gown of white satin embellished with precious stones. My head was dressed in the same manner as had been done at the betrothal ceremony. A white lace veil, embroidered with silver thread, covered my face. The vow was said and everyone waited for my response. But tears left me no reprieve for a reply, and I was trembling all over. Finally, after painstaking efforts, and several clandestine beatings, I said a feeble "aye," thereby winning release from the turmoil and confusion of the moment.

The ladies asked for the bridegroom to appear at the ceremony. Two young brothers of mine, who were about the bridegroom's age, escorted him to his seat in the room, directly in front of me. So copious had my tears been that they had smudged my makeup and ruined my toilette. Raising my head from its sunken position, I looked at the bridegroom in the mirror in front of him. To be fair, he was good-looking and could not be reckoned among the ugly. He had on a beautiful white military uniform, his hair was black and his fair face delicate and attractive. But I never felt that I was supposed to love this youth or be happy to take a husband. All I felt was that I labored under an intense weight, with my heart pounding furiously and my nerves overcome by a strange trembling.

My teacher! Through this union and the happy cries that ensued from it, through all those tumultuous happenings, in the presence of my God and by the exchange of vows which guaranteed my captivity and debasement, they made me the life-mate of this unknown youth whom I did not love, to whose manners I was not accustomed, and of whose way of life I knew nothing. Pleased with their tyrannous accomplishment, even puffed up with pride, they watched my misery with satisfaction.

Oh, what a cursed day, what an evil hour! Never will I forget that moment, when freedom and dignity were snatched away from me and replaced with antipathy and revulsion. Holding that damnable day as the author of my ruin, I will denounce it for ever. In all fairness, however, I should not be the only one cursing that day; that poor youth ought to have felt the same as I did. Just as we shared in the good part of life, so were we partners in misery, and I was as responsible for his suffering as he was for mine.

But I have forgotten to introduce to you this future husband of mine. This young man came from a noble, well-established family and was related to Hedayatollah Khan of Rasht on the father's side and Amin al-Dawla on the mother's side. The boy's father had taken several wives, but his male children had not survived childhood. After the death of several children, this was the only son left. You can easily imagine the depth of the parents' love for this boy. He had been held immeasurably dear by his parents, had even become the absolute authority over them. Fearing for his life, they had demurred from insisting that he study, leaving him free to learn as and what he pleased. Day and night, night and day, he spent his time in play and fun. He surrounded himself with numerous page boys, the sons of high-ranking officials.

The boy's father was the highly regarded commander of the king's special guard and enjoyed the sovereign's trust. The defenses of the citadel and the outer and inner harem were entrusted to his hands. He was honest, truthful, trustworthy, and loyal. The boy's mother also was a distinguished lady of rank, very intelligent and learned. While alive, she had nurtured him with every advantage and benefit and taken good care of him. Although he was her one and only dear son, she was not lenient in his education. After his mother's death, however, in order to forestall his grief for her loss, they had given him a first-rate mansion for himself, along with a nanny, a tutor, a manservant, and a maidservant. From about the age of nine, he had been given total independence.

The boy's nanny was a replica of mine, with the difference that my nanny went to her grave early, without leaving a strong imprint on my character and habits, while his nanny lived long and caused me suffering and provoked my revulsion for many years. Imparting all her uncivilized manners to this unfortunate child, she had raised him to be stubborn, brutish, and ruthless. Everything that one can identify as bad she had taught him, leaving behind a permanent token of herself. Such was my intended husband.

After our wedding I no longer went to school. Instead, I spent all my time bemoaning my plight and reading the poetry of Hafez and Sa'di. Laying aside most of my childish games, I began to read books and novels, which I found enchanting and enjoyable. My mind had ample room for imagination and lofty ideas. I looked upon my childhood captivity with an analytical sense of regret, thinking to myself, "Why should man, who has been created to live free, be a slave to the wishes of others and live his life according to their behest? There are no distinctions among people; all are alike. All can live in natural freedom."

In cold or rainy weather I would see the servants toiling and slaving away in their scanty clothing, rewarded only by adverse comments from their mistresses and rebuked by them for no good reason. This grieved me tremendously and left me heartsick, and I would ask myself, "What difference is there between them and the ladies, except that the latter wear satin dresses and God has chosen to favor them with worldly blessings? So why should the former be the dominated, the latter the dominators? And if one holds authority, why not have due regard for one's kind and be a benefactor to them? Those who look down upon these unfortunates because they are needy would do well to remember that just as the servants are in need of clothing and food and shelter, the masters are in need of their service and cooperation and help. In this world people need and are needed by each other, some for money, others for service. So where is the distinction? Where is the superiority? Why all this harshness and force? I don't understand."

I would hear, for instance, "Why did you break that bowl?" Or, "Why did you use up that much water?" Everyone has an obligation to his subordinates, whether high or low, whether king or minister or lady. What I mean is that anyone who becomes lord of a realm or a city, or mistress of a household, has a certain responsibility, and must make every effort to be good-natured and strong-willed. Determination and perseverance are important, priceless strengths. Resolve and nobility— these exist in order to produce results and benefits. What result do these two virtues bring about? Uprightness and dutifulness. Can one find two words higher and finer than these?

Man responds to this simple impulse with utmost audacity and cheer of heart, and, when necessary, with perfect resignation and acquiescence. A definition of duty, such that it corresponds to reality, is impossible. We look for our sense of responsibility within our conscience. So long as we resist the idea that "From the vantage point of law and conscience, duty is something which we are bound to fulfill," or incline to another theory which says, "That law whose existence and realization are determined by rationality consists of the actions based upon our character and customs," we will fail to apprehend the more profound connotations of duty as we should.

Man finds himself hamstrung by the idea of duty, though the fair-minded and trustworthy person is always prepared to discharge it. One could say that fulfilling one's duty is often easier than knowing it. We can be sure that determining one's duties ranks among the indispensable requirements of life. The duties and tasks that the law sets forth in this regard are the primary political responsibilities of the first importance in preserving human society. These include: "Thou shalt not kill another!" "Thou shalt not usurp what belongs to another!" "If married, thou shalt deal honestly and honorably with thy spouse and educate thy children!"

These stipulations of the law are nothing other than the primary sense of responsibility that everyone acknowledges. Ethical conduct, on the other hand, dictates the fulfillment of many transcendent responsibilities which the law does not recognize and, therefore, cannot enforce. Nevertheless, we have been exposed to a certain dictum of duty which, without any need for external advice, communicates its instructions to our minds and hearts in the clearest possible language, and serves as a guide for our actions and conduct. What obstacles bedevil man in the path of recognizing his duties? What defeats man's sense of duty? Selfishness, sensuality, laziness, fear, a weak will . . . [gap in the Persian edition of the text]

AMUSEMENTS AT COURT

Whatever this youth wanted was immediately made available to him. The announcement of a play raised quite a racket. Everyone was pleased that in addition to their other pastimes, a fresh one had been thought up.

Every afternoon I received five complimentary tickets, sent by the bridegroom to his bride. Most nights, after wrangling permission from my mother, I went to the theater. Often she refused permission, and I would give away my tickets.

When I awoke every morning, the first thing I saw over my head was a collection of fine Chinese vases filled with flowers of every hue and fragrance, sent to me fresh every day. Usually, these were accompanied by brief notes written by the newly-married youth and scented tastefully with rose, very simple and courteous. However, receiving no reply from me, he would content himself with these messages.

Some five or six months passed. The poor boy tried every means at his disposal, but was unable to gain an interview with me. Completely oblivious to all that went on, I did not understand his intentions and was insensible to everything but dolls and the games involving them. One spring night, when the air was warm and mild, the audience chamber was declared off-limits to the public, and I went into His Majesty's company for the evening amusement. That night 'Abdi Jan's troupe had been called so that the harem occupants could watch the show.

Of course, you remember 'Abdi well. Let me, nonetheless, give you a description of his looks. He was a lad of about twelve or thirteen, with large, black eyes, languid and incredibly beautiful and attractive. His face was tanned and good-looking, his lips crimson, and his hair black and thick. Renowned throughout the town, the boy had a thousand adoring lovers. Being a dancer, however, he was unworthy of being anyone's beloved.

Early that evening, about an hour after nightfall, my father went into the dinner room as was his custom. When he went in to have his dinner, the ladies likewise went home to theirs. Finishing their meal in the dark hours, they returned to His Majesty's presence. The festivities and the music that night were more grand and varied than before, beginning at two or three hours after dusk and continuing for seven or eight hours. I had my mother's permission to eat my dinner in the garden, along with my nanny and one of my father's wives, before returning home. Holding my father's wife's hand, I sat near a large pool illuminated by several lamps. A maidservant brought us a portion of my father's dinner and we both ate. Then we went for a long pleasure stroll along the broad garden avenues. Our other companions were eating their dinners and talking, seated where we had left them.

We were both young, I almost a child and she almost an adolescent. In the still silence of the night we walked firmly and quietly on the gravel. Looking at the moon, which shone with a strange glow, each was busy with her own thoughts. Calm and stillness had enveloped the promenade, and the air was so barren of sound that it echoed with our slightest movement, our quietest sound. The reigning silence produced an effect as of nature having gone to sleep and laying its head on the pillow of death's brother. Joining hands with this silence was the darkness of the night, which added to one's fears. The eardrum, straining in every direction, despaired of vibrating with any sound. Only the tree branches waving in the evening breeze punctured the silence with their echo.

For the viewer, the only consolation was the sight of the stars, twinkling irregularly in the inverted azure dome of the sky. The gentle light of the moon, piercing the leaves to fall upon the ground, inspired a sense of fear. The cluster of trees cast further darkness over this fearsome scene, heightening twofold the awful blackness of the shadows.

Suddenly we heard a stifled sound from the middle of the trees. In terror I clung to the young woman's arms, saying, "My dear! Let's go back. Let's go back to our companions. It's been about half an hour that we have been walking about, and we're very far from them. Now that they are looking for us, what will they think of this unexpected absence? Hurry, hurry, let's go back because I'm trembling, though I don't know why. O God! Am I such a coward? Am I terrified by the darkness and silence of the night? No, no! I'm not afraid of these; my fear is that this unexplained absence will cause me trouble."

The young woman smiled and said, "Didn't you notice with what great insistence I asked you to get permission so that we could have our dinner here tonight?"

"Why?" I asked.

"Didn't you take note of why I have chosen to bring us to this dark and quiet walkway?"

I replied in the negative.

The Golestan grounds in front of Badgir Palace in the late-Naseri period. The women of the royal harem were permitted to stroll in the gardens of the outer court during the *qoroq*, when the palace was off-limits to all male members of the shah's court.

Clapping her hands together, she stopped suddenly and said, "I want to talk to you about something important. If you wish, we can sit on the bench near the walkway so I can tell you."

Quite taken aback, I asked, "Was this matter so important that we had to walk all this way, creep through the darkness, hide ourselves from view, and expose ourselves to possible difficulties?"

Putting a finger to her lips, she commanded me to silence. With a deep sigh she said, "Yes, of course this matter is important and demanding of attention! Yes, this is a sad and fearful story. Oh yes! It is so important that for ten days now I have been struggling for the opportunity and the courage to tell you. You must solemnly vow that you will tell no one else, if I tell you. Otherwise, let's go back and leave the subject alone."

"Very well," I said, "let's go. Let's go and sit on that bench by the water. It is bright there, and if anyone else should come by, we'll see him before he can hear us."

She agreed and we set off. Her words had struck the fuse of my imagination like a flash of lightning, kindling all manner of silly notions. The night is inherently a begetter of fears, which are magnified by the particulars of the place. In such circumstances can one limit the scope of one's fancy? Never! One is constantly beset by awe and trepidation, terror and anxiety, caught in the balance between fear and hope, which are counterparts to each other and are considered fundamental in life. And so we both drew near to the bench and sat down. I had a feeling that the words I was going to hear were not any ordinary, routine speech. To prepare myself, I had to call on my courage and fortitude.

"I'm ready," I said. "Please proceed."

She looked at me and said, "Have you any idea?"

قصر بادگير عمارت گلستان

Royal palace of Badgir (wind tower), the centerpiece of the Golestan complex in Tehran. Erected in the early-nineteenth century, it was repeatedly remodeled under Naser al-Din Shah. It housed the Peacock Throne and was the site of Mozaffar al-Din Shah's coronation in 1896.

"About what?"

"About the person who has been hovering around you like a moth around a candle."

"No. Who is this person?"

"An agitated youth who wants nothing from life except you."

"Whom do you mean by this youth?"

She chuckled and said, "Ah, you're feigning ignorance! I don't consider you that slow-witted. Oh no! I see that you understand quite well, but pretend that you don't."

Looking at her in surprise, I said, "My dear! What is it you want me to know? You are well aware that I know nothing and don't understand what you mean."

"Then," she said, "I must explain it to you."

"Certainly."

She went on, "This young man, this unfortunate man, this poor, bereft man whose mother kept him away from you, is now near death. He loves you with all his heart and soul. He has pleaded with me to tell you of his love, and to seek your help and cooperation. Furthermore, I am to learn if you have ever looked upon him with affection and intend to reciprocate his love or not."

I cried aloud, "Good Lord! By what right did you accept such a charge, and why did you tell me this? You know well that I am under the guardianship of a strict mother and a powerful and stern father. Besides, before my Heavenly Father I have contracted myself to another and now belong to him. I have no power or authority; I am quite weak and helpless. What's more, I know nothing of love, for I have loved only two people: my mother and father. Apart from them I will love no one. Oh, oh! God help me if in my condition of captivity and restriction, my mind confused, I should lose the reins of my heart! Madam, madam! I beg you, leave me to myself and do not lead me astray. I forbid you to say such things."

She said, "What I intended by bringing this up was nothing other than that if you also love him and give him a pledge of your affection, he can have your marriage annulled and marry you himself."

I said, "This is impossible. My all-powerful, royal father would never take this step, because kings derive their power and authority from standing by their word. Besides, my sister and this youth will soon begin celebrating their nuptials. Please tell him from me that I do not consent to this and you are forbidden to raise the subject." Then, standing up, I said, "Let's go back."

A total silence, reminiscent of the silence of death, surrounded us. We were each thinking our own thoughts, walking toward the garden path very slowly. All around us, flowers and blossoms were filling the air with their fragrance, and a soft, cool breeze touched my mournful, burning cheeks. I found myself standing at the edge of a bottomless precipice whose opening had been covered up with variegated, colorful flowers; the slightest slip, and I would be sucked in. A new train of thought took form in my mind, appalling and dreadful. My heart was heavy, palpitating so furiously that I could do nothing to slow it down.

In that state, after a few minutes we arrived at the spot where our companions were waiting for me. My nanny reproached me gently and lovingly, saying, "Your absence prompted me to search the entire garden, but I couldn't find you. Where were you? Your mother came and, not finding you, went to look for you. She was upset and in a bad temper."

Feeling a nervous tremor coming on, I replied, "I was near the water, sitting on a bench with that lady, not very far from here. We were watching the moon."

Just then my father emerged from the dinner room. Cheerful and in good spirits, he began to take a walk. When he came up to me, he was infinitely kind and loving, taking a good look at me and my attire in the light of the large gas lamp. Then he put a few gold coins in my hand and began to speak to my female companion.

Meanwhile, 'Aziz appeared out of nowhere and immediately came to my father. After bowing he said, "The musicians are ready. Do I have His Majesty's permission to bring them in or not?"

"Bring them in!" my father said.

As 'Aziz turned to go back, he cast a longing, amorous look at me. Then he recklessly tossed aside a bouquet of flowers that the royal gardener had put together for him from the royal nursery with fastidious effort and at great expense. With his head cast down and his heart full of sorrow, he walked away. We accompanied my father to the auditorium, all of us sitting on chairs behind a screen.

As soon as I had sat down, still deep in thought, I leaned my head back and shut my eyes and allowed my mind to wander. Yes, it had been quite a while that the natural vitality of my wounded, bleeding heart had been obscured by the sands of despair. The light of hope had left nothing but a smoldering glow. I labored under a travail whose name and definition I did not know. I had always had a quiet, peaceful life, spending my days and nights free of mental preoccupation. But at this hour, an enormous tumult and confusion had been interjected into my simple, tranquil life, and a thousand dreadful thoughts ran back and forth through my imagination. This pure, young, newly-matured heart of mine, immaculate and crystalline as the surface of a lake, had been turned enormously murky by the conversation, and remained incapable of any comfort. I felt that I could go to meet death at any moment. The words had been terribly jarring to my ears, and a strong antipathy to this wife of my father's began to arise in my heart, inclining me to avoid her conversation for the rest of my life. While immersed in my melancholy thoughts, highly disturbed and nervous, I felt the touch of an affectionate kiss on my forehead. Opening my eyes, I saw my mother. With a gentle voice that seemed like music to my ears she said, "Are you unwell? Do you have a headache?"

Standing up, I kissed her hand and said, "No, I'm fine."

"Then why are you pale?"

I looked at her as I replied, "Oh no! I feel nothing but happiness."

"Very well, then," she said, "sit down and watch the show."

Her soft, sweet voice soothed the bitterness of my thoughts, and feeling somewhat relieved of the oppressive grief I had felt, I began to watch. But at every moment, it felt as though I could hear footsteps behind me; every time I turned around, this youngster was nearby like a circumambulating pilgrim, and I felt his lovelorn eyes burn into me like a flame. Immediately dropping my head, I would begin thinking again. Until that night, I had never found myself in such difficult straits. The young man's glances were poisoning my life, proffering me a potion mixed with death! I had never been afraid or timid about looking at this youth, and had always watched him freely. From this night onward, however, I was terrified of seeing him and unconsciously avoided looking at his face. A thunderstorm was raging inside me.

My father's wife, sitting next to me, frequently muttered, "Mind you, be careful! Why have you turned so pale and altered? Why are you lost and heartsick?"

I gave no answer, lost in my own thoughts. Meanwhile, the young man was going about with a flower basket full of nosegays, handing out flowers to each of the ladies. When he came to me, he stopped and said in a voice that could only be heard with the greatest difficulty, "Ah, my darling! Take this nosegay and put it on the spot that is constantly throbbing against me."

He gave me the nosegay. Astounded and will-less, I looked at him maniacally and said, "Don't speak to me!"

"I obey," he said, and strew a handful of colorful flowers under my feet.

Ah, my dear teacher! I cannot describe to you my feelings at that moment. I know only this: the nosegay became so heavy in my hand that I dropped it to the ground. All around me, I visualized a wilderness with flickering tongues of fire. At times I saw horrific figures amid the flames, calling to me in their harsh, awful voices. At others, I imagined they were torturing me. Shutting my eyes, I sank back in my chair. Suddenly I heard a voice saying, "You reckless, thoughtless girl!"

I opened my eyes to see my father's wife picking up the flowers. She said, "My dear! What happened? Why did you throw away the flowers? Oh look, look! There is a piece of paper hanging from the nosegay. Did you not stop to think that someone else might see the flowers?"

Wretched me! Not quite relieved of one fear, I was immediately plunged into the next. That night I had encountered so many unexpected surprises that I almost thought I saw a tub of blood before my eyes. My temples were convulsed and throbbing incessantly, and I felt a painful spasm as of someone about to go mad. My ears were constantly ringing. Fiery torrents of blood gushed painfully in my head, and through all these internal convulsions I repeatedly heard the words, "Take this nosegay and put it on the spot that is constantly throbbing against me."

I took the flowers and looked at them. Among the flowers was a little card with only the words, "I love you!"

This was the second time that night that I was hearing the word "love" from someone other than my mother or father. It seemed as strange and repulsive in my sight as did the guillotine to the condemned.

Tearing up the card, I hid the shreds in my pocket and continued to watch the show. Those beautiful instruments, those pleasant games, all seemed tiresome to me. I wanted to go home as soon as possible to get away from the clamor and the crowd and think only my own thoughts about the night's eventful developments.

The show finally came to an end and we went home. This was the only night that I had no sleep, the first time that the sweet, delightful slumber of childhood had become bitter and unpleasant. I was now a captive of never-ending sorrow. Henceforth, as far as lay in my power, I denied my father's wife any opening or opportunity to talk to me alone. I was particularly careful never to hear those words again.

Days and nights passed by in a flash. Soon my sister's nuptials were to be celebrated with all due splendor. I was nearly eleven years old. Despite all my coldness and silence, the young man's ardor had not cooled. In fact, his energy never flagged and he spared no pretext to express his love, devotion, and obedience. Little by little, my mind was stirred, and I began to watch him with attention. His face was not comely or lovable, but his looks struck at my heart like poisoned arrows—and there was no avoiding them. I began to feel equally interested in seeing him. If one day I was in His Majesty's presence and he was not, I felt like I had lost something. Sometimes I would be so engrossed in watching him that I would be unconscious of the talk around me, hearing nothing. And when I was asked, "Who was there in the chamber?" or "What happened at your father's court?" I could only answer, "I did not pay attention!" And, in fact, I had not, because my gaze had been directed at one spot. It was never possible to talk to him, however. And it was absolutely impossible for me to write. I never told him that I loved him—I did not know what the word meant.

The child bride's wedding began with pomp and ceremony. Receiving a hundred gold coins from my father for the wedding expenses, we prepared the bride's trousseau. At the wedding, the youngster could only send me a note in which he complained of all the woes and torments he had suffered and was suffering.

After the wedding my father set off on his travels, spending some four or five months away. I saw neither hide nor hair of the youngster during this time, because he had accompanied my father. I had a difficult time of it, because my father's wife, my constant companion, was also away. Since my brother was too young, however, my mother did not go, remaining in town with the rest of the harem residents. A few months later they returned. I was delighted to visit with my father's wife again. She told me of the promenades, the beauties and the delights of the trip, while I told her of my loneliness and grief. Finally she gave me a white, bloodstained handkerchief and said, "He has sent this souvenir for you with the words, 'The handkerchief is stained with my tears of blood.' The stains are from when he was greatly distressed and slashed his own hand."

Deeply horrified at the sight of this dreadful thing, I was woefully distraught. That night I saw the youth again for the first time in several months. During the trip, this unfortunate lad had been unable to contain himself and had acted like a lunatic. Most of the ladies had learned where matters stood. Soon, the talk swirling around the subject had risen to a chaotic murmur. However, out of fear for my father, no one had said anything explicit.

An orchestra had been brought to the orange grove, and all the ladies gathered there after dinner. It was a beautiful, pleasant night. I was delighted to see my father and the company again. During his absence, I had spent my days in lethargy, with nothing to occupy my mind. All the ladies were happy, laughing and strolling about the grounds. The orchestra was playing. Joy and vitality emanated from the very walls, and everyone was united in happiness.

The youngster came and stood among the group. He bowed pleasantly to me and said, "Ah, madam! I do not know how to befittingly express my regrets to you for your absence during this beautiful trip, which extended as far as the seashore. But even if you were not present in person, believe me, you were always present in my mind and heart, and I thought of no one but you."

Then he made a beautiful, reverent bow and walked away. Rooted to the spot, I was dumbfounded. These few simple, clear words from him had a strange effect on me. I could neither see nor hear anything. Leaning against the wall, I buried my face in my hands. After a while, when my condition eased somewhat, I saw him at a distance, leaning against an orange tree. Watching this emotional maelstrom within me, he was ruthlessly plucking leaves off the little tree that nature had placed at his mercy.

That exchange and the ensuing emotional upheaval immediately became the talk of the ladies, each one offering an explanation or positing an opinion. I felt trampled under the weight of the glances that rained on me like bullets from every direction. Everywhere I turned, my gaze fell upon incredulous eyes whose curiosity was transparent. Unlike earlier in the evening, when I had been happy, I was once again immersed in anguish. Every moment I encountered a fresh, unknown affliction, while the agony my counterpart suffered was no lighter than my own. And so another night came to an end.

At about this time, my prospective husband's family sought my father's permission for the nuptials to proceed. This was unbearably painful for the youngster. My father, however, refused permission. In fact, he was quite upset. "The girl is too young," he said. "It will have to wait." There was a reason for this attempt to obtain permission. The following year would witness the Shah's jubilee. Of course, at such a great celebration everyone would enhance his power and privilege according to his deserts. Since from the very beginning my father-in-law-to-be had sought me for his son with this idea in mind—in the hope that he would make dramatic gains in position and prerogative—there was no better time for the nuptials. The new bride would inevitably enjoy His Majesty's favor and all her wishes would be granted immediately. I had forgotten to mention that when I was betrothed, my future father-in-law was honored with the title Sardar-e Akram (Most Distinguished Commander), and titles in those days indicated great status; hence, he was a commander of the highest, most accomplished rank.

Suitors who asked for our hand, whether for themselves or their sons, were principally motivated by their own benefit.

Having a daughter of the sovereign in the family empowered and authorized one to perpetrate any transgression against people's lives, property, and honor with impunity. We unfortunate ones were tools in their hands—weapons that nature turned against ourselves. I often think and see how man slumbers heedlessly, how distant he is from God, how helplessly a plaything of strange desires and hopes. Never satisfied with the course of events, he always resists nature, oblivious that it works its will whereas he languishes in the valley of blighted hopes and disappointments.

What is life but a trail of fast-sinking hopes and desires? A sage Arab poet-philosopher has said, "Life is pain and torment from beginning to end. I wonder not, except at him who wishes to prolong this lifetime of suffering." A momentary pause shows us that this definition is not an exercise in fantasy or oratory. Not a day or an hour passes without numerous proofs and reinforcements of its validity. Has not everyone passionately explored life's battleground of struggle? Day and night people are mounted on the lightning steed of effort and action, striving to find ease in unease, happiness in suffering, safety in danger. Yes! These struggles, these suicides, these reversals are the foundation of the world's equilibrium and the raison d'être of order in the mill of creation. Were it not for mankind's perpetual struggle, the thread of order in the world would have snapped, creation would have ceased to make progress, the great and the insignificant would have been indistinguishable, and the beautiful could not have been told apart from the ugly.

If we consider the first epoch of man's existence, we will discover a strange form, wandering hungry and naked in the wilderness, going nowhere. The signs of abasement and destitution are evident from his carriage. He is continually thinking of laying hands on something to appease the tortured inferno that is his stomach. Then, crawling into mountain gorges or caves, or under the shelter of rocks, he passes the night. His body trembles with fear of beasts. They have been endowed by nature with covering; he is naked. They are armed with claws and talons and teeth; he is defenseless. They move together in packs; he is alone. The only thing that protects him in this bewildering, perilous environment is his power of intellect and cogitation. Once it transcends the condition of savagery and hostility, we see that this very same human race has begun to prosper, to claim supremacy, to build mansions and palaces, to take possession of the earth's abundance, to fix the position of the heavenly horizons, to make the surface of the sea and the expanse of space the thoroughfare of his ships and airplanes, and to subjugate the invisible forces of nature to his will. Is this capable, talented man the same abject, timid, impotent creature that roamed the wilderness with the animals? Yes, he is! When he became fed up with his state of helplessness, necessity, his persistent tormentor, further robbed him of his strength. Resigned to toil, he strove to the limit of his ability until he found the path to betterment. For many a day he endured this manner of living, until, over several millennia, the early signs of collective civilization began to appear and, little by little, man rose to his present state.

I must not, therefore, marvel at people's greed and ambition today. The more extensive man's reach becomes, the more his needs increase. No matter how much progress he makes in luxury and opulence, he seeks something still better. The hawk hunts the sparrow, paying no heed to its cries for help. Man decapitates the suckling lamb and captures the fowls of the air and the fish of the sea to consume them for his nourishment. When animals find a tasty morsel or a verdant pasture, they fight each other. It is no wonder then if, in order to gain authority or rank, men choose a sultan's daughter for a bride. What is amazing is that they never attain their goal. Likewise, this poor man did not gain the object he had in view. An unexpected turn of events shattered his dreams: the assassination of my father, which occurred the following year.

At about this time, my father fell in love with a twelve-year-old girl. This girl, the sister of one of his wives, was the daughter of a gardener whose first daughter was already a partner in the throne of Persia and whose second daughter now seemed poised to increase the family's stakes. The younger sister was the same woman who, for many years, enjoyed the sovereign's affection and could do as she pleased. As a girl, she was rosy-cheeked, with large, black eyes. Somewhat deranged, she often made bizarre requests. Her name was Mah-Rokhsar (Moon-Faced), an almost apt name for she was incredibly beautiful. Her speech was so sweet that she drew his attention in spite of himself. At first his love for her was a mere whim. Gradually, however, it grew to unexpected proportions.

The older sister became jealous and stubbornly set herself to reverse the situation. Not having anticipated the speedy march of royal ardor, she herself had been the means of bringing them together. When she saw that his passion was leading to a love approaching mania, she kicked up a raging fuss and employed every artifice known to woman. My father paid her no attention at first. Ultimately, however, he was forced to bring in a third party to mediate the situation satisfactorily and quietly. Every day the sovereign showered new favors on the older sister, sending her large sums of money and expensive jewelry. However, the humbler and more submissive she saw him, the more intense her machinations became and the more strenuously she worked at keeping her sister away from my poor father. The several mansions she was given all to herself, the profitable lands transferred to her ownership, the magnificent houses purchased for her abroad—none of these swayed her in the least. My poor father considered himself the most wretched of the world's kings at this time, and had lost all reins of authority. When His Majesty the sovereign was downhearted, the entire palace was downhearted. The matter had assumed such proportions that there was talk of it in every nook and corner. The remarkable thing was that this twelve-year-old girl never shied away from expressing her love for my father, giving evidences of her affection with childish gestures that grew out of sincerity and honesty. For instance, despite the restrictions and impositions placed on her by her elder sister, whenever she saw my father she would run to him, throw herself in his arms, and say through her tears, "Ah, you're here? I'm so glad you came. Today they beat me ten times more than before, because I missed you and cried for you and kissed your picture."

I could see clearly what effect these simple words had on the poor man's heart, and how he struggled to contain his love through his majestic dignity. How sad I felt for my poor father, who involuntarily kissed her in everyone's presence and said, "Continue to love your king, my dear, for he loves you, too!" Then the girl would begin her childish play, fondling my father's head and face and throwing herself in his arms to sleep. As soon as they tried to take her away from him, she would begin to cry.

My dear teacher! Do not look down on my father; he was rendered helpless by this love. These unfortunate monarchs are foremost in misery among the people of the world. From

Khanom Bashi (right), one of Naser al-Din Shah's later favorites, known as "the Chief Gardener's daughter." A close ally of Amin al-Soltan, she was allegedly an inadvertent accomplice in the Premier's palace machinations. The young girl to her right could very well be her sister, Mah-Rokhsar. Barely into her teens, Mah-Rokhsar apparently attracted undivided royal attention on the sole merit of a close resemblance to the shah's early love, Jayran Forugh al-Saltana.

early childhood they hear and see nothing but lies, hypocrisy, and deviousness. Every person who bows to them does so out of fear or necessity. Anyone who shows them affection is after money or jewelry. Every service performed for them is motivated by the hope of prestige or preferment. It should come as no surprise that, in contrast to the poisonous words of hypocrites and schemers, the sincere prattle of this child won my father's heart. Welcoming her love at this late stage of his life, he reciprocated it ardently. This double-sided love—one side motivated by sincerity, the other by a distrust for humanity—gave the elder sister unimaginable power and independence. Indeed, the true sovereign of Persia at the time was this woman, doing what she wanted and saying what she pleased.

Amid the hubbub generated by the love of a woman at such an august court, the opportunists found their chance and, galloping into the arena, had a field day. My father's inner confusion and emotional turmoil had left him no leisure to attend to his affairs. The reins of state had fallen into the hands of two individuals who were hostile and inimical to each other. One was my brother, Na'eb al-Saltana; the other was Mirza 'Ali Asghar Khan, the Grand Vizier.

THE GRAND VIZIER

This Grand Vizier, this first subject of the realm, was the grandson of a Zoroastrian named Zal. On the mother's side of the family he was Jewish. Early in my father's reign, his father had been a butler, a man of no ability. Working his way up through the butlery, he had risen to the rank of Amin al-Soltan (Trustee of the King).

Do not be amazed that the son of Zal became Amin al-Soltan at the court of the Persian sovereign. This was one of the great tactics my father had thought up to ensure the independence of his throne: to elevate base, ignorant men to positions of authority. He must have read the history of the French Revolution several times to learn that great families should be annihilated, and the power of knowledge vanquished and eliminated through ignorance. He must also have forgotten that ignorance flourishes only briefly, after which knowledge once again raises its head irresistibly and yields its results. In the same way, when the shining orb of the sun strides majestically across the threshold of the empyrean to its retreat in the west and hides itself from our eyes in the depths of the boundless horizon, darkness envelops the surface of the earth. But the eastern gazelle of the dawn raises her luminous head from her fiery chamber and drowns the world in the golden waves of her glow, rendering every atom in creation grateful for her outpouring of light and warmth. The birds in the trees burst into song, the variegated members of the vegetable kingdom raise their heads from the night's ponderous sleep to usher in the monarch of the stars, the queen of flowers adorns the emerald expanse of verdure with her winsome beauty, dewdrops tumble along the azure of the leaves, hill and dale, valley, stream, desert, sea and vista present their views to you, the watchers. The sleeping world awakens in you and every life form on our teeming planet resumes its work.

After the death of Amin al-Soltan, the same Mirza 'Ali Asghar Khan first inherited the rank of Amin al-Soltan, and later assumed that of Grand Vizier. Soon he forgot his patrimonial ice bucket and set himself up against my brother, who was Vice-Regent, Supreme Commander, and Minister of War. This Grand Vizier and first subject was a boundless, inexhaustible conflagration. The nation's entire wealth was held in his purse and in that of his brother, Amin al-Molk; and yet, after all his efforts to this end, would he be sated? His excesses transcended the realm's frontiers, and many others shared in his exploits. He harbored a peculiar love for the country's denigration, striving to lay its future basis firmly, and he spared no effort to oppress and persecute the subjects of the realm. With incredible mastery he was able to lay the blame for his actions at my dear brother's doorstep and raise the ire of the populace against him. Among the things he did in his lifetime was befriending and helping the poor and the sayyids and establishing fees and salaries for the sacred shrines. He freely spent and dissipated the wealth of the populace as though it were a bequest to him from the late Amin al-Soltan, all the while oblivious to the fact that government functionaries had extorted this money from peasants and laborers by the stroke of the whip. Any matter that smelled of intrigue, he indulged in without the least remorse, with a view to winning popularity among the masses.

The Grand Vizier's conduct was not unlike the man who, on the night of Alexander the Great's birth, set fire to the temple of the goddess Diana so that his name would be recorded in the pages of history. He lost no opportunity for intrigue to wreak the nation's ruin and the monarchy's overthrow, unlike my brother who maintained an impartial and independent stance. The land of Persia and her people were, indeed, the playthings of this Grand Vizier's whims, and awaited a grim future. Today we clearly see the results of his acts.

He was uncommonly fond of women, whom he received in great number in his gardens and apartments. All these women had been bribed with enormous sums of money to cast aspersions on my brother, to speak well of himself, and to report all the news from the evening meetings. One might say he commanded a secret police force comprised of prostitutes who

Kamran Mirza in all his glory, with an assortment of decorations from home and abroad. The vice-regent (*na'eb al-saltana*) was renowned for his resemblance to his father, Naser al-Din Shah.

relayed all the activities and ideas of the people to him in detail. He spent most nights gambling, and if he happened to gamble away several pounds one night, he would dismiss and replace the governor of Shiraz the next morning, receiving a hundred thousand *tuman*s in the bargain. Or he would accuse a well-established, wealthy family in His Majesty's presence and have them imprisoned, consenting to their release only after payment of exorbitant ransoms.

He put one in mind of the Roman emperor Caligula, who was from the family of the famous Caesar and who ascended the throne after Tiberias. Initially, he treated his people and soldiers well, freeing the prisoners and showering his people with kindness. Before long, however, he underwent a complete change and became ruthless and bloodthirsty. He took his own sister to wife, and after her death had statues of her installed in the temples and commanded the people to worship her as a goddess. He even raised his horse to the rank of an oracle. He seized people's wives and then let them go. He is known to have said, "I have the right to do anything to anyone." One day he invited all the grandees and notables to a banquet. Suddenly he burst into laughter. When asked why he laughed he said, "I laugh because in the space of half an hour I could have all of you beheaded." One of the strange statements that has come down from him is this: "Oh, how I wish that all the people in Rome had but one head, that I might strike it off with one blow!"

The Grand Vizier and first subject was of the same persuasion. Stranger yet is this, that he accomplished it all: he had my father killed, my brother dispossessed, and the government of Persia sold to foreigners.

While this man was busy oppressing the people and despoiling the country, there were also dealers of destruction

Amin al-Soltan's residence in Tehran, known as Park-e Atabak. Built sumptuously in the style of a French mansion, it was furnished with items brought back from the Grand Vizier's several foreign tours to Europe and the Far East. Some years after his assassination, the residence became the compound of the Russian embassy.

on the opposite side. One of these was a certain Aqa Bala Khan who enjoyed my brother's love and esteem. With my brother's encouragement and cooperation, he laid unjust hands on people's property and lives, assaulting the wretched subjects repeatedly and mercilessly. He had no compunctions about murder, pillage, theft, and avarice. From another direction, the clan of the Taleshi, to whom my father had given his loving support, plundered the subjects' property, reducing them to total wretchedness. From yet another direction, the governors of the realm refused to stop at people's lives and property, but did every blessed thing they pleased. And finally, another brother of mine, Zell al-Soltan, did little to stem his own cruelty and tyranny toward the subjects, and made numerous enemies among the tribes for the royal family.

The kingdom was in the throes of death, the subjects wretched and destitute, the governors busily wreaking oppression with full force. Persia's political landscape was so bleak, and the people so heartsick and disgusted, that in everyone's face one could see the unmistakable signs of disaffection. The nation was edging close to the time when the thunderous clamor of the multitudes would tear down and demolish the pillars of monarchy and release the people from the yoke of continuous oppression.

In these latter days, intermittent noises were heard here and there, but these were quickly silenced by my father's delicate balance of unity. Among them were the Régie and the situation with Aqa Sayyid Jamal the Afghan, the latter culminating in catastrophe. Meanwhile, Malkom Khan was sending up sparks abroad, and Amin al-Dawla was busy effecting a general awakening. Outwardly, it was still the same king, the same monarchy. Inwardly, it had rotted and was drawing closer to destruction day by day. If a man of foresight had looked at the

"The Shadow of the King," Prince Zell al-Soltan in his Kaiserian attire with the Aqdas medallion featuring a portrait of his father, Naser al-Din Shah. The emblem of the lion and the sun on his helmet was symbolic of the mighty army that he created on the German model.

situation carefully, he would surely have said, "I bid farewell to this monarchy in decline."

While beset by this chaos and all these unpatriotic enemies, my poor father was deeply in love and engrossed with matters of the heart. Owing to this love and the family's confusion, Mirza 'Ali Asghar Khan, the Grand Vizier, not only gained the upper hand over my brother, but he also discovered all the royal secrets. Guided by instructions from a foreign master and using the suggestion of imminent bloodshed as a weapon, he added to my father's troubles every day and enlarged the scope of his corruption, hypocrisy, and activities harmful to the state.

My father had been reduced to exasperation by the over-bearing conduct of the woman who had once been his favorite, whom he had long loved from the depth of his heart, and whose sister he now had the misfortune to love. Weary of face-to-face encounters with her, he had delegated such tasks as a formal duty to this same well-intentioned Grand Vizier, making him the means of resolving the situation. My father authorized him to speak to the woman (known as "the Chief Gardener's daughter" because of her father's occupation) and use all the means necessary to win her consent to the marriage between my father and her sister. Delighted with the turn of events, the Grand Vizier agreed.

During this time my father heard reports from here and there that the Grand Vizier had received large sums of money from overseas and was hatching a conspiracy. All his treacherous conduct toward the government and the nation had come to light and reached the sovereign's ears. But one could not simply dismiss or execute a grand vizier with no evidence, although there was a buzz of rumors about his dismissal and execution. The Grand Vizier, for his part, needed to gain access to royal secrets, and Mah-Rokhsar provided him with the means. This man, who was the confidant of the throne and the realm; who held in his grasp the reputations, lives, property, and honor of the nation; who was so trusted by His Majesty that he had been given permission to enter the harem—this noble, benevolent personage so conscious of his indebtedness dealt so masterfully with my poor father's wife that the wisest of women would have been tricked into disclosing her secrets. In the course of fulfilling his conciliatory mission, this wicked Grand Vizier learned all the privy affairs of government from the unsuspecting lady. She had no idea that her answers to his questions would ultimately roll up the curtain over a bloody scene.

Since this lady had been especially loved and trusted by my father, whenever he read important correspondence she stood behind him holding the lamp. My father did not imagine that she was capable of reading all the various styles of handwriting; or perhaps the sheer force of his love blinded him to the possibility that she might betray the secrets of government. Whatever the case, he was not very careful. He would read all the documents in the privacy of his bedroom at night, and the next day the Grand Vizier would extract all the information from the poor lady in his interviews with her. In addition to benefiting from the information, he extended the sphere of his mischief in order to work my father's ruin. While he was busy with his schemes, he also secured jobs for two sisters, Fatima and Nosrat, in the harem so that they could report to him twenty-four hours a day.

None of this is strange. The viper becomes deadly when it senses that its fangs are about to be extracted. Yes! In times of happiness and prosperity, the abasement and deprivation of a former time are forgotten. The butlery and the ice bucket are consigned to the shelf of oblivion. Obviously, authority, riches, property, and power wipe out one's sense of gratitude, replacing it with tyranny, injustice, bloodthirstiness, enmity, and hard-heartedness. The power to issue unquestioned orders and to command obeisance and undeserved respect engenders cruelty. This greedy and ambitious man was not at fault and should not be condemned if he sacrificed my father for the continuance of his ruthless authority. Rather, my father should be blamed for appointing a grand vizier and first subject who brought ruin upon the country, murdered him, and darkened Persia's future. Had this Grand Vizier been appointed to his position by virtue of merit, had his parents been from a decent family, and had he been educated, let us say, in law, perhaps he would not have been so inherently perfidious. Even if he betrayed the generosity of his lord, he would at least spare the nation. If he considered the monarch to be murderous and worthy of death, he would desist from selling the poor, wretched, hard-working peasant to foreigners. The very mention of treason would be a grave sin to him, whether with respect to the government or the people. But alas! This man was a gullible, ambitious, evil-minded commoner who spared no effort to bring destruction on Persia.

Every daughter has a duty to mourn the loss of her father, and I grieve for mine as a daughter should. But I am infinitely more unhappy and heart-stricken for this soil, this land of my birth and upbringing. Now, as I write this, it seems as though the veil of ignorance is lifted from my sight and all the events of the past are marching before me in a procession. O woe for the country and nation that was made a sacrifice to one man's avarice!

But believe me, my teacher! Today I take pride in such a father and consider him absolved of all blame and guilt. The poor man was but one person, and could do no more than he did. Had be been given the chance, he would have emancipated his subjects during the jubilee celebrations and provided a firm constitutional basis for Persia. The Grand Vizier's misdeeds would have been proven through a legal process before a national parliament and the guilty man executed. But alas! Soon—much sooner than he could have anticipated—the premier caught on to the situation and forestalled his lofty intentions, tossing the wretched nation into the shattering storm of defenselessness.

Having extracted a good deal of important information from the lady (after prolonging the matter for a few months) he had finally convinced her to consent to my father's marrying her sister. But there were numerous conditions. Among them: after they were married, my father must not keep Mah-Rokhsar in the harem, but house her elsewhere. This was a strange plan, a gross example of impudence, but it worked. This poor father of mine who, blindly and unconsciously, disclosed all his royal secrets to this traitor of a grand vizier, viewed the plan as a great indulgence to himself; he agreed to have her live outside the harem. Women say, "Let our beloved husbands do whatever they like, so long as they do it outside and not to our faces." They forget that the husband's life and property, to say nothing of his honor, must be guarded both within and without.

Well, a house was found outside the harem and the girl was contracted in a temporary marriage and taken there. What was the Grand Vizier's objective in having Mah-Rokhsar leave the harem? His chief purpose was this: my father, being the sovereign, could not abandon affairs of state during the day and go to his beloved's house in full public view to indulge his pleasure; he would have to go at night. If he went back and forth during the day, the Grand Vizier could turn to the people and say, "Your king is a thoughtless fellow who ignores matters of national importance to lose himself in dalliance." My poor father had understood the situation and planned all his movements at night. Inevitably, he would go without his royal entourage; there would be no armed escort. He would be alone or accompanied by only one servant, both traveling in an ordinary carriage. On the way there or back, the lackey could have seized the opportunity to murder him. It was truly a well-conceived plan. Why it did not succeed I do not know.

PREPARING FOR THE JUBILEE

The Shah's jubilee was approaching, now only a few months away, and the ladies were all busy making preparations. Owing to the peace between the lady and Mah-Rokhsar, and the fact that my father had attained his goal, the sorrowful dreariness that had enveloped us all dissipated. Cheerfulness and joy returned and life began anew and a new court was convened. My beloved father was so ecstatic that one could not conceive of any limit to his happiness. He was kind and generous to the guests, one and all. Unable to conceal his joy, he granted them everything they asked for. This was especially true when, instead of the usual volume of importunate petitions, he received a love letter.

During the time that unhappiness had held sway at the royal court, both within and without, and everyone had antic-ipated matters coming to a head moment by moment, I spent many a weary day. I was on my way to finding out what love meant, what attachment was. I felt deeply that I was in love with the youth, but I never violated my obligations or over-stepped the bounds of decency and lawfulness; I kept my composure and never disregarded caution. Not a soul had an inkling of my love for him, not even himself. But he was not at all concerned whether I felt toward him as he did toward me. Through all my inner turmoil he never stopped using the word. Ten times a day he would send me messages through anyone and everyone, saying, "I love you." All I did in response was to heave a deep sigh and turn my teary eyes skyward.

Before long, this youth lost all his self-restraint and could no longer conceal his pain. All the residents of the harem were witnesses to his tempest of love and whispered about it among themselves. Circumstances, too, appeared to cooperate with the poor young man. Every minute of every day there was a new occasion to celebrate. The ladies hosted grand parties in their homes every day, and in all the sovereign's private mansions or in the government house or in the White Hall there would be no end of music and theater and orchestras and shows. The stricken lad had many opportunities to see me, often watching from afar.

My father at this time had become completely like a child. So great was his joy that he found a fresh amusement or cause for celebration every moment. Many a night he would urge everyone to walk about in total darkness. He had previously equipped numerous page boys and eunuchs with masks and told them to appear suddenly and frighten the ladies, who, screaming and running helter-skelter, would fall to the ground and afford him a good laugh. Gambling sessions were held almost every night. He would pull new money out of his pocket, shiny bright coins, and distribute it among the ladies, and the games would begin.

One of the games which I was particularly fond of and never missed watching whenever it was played was one

invented by my father and called "lights out." There were a
hundred or so gas lamps in the *andarun*, but the electric lamp
was a recent invention and all the royal mansions had been
equipped with it. The venue of the game was the White Hall;
my father had chosen it because it was large and spacious.
Whenever the game was to be played, the ladies would be
informed in the afternoon that there would be "lights out"
that night. Respected women and ladies of birth usually
demurred, considering it a great loss of dignity for themselves.
The others, however, were keenly interested and would begin
to play with immense enjoyment. This game, so important, so
loved by all, was outwardly a childish pastime. In reality my
father had serious objectives in promoting it: first, he wanted
to know everything about the inner workings of the harem;
second, he wanted to know which ladies were enemies and
which were friends. This was the best way for him to find out.
The ladies not only failed to catch on to his true intentions at
first, but even at the end they had no idea what he was trying
to accomplish. On the surface of it, the game seemed to them
no more than an imaginative diversion.

The game consisted of turning out the lights. In the
darkness the women had absolute freedom and license to kiss
each other, beat each other, bite each other, blind each other,
or break each others' heads and limbs. At the beginning of the
game the ladies would all sit in the middle of the hall, talking
among themselves. My father would sit on a chair near the
light switch. As they were busy in their conversation, he would
turn out the light. Suddenly all hell would break loose.
Screams, cries for help, oaths, curses and wailing would be
heard everywhere. Everyone was up to something. The
dignified ones crept into corners or hid under a bench, a table
or a chair to find safety. The wild ones doled out and received
their beatings. Of course, as you know, it is the wicked who

His Majesty's Bed Chamber (Khwabgah), one of Naser al-Din Shah's prodigal additions to the Golestan royal complex in Tehran. Erected in 1886 to replace the older *andarun* structure (see page 123), it was inspired by the architecture of the Dolma Baghcha palace in Istanbul which the shah had visited some years earlier. The venue of Naser al-Din Shah's nocturnal amusements, it also housed in the basement the shah's private treasury. The building was the victim of Reza Shah's anti-Qajar grudge. In the late-1930s it was demolished overnight to make room for the Ministry of Finance.

form the majority. Amid this pandemonium of keening and wailing whose effect was heightened by the absolute darkness—presenting a bizarre spectacle to the observer, as of a corner in hell in which a thousand perils awaited man—the lights would suddenly come back on, catching everybody in some act. Usually the clothes would be ripped to shreds, the faces and cheeks bloody, the bodies obscenely exposed; the beatings had been so severe that the largest stitch of clothing on anyone was no bigger than a quarter meter. The women's faces were grotesque, their hair disheveled, their eyes bloodshot and filled with rage. As for those who had preferred caution, they were a strange sight to behold, hiding under tables and chairs with their arms and legs thrust out.

The wonder of it all was this: as soon as the light was turned on everyone began to laugh, and the game would begin all over again. After some two or three hours of this game, my father would finally take royal compassion on the bruised and battered participants; those whose dresses had been shredded beyond use would be honored with money for new clothes. The session concluded, the poor women would scatter to go home, where they attended to their appearance until morning. I am amazed that when it was time to resume the game, they were eagerly prepared, and gleefully submitted to an orgy of punching and kicking.

On these nights I would stand behind my father, where I was safe from all mischief-makers. Until one night, as I stood there confidently, my hair was suddenly grabbed from behind by a powerful hand, and I was pushed with extraordinary force to the ground. My hair was being pulled and wrapped around my throat with great energy, stifling my desperate screams. I was not far from being strangled to death when suddenly the light was turned on, and everyone saw me half dead. The perpetrator made a quick getaway, but she was found out. This was a Kurdish slave of my father's who was attached to my sister, the wife of 'Aziz. Incited by greed, she had taken a bribe in exchange for hurting me. In her zeal she had attempted to dispatch me once and for all, and to end all my troubles as well as theirs. But since God had not willed it, I survived to watch the great drama of life unfold.

After this episode the game was discontinued. A feud broke out between my mother and my father's wife. Finally, 'Aziz's mother-in-law sent my mother a message which can be summarized as follows: "My son-in-law is in love with your daughter. If you do not find a way out of this, I will take my complaint to the king." Out of fear of her mother, my sister had laid all the blame on me—poor, blameless me! I had known nothing about any of it and had no conception of what they had in store for me.

My mother had said in response: "I am sure of my daughter. But if I see that it is true and you are in the right, I will kill her myself and set her corpse on fire." She betrayed nothing to me, however, and told the entire household to keep it hidden from me so that I would be unaware that she had found out. She guarded me jealously herself, ensuring that I could never step out alone and without her for a moment. Wherever we went for a walk, whatever recreational activity we had, my mother was with me night and day, doing everything she could to prevent my conversing with anyone.

Free of fault and devoid of any important business to accomplish, I was glad to be with her and did not mind her company in the least. But my jealous and heartless enemies stopped at no insinuation. Never could they be content to leave me (poor me) in peace. They embellished every childish gesture of mine, attaching bizarre meanings and interpretations to each of them.

Finally my mother was left with no choice but to take away my beautiful, gorgeous clothes and put me in a simple, unadorned dress. She could not find a dress to please her in my wardrobe; all of them were pretty and expensive. So she had to give away one of these beautiful dresses to a playmate of mine in exchange for her dirty dress, which she then put on me. She commanded me to go into my father's presence that day and ask for a simple piece of cloth from which a new dress could be made.

I was tremendously distressed and disheartened at this unexpected turn of events. In a fit of lunacy I began to spout blasphemy and broke down in tears. "I will never leave the house in such a filthy, tattered dress and appear in that large company," I said. "I will not even step out of my room."

They told my mother that I had ripped the dress off my body and tossed it away, swearing that I would be buried alive before I left my room. My dear mother recalled all the ugly things people had said and, using my latest reaction as a pretext, came to my room. She was transformed from her natural self by the intensity of her rage. As soon as she had entered the room, she bolted the door from the inside and, without further ado, proceeded to punish me—or to put it more plainly, to beat me savagely.

Ah, poor me! Wretched me! No way of escape did I have from that room, no one to answer my pleas for help. Bruised all over my head and face, I was bloody, my hair torn and bedraggled, my dress in pieces. Nor did this heartless mother of mine abate in any way the intensity of her unceasing blows. Fallen to the floor, barely alive under her hands and feet, I was close to being killed. The servants forced the door open with a rock and rushed into the room to rescue me from her. All my father's wives who lived in our part of the courtyard gathered in a group and reproached my mother for inflicting such injuries on her innocent and blameless child for no reason. They led my mother away and I fell lifeless into the arms of my wet nurse. I could not hear anything that was being said around me; everything I saw was a blur.

My teacher! You will surely be moved by this act of savagery on my mother's part. But when we look at the individuals who make up a society, be they good or bad, we see that their moral values—whatever those may be—determine the morality of the larger group. Sociologists disregard individual idiosyncrasies and pay attention only to shared character traits, calling these commonly-held qualities social behavior. Social behavior is not an individual acquisition. It is transferred to man by inheritance, and commingles with his nature. That is why scholars have called it "intrinsic attributes." This science has decidedly nothing to do with traits that distinguish individuals, only examining group attributes in detail. Absolute attributes consist of qualities and potentialities. The science of alchemy, for example, studies and analyzes the qualities of compounds from a particular point of view.

The most important ties that bind people together and connect them like the links of a chain are those of character. This issue is so closely linked to other areas of life that we cannot single out any particular one as more important than the rest. Great philosophers who have spent years of their lives studying this subject have been unable to step outside the orbit of this interdependence.

But why write to you about philosophical theories? You yourself are conversant with history. The history of the world shows us how far absolute authority corrupts one's values. When a mother shuns her child from the hour of its birth; neglects both its moral and physical education; personally fails to provide the necessities of life for her infant; grudges to breast-feed her suckling babe out of regard for her own tranquillity and, depriving it of its natural food, puts it in the care of a foster-mother—it is obvious that the child cannot profit from its father's love and is banished from its mother's edifying influence. When she grows to adulthood, aside from being unintelligent, ineffective, and weak-willed in the affairs of life—no doubt, because her mother showed her no intimacy or warmth—she in turn will not care for her offspring with a sincere love.

Therefore, it is no surprise that wretched I, deprived of character training and human warmth, through no fault of my own should receive a severe beating; rather, you should marvel that I was not kicked to death and that cruel treatment did not end my life. Nobility of birth and greatness of rank, when coupled with freedom of action, breed a deep-seated harshness within the human soul which is only exacerbated when a mother parts with her offspring at the outset and remains a mother in name only.

That very day, one of my father's wives told him what had happened. Not only did she recount this particular instance of my mother's cruelty, but she told him the entire story from the beginning. Extremely displeased, my father summoned my mother to his private quarters and chided her for being so gullible as to act on the advice of a self-serving enemy and treat me the way she did. He strictly forbade her from divulging the matter and imposed a complete ban on the subject being discussed outside. He also forestalled the other perpetrators with numerous threats, swearing that if anyone breathed a word about this matter, he would not only expel her from the harem, but would have her locked up for life.

As I lay fallen and hurt, a eunuch came and summoned me to my father's presence. In that miserable state I put on my clothes and went to him. Never will I forget the hour when my poor father caressed me for the last time. After that night I no longer had a father—because a month later he was murdered.

Oh, what an anguished face my father had, what a fine figure, what a loving, gentle voice! Although I was no more than a child then, I have not forgotten the sweet melody of his speech; I have continued to hear it all my life. He was half-dressed, praying in a beautiful, melancholy tone. Every time he raised his eyes heavenward, a certain humility and submission, supplemented by a complete air of detachment, came over his face. The intensity with which he invoked God I have never heard or seen in anyone but him. I was standing before him, watching my sultan, my lord, whom I loved beyond measure. For as long as he lived I saw nothing but love and respect from him. He gazed at me and I returned his glance shyly. Our eyes met. Finishing his prayer, he chuckled, called me by name and sat me down in front of him. Stroking my head lovingly and looking kindly into my eyes he asked, "Where were you?"

"At home."

"What were you doing?"

Choking with sobs, I replied, "Nothing."

He took a long, deep look at me and said, "I will have you married soon. I will come to your home often and you must serve me." He put his lips to my forehead and gave me a gentle, affectionate, prolonged kiss, all the while holding my head in his hands.

Oh, my dear teacher! In remembrance of that moment my heart has stopped; the pen weighs heavy in my hand and I must interrupt my labor of writing for an hour to calm myself. Dear God! Even after twenty-seven years, I still feel the warmth of my dear father's lips. Oh for that kiss that sent a shiver through the fiber of my being and thrilled the blood in my veins, so intense was my joy! My tongue was speechless, my eyes could not see, my ears heard nothing. Love—a pure, grand, majestic love—severed my lifeline at that moment. My breath labored through my straitened throat and a thrill of delight possessed my entire frame. O my teacher! If the opaque veil of oblivion did not descend over life's incidents and blot out the hardships from the pages of memory, human life would be fleeting and transitory indeed! O would that the temple of my life had crumbled to dust at that moment, or that a propitious fate, a favorable providence, had filled the cup of my life to the brim and given me release from the burden of fatherlessness, before I had to swallow the bitter draught of separation from such a sire. Would that at that hour a sudden, violent fever had gripped me and sent me instantly to the darksome abode of nothingness. Alas, though man travels to the realm of eternity without hindrance, no such burning fever, no lethal disease, came to hang upon me. Even should he choose to, man cannot readily drift into death. The blood continues to course through his veins and the body to perform its functions.

At any rate, happy and at ease, I took a walk that night, no longer troubled by this saga. The boy, too, abandoned his lunacy, and I now looked upon him with revulsion and distaste. Thus did the matter come to an end. Not another word was said about it, and this story of puerile love was consigned to the shelf of oblivion.

Naser al-Din Shah Qajar in his mid-fifties (during Taj's childhood) in an official portrait. In the center of his medallion sits an imaginary portrait of 'Ali, the first Shi'ite Imam, whom Naser al-Din adopted as his patron saint. The medallion was created by the shah himself on the occasion of the short-lived conquest of Herat in 1856. The dazzling array of royal jewels, fastidiously self-chosen, betrays an almost narcissistic concern with appearance.

Everyone was preoccupied with the festivities and the preparation for the jubilee, and people's joy knew no bounds. The only topics of discussion were the celebration, the dresses, the ornaments, the jewelry. Morning and evening the ladies were busy buying fine clothes and expensive jewelry, allowing themselves no moment of respite from these preparations. Each night they submitted their day's work to His Majesty and brought forth their jewels. Despite all this happiness, however, there was a certain nagging feeling in the air, the reason for which remained elusive. The signs of doubt were visibly evident on all these cheerful faces.

One night my father walked into the harem very happy and jovial. After he had said his prayers, he began to talk to the ladies there. The eunuchs brought in the clothes he was to wear on the day of the jubilee. These were made of the finest black felt and studded with large pearls selected by himself. The clothes were accompanied by an exquisite crown, also covered by pearls. The ladies, all aflutter with compliments, converged to view the clothes. Laughter filled the air. The only quiet person in all this to-do was Anis al-Dawla, watching her peerless husband with a despondent trepidation. She was absolutely dejected and wonder-struck at his unconcern, to the point of losing her equanimity.

This faithful woman, this chaste woman, this woman who loved her husband with all her heart and soul, this woman who quickly followed her husband to the grave, had had a premonition. Suspicious of the Grand Vizier's frequent visits to the chief gardener's house, she had somehow persuaded one of his attendants to tell her of their confabulations. The servant had obliged and had told Anis al-Dawla everything, detail by detail. Confirmed in her suspicions, this noble woman had also made inquiries about the Grand Vizier's activities abroad through Bahram Khan the eunuch, and was watching his moves carefully. One step away from discovering something, she had shared all she knew with her beloved husband. This is not to say that my father trusted this man. No! But he did not want to lose his self-possession and exercise his royal authority on a woman's word. Disregarding her advice, he had told his dear wife, "You're mistaken. For several reasons you labor under a misconception. There's no truth to it."

Despite such a rebuff, the poor woman, though outwardly silenced, had secretly resumed her investigations, never letting up in her efforts to gather information.

It was at about this time that, after having left the country for a while, one of the victims of Aqa Bala Khan's sword of tyranny came to Tehran on the orders of Sayyid Jamal the Afghan. He carried a letter from the aforementioned sayyid to Sani' al-Dawla. Fearful that the letter delivered to him might be discovered, Sani' al-Dawla sent the man to the shrine of 'Abd al-'Azim, instructing him to remain there until further orders. Then he gave the sayyid's letter and the whereabouts of the man to the Grand Vizier. The Grand Vizier found no better instrument to advance his secondary objectives than this man, whom he beguiled into killing my father. Although the man had struggled to reach Tehran for the very same purpose, the Grand Vizier's promises and his ceaseless offers of protection nurtured the idea further in his head and prepared him for the deed. No doubt, my teacher, you are aware that whenever a man attempts to do something, he will accomplish it if he feels heartened. It is likely that but for the promises made by this trusted servant of my father's, the man would not have acted so rashly. Or if he had, his shots would have misfired.

I must tell you something about this man. When Aqa Sayyid Jamal had been in Tehran, detained in Amin al-Dawla's house, this man became his servant. Little by little, he was won over to all of Sayyid Jamal's opinions, which were neither theological nor ideological; he was against all religions and ideologies. Today we have no school of thinking more uninhibited and broad-ranging than socialism. His ideas were far broader and freer than socialist thought. Opposed to all bonds of temporal authority, even a mother's love for her children, he encouraged people to return to societal behavior that was prevalent at the dawn of creation. He was neither a supporter of the government nor a defender of the nation. He had his own peculiar, half-witted system of beliefs.

I know little of his history, but what I do know provides enough of an introduction. After being exiled from Persia, he had traveled throughout Europe. In the cathedral of Notre Dame he had spoken out against the republican government of France. Expelled in disgrace from that country, he had traveled to several others, everywhere earning the antipathy of the people, who considered him mad. Then he went to Ottoman Turkey, where he rose in the Sultan's esteem and won himself a high-ranking position. In his efforts to draw closer to the person of the Sultan, he overlooked no cruelty, injustice, or savagery toward the Ottoman subjects. Aided and abetted by the Sultan himself, he afflicted the Ottomans with unbearable hardships. Finally he had committed treason against the Sultan by organizing conferences overseas to plot his overthrow. The Ottoman grand vizier got wind of the situation and presented his findings to the Sultan. The sovereign, however, owing to the trust he had in Sayyid Jamal, refused to believe anything and actually threatened his minister. The premier then said, "One day when Sayyid Jamal is in Your

Majesty's presence, order for his writings to be brought forth. Then you will know."

The Sultan agreed. On the day that Sayyid Jamal was at court all his writings were brought in. On perusing them, the Sultan realized that the premier had been right. However, unable to have Sayyid Jamal executed outright, he had him poisoned instead. The poison did not result in death instantaneously but over a course of time. Detained for over a year in the house that served as his residence, Sayyid Jamal finally lost his speech to a debilitating condition, his ears fell off, and he died.

While Sayyid Jamal was detained in Istanbul, slowly succumbing to poison, this man (called Mirza Reza) went to him. Describing Aqa Bala Khan's cruelty, he wept and complained before Sayyid Jamal, who replied, "Go and pull out tyranny by its root. So long as you don't, and the root rests in water, the stem has the promise of bearing fruit. For every one of its branches that you hack off, it will spring two new shoots."

Determined, this man came to Tehran and gave Sayyid Jamal's written instructions to Sani' al-Dawla. Housed in the shrine of 'Abd al-'Azim, the man was strengthened in his resolve to murder my father. The oppression the man had suffered from Aqa Bala Khan was truly beyond human endurance. Arrested as a Babi, he was kept in prison for many years. In his captivity, his daughter was violated before his eyes. His son, too, was raped and whipped. There were several other atrocities that Aqa Bala Khan committed. After the man was released from government detention, he threw himself under my brother's carriage and ripped out his own bowels with a knife. Instead of listening to his grievances, my brother had him imprisoned again. After several years he was again set free, whereupon he went to Sayyid Jamal. Now he had returned.

On the morning of the day that he was assassinated, my father saw Anis al-Dawla as he came out from the bath. Waiting for him to get dressed, she requested permission for a private audience. They went into a room. Throwing herself at his feet, she pleaded, "A soothsayer has told me that for three days you will be threatened with danger. Be merciful to yourself and this handful of subjects. Cancel your plans for today and refrain from going to the shrine of 'Abd al-'Azim."

Sinking into thought, my father finally raised his head and said, "If my subjects look with the eye of discrimination and fairness, they will see that I have not been a bad king. Throughout my reign I have not wasted a single life or fought even the most trivial of battles with neighboring states. I have always preferred the peace and prosperity of the nation over my own. I have not spent the nation's wealth wastefully and I have not usurped people's property. Today there are millions in the national treasury, and chests full of jewels in the royal vault. Throughout my reign it has been my endeavor to secure Persia's wealth. Now, with all the plans I have drawn up and all the provisions I have made for my subjects—giving them their rights after centuries, abolishing their taxes, convening a consultative assembly for them, admitting regional delegates to represent them—I don't believe their welfare lies in my death. Suppose all my services to the people of Persia went unacknowledged and they truly intended to murder me. If I don't go out for three days, they will kill me on the fourth day when I do step outside. So let them do it. After my death they will see all the labors I have undertaken for them and through their suffering they will appreciate me better."

Kamraniya, country seat of Kamran Mirza in the northern resort of Shemiran, where the prince occasionally detained political suspects in the basement of an otherwise serene dwelling.

He also told Anis al-Dawla, "I'm not afraid at all. But I feel sorry for the people of Persia, because my son is incapable of being a ruler. All that I have stored up for Persia's rainy day with infinite pain over this half-century he will squander in a few years."

Tears filled his eyes and he wiped them with a handkerchief. Anis al-Dawla cried, "Oh! You are a king, and yet you weep? You are powerful, yet you bemoan your helplessness?"

He replied, "No, Anis al-Dawla. It's not for myself that I feel regret. It's for this land."

Anis al-Dawla said, "My lord! Don't accuse the people. All of them love you. The one who has betrayed you is he who has been nurtured by your own generosity. This man is the unworthy one whom Your Majesty has raised to such rank that he now flouts you. This treacherous man cannot be considered one of the noble people of Persia. He's but one man, and one man's transgressions don't stain an entire nation."

After some thought my father said, "If you're referring to the Grand Vizier, he will reap the punishment for his actions. I have planned his punishment to take place after the jubilee. But since you insist, I will have him arrested tomorrow."

However much my father's wife insisted, saying, "Cancel your ride today; first attend to this matter, then perform your pilgrimage next week," he did not listen. He went ahead, and was murdered by that man.

After my father had left the harem, the ladies returned to their homes to resume their daily tasks.

A few days before this, the Grand Vizier and Sani' al-Dawla went to the shrine of 'Abd al-'Azim and spoke at length with Mirza Reza at Jayran's grave. On his return, Sani' al-Dawla realized he could not bear the burden of this enormous treachery. He died of a heart attack. The Grand Vizier, on the

Entrance to the shrine of Shah 'Abd al-'Azim in the south of Tehran, the scene of the assassination of Naser al-Din Shah. The inscription above the gateway bears the name of "the king of the happy conjunction, Naser al-Din Shah Qajar."

other hand, awaited the outcome with full confidence and assurance.

Because Sani' al-Dawla had left behind no children, all his money was seized and brought to the harem. In the harem my father had a little vault entrusted to a Kurdish slave woman named Fatima. He also had a little booklet under lock and key in which he kept account of all the royal wealth and jewelry and recorded certain secret matters; he always wore the key around his neck. It took four or five days for bearers to bring all of Sani' al-Dawla's money in sacks and deposit it on the floor of a room with grated iron windows. I do not know the exact amount of these gold coins, but I do know that one corner of the room was piled high in a little mound of gold. It was said that he had several times as much in the bank. These gold coins—the commissions he had received from people in lieu of titles, positions, and offices—he kept at home for his enjoyment. He also owned an exquisite, priceless book worth several times the value of his money. Unhappy people of Persia!

THE ASSASSINATION OF THE SHAH

That day at noon there was a major commotion in the seraglio. Despite the Grand Vizier's explicit instructions that the news should not be spread in the harem just yet, the eunuch had been unable to restrain himself. Word had gone out that the Shah had been fired upon but the bullets had missed. All the women, with disheveled hair and frightful looks, poured out of their rooms in a torrent and ran to the government house. "We want to see the Shah," they screamed.

We were told that he had been wounded and was in the White Hall. The women's screams rose to a higher pitch. The eunuchs came in and said, "The Shah is well. Any moment now he will come in through the large door of the harem." The wretched women ran as fast as they could to the door, and their cries abated somewhat. After waiting for a while, they saw that there was no sign of the king. Without either *chador* or veil, they were prepared to run out into the streets. There was no way for the eunuchs to restrain this fire storm of anguish, this lightning bolt of grief.

My teacher! I will now recount a ludicrous story with the plea that you take some pity on my misery, for, on this very ill-fated day which plunged me into the abyss of misfortune, I was overtaken by a fast-moving cataclysm. The women in the harem had recently learned to dye their eyebrows black. The dye was made of silver nitrate, which, as you know, makes eyebrows doubly dark and cannot be wiped away; a few days have to pass before it is possible to clean it off. That morning, wholly ignorant of the course of events, I had daubed a large quantity of this dye on my eyebrows. I never tampered with my eyebrows because they were sufficiently full and dark. On this day, however, overcome by a childish impulse, I had dyed my eyebrows black.

On hearing the clamor, I rushed to join the crowd, running hither and thither. The dye, meanwhile, had become stronger and had turned jet black. In my state of anxiety and fear, wondering if my father was dead or alive, I was taken by surprise by a slap on the face. A gush of blood flowed down my nostrils. I turned around to look for the aggressor when I was struck again. Startled, I thought, "Why, amid all this confusion, is someone hitting me?" Perhaps, I thought to myself, it was appropriate to beat fatherless children; this would explain why someone was hitting me. Finally I heard my mother's harsh, incoherent voice, saying, "Was this the day for you to blacken your eyebrows, and in such a manner?"

Nearly out of my senses, I cried, "How was I supposed to know about this? Besides, you yourself told me to do it. What is my fault?"

"Go on," she replied, "go wipe your face and shut up!"

Amid all this bewildering confusion and lamentation I went home. In tears I began to wipe my eyebrows with vinegar and oil, but that proved to be of no use. So I shaved them off completely. With my eyebrows gone and my face downcast, I was a picture of ludicrousness. I ran back to join the crowd again to learn if my beloved father was alive or dead. Towards late afternoon, the ladies' state of doubt was resolved and their unspoken fears confirmed: their beloved husband had been murdered . . . .

No hand or pen of mine could possibly describe that bloody scene to you. If you think about it carefully enough, you will understand.

> Say not, "Kings occupy the highest rank,"
> For none is loftier than the dervish.
> Untrammeled with weight, one makes better haste.
> Such is the truth; pay heed, O men of insight!
>
> The pauper grieves after a piece of bread,
> The monarch after an entire realm.
> The beggar who dines on a loaf of bread
> Sleeps as soundly as Syria's king.
>
> Sorrow and joy alike do end
> (Death drives them forth from the mind)
> Whether for him who wears the crown
> Or him who bears the yoke of taxes.

Inner courtyard of the shrine of Shah 'Abd al-'Azim, with the veranda *(ivan)* leading to the shrine where Naser al-Din Shah was shot at point-blank range. The crowd lining the passageway, in this drawing from a photograph by S. G. W. Benjamin in 1882, was not much different from that into which, on the eve of his jubilee, Naser al-Din ventured for the first time without having the area declared off-limits.

If a proud man commands the universe,
Or if one humble languishes in jail,
Once the hosts of fate are done with them
Neither can be told apart from the other.

All that night one could hear weeping and moaning every-where. No one had any peace or respite until the morning. Then all the ladies congregated in Anis al-Dawla's house and the outpourings of grief began anew. While they were thus engaged in bemoaning their husband's loss, word spread that the assassin was Mirza Reza of Kerman, the brother-in-law of the well-known *mirza*. Fearsome shouts rose everywhere. Some mentioned that Nosrat and Fatima were related to Mirza Reza.

No sooner had these words been uttered than all the ladies of junior rank ran to the courtyard to find these two girls. One of them was in the bath; apparently she had been preparing herself for such a situation, and had made the bath her sanc-tuary. The other girl had hidden in the posterior courtyard. When they pulled the girl out of the bath, she was practically naked. Whatever people could lay hands on—stones, sticks, knives—they used to attack these girls, wounding them in the head, face, and body. Bleeding, injured, and scared out of their wits, the girls were angrily brought to Anis al-Dawla's house. Anis al-Dawla quieted everyone down and said, "Please don't tear them apart or kill them yet. Let them be subjected to questioning. If they're guilty, it will then be an easy matter to put them to death."

The two girls were taken away and locked up in a room. Later a eunuch came to Anis al-Dawla with a message from Mirza 'Ali Asghar Khan, the Grand Vizier, which said: "I have heard that these girls are guilty. Since this is official govern-ment business, it would be appropriate for you to send them

میرزا رضای کرمانی که مرحوم ناصرالدین طیب ا؟ مقره شهید کرد

"The late, blessed Mirza Reza [Kermani] who martyred the late, blessed Naser al-Din Shah, may God purify his tomb" reads the caption on this revolutionary postcard from the 1910s. The dual homage to assassin and victim is indicative of the remorseful ambivalence of the post-Constitutional period, elevating Mirza Reza Kermani to the status of a precursor of the revolution and Naser al-Din Shah to that of the "Martyr Shah" *(shah-e shahid).*

to us for questioning." Anis al-Dawla agreed, and the girls were taken away and put in another room.

The official period of mourning lasted three days. Every morning people would gather in Anis al-Dawla's house and stay until evening. At night they would go to their own houses. After the three-day period people continued to mourn in their homes. The absolute ruler and the power behind the throne at this time was the Grand Vizier. Everyone awaited the arrival of the crown prince, wondering how the new sovereign would treat his subjects and rule his domain.

Days and nights passed by quickly. The majestic palace that had been steeped in happiness and pleasure all hours of the day or night now wallowed in a fearful, agonizing sorrow. No sound was heard except that of weeping. All those pretty faces were withered, the complexions clouded, the eyes dimmed. Clothed in black, the women seemed like statues to observers. That grandeur and majesty vanished so rapidly that one would think it had been no more than a dream, a figment of the imagination.

"If centuries pass, well, let them go! Why fear?

But thou, like whom there is none so pure, do thou stay."

A few days later, Amin al-Molk, the Grand Vizier's brother who was then the master of the treasury, came to the *andarun* with the Grand Vizier to look at the coffers. On the pretext that Mozaffar al-Din Shah was in debt and needed to be sent some money in Tabriz, they took out a large sum of money; or, to put it more accurately, they emptied the coffers. For eighteen days, some thirty or forty servants labored from morning till evening to carry away the bags of money to treasuries outside the palace. From these treasuries the money was stacked into cartridges and carted off to Amin al-Molk's house. A small amount was kept, and the rest transferred to the *andarun* in the Grand Vizier's house.

Once the money was taken away, they left the harem alone, except for the matter of the jewels and money left in Fatima's keeping. Before the strong-box was reclaimed from Fatima, every time she was served her dinner at night and the empty dishes were taken away, she would fill them with gold coins and cover and seal them in a tray. Thus everything would be taken away, with Fatima's brother standing at the door to receive the tray. By the time the Grand Vizier had finished with the money in the treasury, Fatima, too, had stolen substantial amounts in gold coins. Since the account book for these monies was in Fatima's own possession, she removed all the pertinent information. And when she did hand it over, the Grand Vizier also tore out pages of information pertinent to himself, thereby almost destroying the book completely. Since this account book and everything in Fatima's keeping were apart from government possessions and pertained to individuals, they were considered "personal wealth."

While everyone was occupied with his own thoughts and busy with his own concerns, I was lost in bewilderment and watched the proceedings as if in a dream. All the women were bustling about, getting their money, jewels and other valuables out of the harem by any means possible for safe keeping outside. My mother was an exception; lost in her sorrows and cares, she took no thought for possessions and money and jewelry. Besides, we did not hold any crown jewels or government wealth; whatever we had was bought and paid for.

My teacher! As I think back to those days, I begin to tremble from head to toe. I am lost in wonder at the world's fickleness. All the power, the privilege, the glory, the wealth and the diversions of people seem abhorrent to me. There has never been a power, a splendor or a glory to match that erstwhile majesty. And what happened to that? Where did it all go? What did my father gain from all that he had? It is so true when they say, "Should a man leave behind a fair name, better it is than that he leave behind a gilded palace."

Not long after, news reached us of the new king's arrival. The effect was of a jolt of lightning, and the wailing and keeling rose to a crescendo. The day arrived when he entered the capital and took up his place in the seat of government.

Let me not forget to write this so you know: not a soul interrogated the assassin, Mirza Reza, or put him on trial. The man had been committed to the care of Haji Hosayn 'Ali Khan, the Grand Vizier's uncle, and was treated quite well. The two girls had been taken away and had been given not only rewards and new clothes from the Grand Vizier, but also annuities. This should tell us something about the degree to which the Grand Vizier cared for them and protected them.

The new king arrived. The next day he visited the *andarun* and showed the ladies much kindness, offering sympathy and condolences.

PORTRAIT OF THE NEW SHAH

My teacher! Although you are quite familiar with this new king of ours, nevertheless I find it necessary to describe him. This dear brother of mine was very simple, pure, kind and soft-hearted. His family was limited to seven wives and a few male children, namely, the crown prince, Sho'a' al-Saltana, Salar al-Dawla, Nosrat al-Saltana, and Naser al-Din Mirza. His daughters were 'Ezzat al-Dawla, Fakhr al-Saltana, Fakhr al-Dawla, Shokuh al-Dawla, Nur al-Saltana, Aqdas al-Dawla, and Anvar al-Dawla. All Turks, his family was completely deprived of proper manners. This poor brother of mine had been created to be a good father, to head a decent household, but in no wise could he be considered a king. So shy, meek, and prone to embarrassment was he that the hardest of hearts would bleed for him. Very changeable, he listened to everyone; weak-willed, he allowed himself to be guided by the will of others. He was timid and simple, worshiped flatterers and loved sycophants. His retinue and court were comprised entirely of base, vile, vulgar, and contemptible young men, simple and rowdy; himself fearful, irresolute and extremely gullible. From the time of his arrival he began to dismiss all the accomplished, hard-working servants of the court. He also dismissed all his father's attendants, placing the reins of authority in the hands of his own. Here we might handsomely laud this sovereign's gratitude for not forgetting the services of his attendants. But we can also find fault with him. It would have been so much better if he had found some way to entrust duties to his father's honest, trusted and highly esteemed servants and to salve their inner wounds with the balm of money. Instead, he gave over the affairs of state to a bunch of hungry, upstart men who brought ruin and beggary upon the nation. He could have chosen among all his father's upright, trustworthy servants; yet, the only person he chose to keep was the Grand Vizier. This charlatan passed himself off as honest and trustworthy, claiming that but for him the throne would not have gone to the new king and that all his aims would have been thwarted. By a thousand oaths and testimonies he established himself as a loyal servant. This is not to suggest that his treachery was so well concealed that my brother was in the dark. But the new king had suffered no loss by this treachery; quite the opposite, he had acceded to the throne. Besides, his unfamiliarity with affairs left him, at least for a while, in need of the man who had held the great office of the grand vizierate for years.

Finally, after a week, an edict came down from the new king: all the ladies had to leave the harem with all their possessions, except those who had children. These would be sent to Sarvestan, where Monir al-Saltana, the vice-regent's mother, lived. She had evacuated her home and moved to the vice-regent, my brother's. The unfortunate women, now widowed, left their seat of grandeur and comfort en masse, with a thousand sighs and groans. Only a few had children, such as my mother, Yamin al-Dawla's mother, 'Ezzat al-Saltana's mother, Qodrat al-Saltana's mother, and Sharaf al-Saltana's mother. Farah al-Saltana, 'Aziz al-Saltana, Sharaf al-Saltana, 'Ezz al-Saltana, Qodrat [al-Saltana] and I were quite young—the oldest of us was not yet thirteen—and we also had two younger brothers. The courtyard at Sarvestan was divided into sections, and we were housed there like captives and prisoners. My sisters and I would join together every day in weeping, importuning our mothers and asking for our father.

A few days passed and the coronation ceremony began. The new royal family all arrived from Tabriz. Amid these transformations I was in profound anguish, fully aware that my father was no more. Every night I cried profusely before falling asleep and had recurring dreams about him. Most nights I would wake up at least ten times before dawn and weep aloud. So grieved and heart-broken was I that nothing could assuage my sorrow. My mother had taken a section of the courtyard close to the outside, apart from my sisters; this was so that she could visit her father and brothers. My grandfather and uncles came over often and diverted my childish mind with a thousand distractions. Yet I was always dejected, feeling that I was close to death.

Mozaffar al-Din Shah and his entourage, c. 1902. Amin al-Soltan (standing to the shah's immediate right) was the architect of the new monarch's accession to power, aided by the chief of the Cossack Brigade, General Kossakowski (standing in the back row, second from the right). The shah's son, Salar al-Dawla (standing to his left), later led an anti-Revolutionary force against the young Constitutional government in 1911.

It was then that my father-in-law-to-be was appointed minister of war and commander-in-chief, and therefore spent all his nights in the barracks. My future husband sent me letters all day and often came to see me. But I was so downhearted and distracted, mourned my father so profoundly, and felt so sorry for my father's wives, that I never wrote back to him, nor did I take any pleasure in his visits. The only person to whom I was somewhat close was my grandfather. This venerable old man loved and respected me beyond description. I was always delighted to see him. Sitting in his lap, I would throw my arms around his neck and kiss his white beard. Then, tears filling my eyes, I would ask, "Am I never going to see my father again? Will I always be a prisoner in this little courtyard?"

The poor old man would clasp me to his breast and kiss my forehead, tears streaming from his eyes. He would say, "My love! God is great. You command more respect than that. Your life has just begun. No, you won't always be a prisoner here."

Soon a eunuch came from my brother with a decree about our stipends and annuities and three pieces of jewelry. The stipend for my mother, my brother and me was set at eight thousand *tuman*s per year, paid in monthly installments. I received a diadem, my mother a . . ., and my brother a pair of ornamental buckles. We were instructed to put away our mourning attire, since it was time for the coronation. The next day I was brought a purple dress and told to put it on. I asked, "Why are you changing my clothes? After my father's death shouldn't I always be dressed in black, like an orphan?"

My mother kissed me and said, "My dear! Your brother is the king. This is a coronation. You must go into his presence. You have no choice but to change your dress."

"But what does my dress have to do with my brother's coronation?" I asked. "It isn't two months since my father died. Why must I change my clothes?"

Three of the younger daughters of Naser al-Din Shah. Though they are not identified, they represent Taj's childhood sororal environment.

Despite all their insistence I held firm. Finally I broke down in tears. Running to my grandfather, I threw myself into his arms and said, "Grandfather! Tell them not to change my clothes. My father has just died. I can still see him; he still talks to me."

The poor old man's complexion darkened and he said, "My dear girl! Do as you wish. You're in the right." He would not let them change my clothes, and made every effort to calm me down. But I would not be soothed. Walking into my mother's room, I would pick up my father's portrait, take it to my room and hide it in a corner. Whenever I was left alone I would hug it to my breast, kiss it and weep so copiously that I would fall asleep as I was. Ultimately, these adversities took their toll, leaving me weak and emaciated.

Several days later a eunuch came from my brother and summoned us into his presence that night. I tried to desist from going, pleading that I could not bear to see my father's house. My mother used every means she could to persuade me to go. An hour after sunset the eunuchs came and opened the courtyard gates and led us away to the king. The little compounds were all connected to each other, but an inspection of the confinement camp would reveal all the gates to be locked, the keys in the pockets of the eunuchs. When it was time for an audience with the king, they would open the gates and lead us away.

That night, for the first time after my father's death, I saw the residence he used to live in. My poor sister Farah al-Saltana, a year older than me and a mild, sensible, well-educated, well-brought up girl, was quite close to me. Holding each other's hands, we followed of our orphaned younger brothers and sisters as the eunuch led the way. Every so often this sister and I would kneel on the ground, throw our arms around each other, and burst into tears. The younger children would gather around us, making an industrious effort to separate and raise us up with their little hands. Holding them in our arms, we would stroke and kiss them. Resuming our journey, we would walk a few steps before once again embracing each other and giving vent to our grief. Finally we reached the large courtyard and heard music and singing. I broke into a sudden run and my older sister joined me. Despite all the eunuchs' and servants' entreaties for us to go to the king, we refused, saying, "Where there is music we will not go." They had to drag us.

Alas! Why did my life not come to an end right away? Why did I not breathe my last then, but continued to draw breath? Wonder of wonders! Man, my teacher, despite the delicacy of his nature and his nobility is harder than rock and more unyielding than cast iron in the face of adversity. No pen or tongue of mine can tell you of my anguish and helplessness. These matters are beyond the pale of description; one needs to see in order to understand. Had people's minds and modes of thinking changed so much? Had attitudes and tastes altered so drastically? Welladay! A father as grand as he had been was no more, and the majesty of the throne had gone up in smoke. Now who was this and what was he? Where did he come from? Was it a dream or reality? I could not understand.

In a long, wide avenue was set a dais draped in rugs, with a chair at one end. The sovereign was sitting in it, dressed in jacket and trousers, his head bare and bereft of the royal crown. His family, women, children and more distant kin, were sitting in a group. Maidservants, stewards, and eunuchs were milling about in confusion, completely unmindful of royal protocol. Around this king were scattered two or three groups of female minstrels, while women of ill repute sat on the fringes of the rug. In the middle, a number of heavy, unshapely women were dancing and making vile gestures or lewd comments. Awful screams of laughter and insane, ludicrous shouts could be heard on all sides. Staring in awe at this banquet, we were so upset and distressed that none of us had the strength to utter a word. As soon as we had arrived, the sovereign, our esteemed brother, had risen to his feet to embrace and kiss us one by one. Then he had granted permission for us to be seated among these dregs of society and turned his attention to his own amusement.

Seated among the guests was Prince Jahansuz Mirza, son of the late Fath 'Ali Shah. Actually this was not a royal feast; it was a gathering of relatives—and very mean, second-rate relatives at that. My father's palace arrangements passed before my eyes, and I could not help but notice the difference between my father and my brother. For as long as I had been a conscious, intelligent being, I could not remember female musicians in my father's harem, with the exception of wedding feasts, and then it was only male musicians. It was impossible to find a single whore among them. Besides, my father was so majestic and inspired such awe that no soul dared to speak loudly in his presence; nor could maidservants, eunuchs, or others approach his person. Not to mention that I had always seen my father in gem-studded clothes and imperial crowns, never underdressed in jacket and trousers. Upon my arrival on this scene, I had not been able to tell the Shah from the rest or discover where he was. He evidenced no sign of royalty, either in his bearing or in his clothes.

At any rate, I sat down and observed this jarring scene with a mixture of aversion and wistfulness. All of a sudden, I felt a hot liquid on my hand. Raising my head, I saw that an impudent slave girl had lit a candle and, holding it over the king's head, was watching the dancers. The hot wax from the candle was dripping in large drops on my brother's shoulder, and from there onto my hands, head and face.

Several hours later, this bizarre reception came to an end. One of my particular memories from this night was a royal utterance, which I can almost hear even now. The words were so incongruous that I have retained a bewildered memory of them. The king said, "Prince Jahansuz Mirza! My father was a powerful ruler, but his affairs were in disarray."

The king's dinner was brought and served in his apartment. A black slave woman, who had taken the title Khazen-e Aqdas and who enjoyed my brother's special affection, came in and announced to the king, "Sir, your dinner's ready. Gracious God, bless your soul! Aren't you tired? Get up, the food'll get cold. Take your sisters to eat supper with you. We'll go into the other room to eat."

Dumbstruck with wonder, I watched as the curtain rose on this drama, unfolding scene by scene before this poor nation, and shook my head in amazement. My astonishment drowned out my brother's voice as he said, "Come and eat supper with me."

Stupefied with distress, I walked like a drunkard up the steps of the mansion and entered the corridor with the others. A large trencher placed in the room held the king's supper. Sitting at the trencher, we began to eat. All that this mournful ceremony lacked was music. Having finished our meal, we rose and, requesting permission, took our leave.

This final torment robbed me of all strength, rendered me helpless, and confined me to bed. Ravaged by the measles, I was so ill that I almost died. For almost a month I endured great pain and discomfort. After the illness had abated, the Shah issued orders for my nuptial plans to proceed. Lost once again in the valley of bewilderment, I saw no way out of my quandary.

There were several occasions on which we were taken into the royal presence. Little by little, that world of savagery and barbarousness was beginning to civilize and refine itself. Nevertheless, none at court knew how to treat guests properly and send them away from the palace happy and satisfied.

The chief hostess for general events was Hazrat-e 'Olya'. This very distinguished lady was a noblewoman and a princess, descended from one of the ancient families of Persia. Her ill health, however, had made her completely averse to society and companionship. The respected lady was so heartsick and weary of all the entertaining that she finally abandoned it altogether and delegated it to others. Whenever she entertained, the guests usually found themselves wandering about aimlessly, with nothing to do from morning to evening. On taking their leave, they would often find their wraps resting in greasy food trays. With a world of regret for this signal honor, they would go back home.

My father's lordly palace had now changed beyond recognition, with no trace of royal etiquette. In contrast to the bygone glory of his household, this family was very simple. Never mind that all the crown jewels now glittered on the heads and arms of high and low, lady and maid, alike. The consummate man does not judge others by outward appearances, but by the accomplishments within. Notwithstanding all their trappings and frills, these people were completely unworthy of attention and unfit for association, while being eminently suitable for avoidance and contempt. Any sensible, right-thinking person would take one look at this royal system and, with philosophical scrutiny, recognize at once the result of this manner of living and its ultimate end.

After Hazrat-e 'Olya', the task of entertaining was divided among Nezhat al-Saltana, Nur al-Dawla and Khazen-e Aqdas. Nezhat al-Saltana, the mother of Sho'a' al-Dawla, was prettier and more civilized than the other ladies. Nur al-Dawla, the mother of Salar al-Dawla, on the other hand, was a tribeswoman from Azarbaijan, quite plebeian and not particularly attractive. As for Khazen-e Aqdas, she was a negress; one of the servants of the late Shah's mother, she was formerly called Olfat. On one of the Crown Prince's visits to Tehran, he was given Olfat and her mother, Delpasand, as gifts. Taking Delpasand as a temporary wife—she being white—he made Olfat the chief of the butlery by virtue of merit. After the Crown Prince's divorce from Omm al-Khaqan, the mother of Mohammad 'Ali Shah, Delpasand assumed the title of Mo'azzaz al-Saltana and the guardianship of E'tezad al-Saltana, the very same Mohammad 'Ali Shah.

When the telegraph announcing my father's assassination reached the Shah and he prepared to leave for Tehran to ascend the throne, he immediately bestowed titles on all his family, young or old. It was at this time that Olfat became Khazen-e Aqdas (Most Blessed Confidante). Enjoying the king's special favor, this lady had his ear and wielded considerable influence. It gave me great joy to see my beloved nanny's cousin covered with diamonds and crown jewels. As you know, my dear teacher, being an artist yourself, a black face is nicely enhanced by white jewelry, particularly if it is shiny. But what brought me the greatest inner happiness, my teacher, was the fact that this woman had retained her accent; most of her words were identical to my nanny's, very funny and sweet.

These ladies, guided by their own particular tastes, had chosen whom they wanted to entertain among the ladies of rank and daughters of the Shah. All those who had to come and go were thus divided into three groups, each group owing allegiance to its hostess. One of the differences was that this palace never saw the same kind of freedom of association that had reigned in my father's time. The earlier entertainers had spent all day attending to their guests and looking after the venerable and high-born ladies who came, unlike the present set who fled from their guests, limiting their association with ladies of status to festivals and formal occasions. Besides, they also harbored several meaningless secrets, which they were unwilling to share with others.

Among the many immoral things that stirred murmurings and caused wonder was the constant coming and going of female musicians and prostitutes who disguised themselves as musicians. For a while my brother's attention was drawn to a paltry, ugly girl from the troupe of Haj Qadam-Shad. The girl went by the name Keshvar Shahi, and several thousand *tuman*s in government funds were lavished on her worthless person.

My teacher! Surely as you think about it now, you must be very surprised at the idea of a king, for whom anything is possible, submitting to such baseness and choosing his mistress from the troupe of Haj Qadam-Shad; whereas one look from the king, or the mere drop of a handkerchief, is enough to awe the proudest of women into submission. Do not be surprised, however. Kingship is no more a guarantee of good character than are parents a guarantee of nobility. These must come from education, good teachers, and learning. The kings of Persia, unfortunately, have been woefully deprived and most unlucky in this regard. From the hour of their birth they have seen and heard nothing but lies, flattery, and insincerity.

As a child I heard my mother telling a very highly respected guest a story she had heard from one of the other ladies. This concerned a photograph taken of this king [Mozaffar al-Din

Shah] by the great Amir Nezam in Tabriz and sent to my father. To this day I consider this an exaggeration born of malice. Others, however, have sworn to the truth of the story. The picture, taken with great difficulty, showed my brother copulating with a mare. If we acknowledge this to be true, then we can no longer fault the "country." Such was the palace; now let me write you something about this king's private quarters and his court.

The former grand vizier had become atabak, Amir Bahador had become commander of the royal guard and Hakim al-Molk had become minister of the court. Aqa Vajiha had been promoted to commander-in-chief. The king's private functionaries were: E'tesab al-Molk, Mo'tamed-e Khaqan, Amin al-Molk, Loqman al-Dawla, Nezam al-Soltan, Hesam al-Saltana. They were later joined by Mokhtar al-Saltana, two Jewish dancers named 'Aziz and Habib, and others of the same ilk. All these private attendants spent the entire day making music or spewing out idle talk and jokes. In private, shameful things went on. For example, all of them were good looking, so they had no choice but to serve as instruments of enjoyment and diversion for others. From the inception of the Qajar dynasty to that time, never had such a scandalous court been convened. It was not long before the crown lands were turned over to these people, and all the taxes levied went into the pockets of base riffraff.

I have forgotten to mention some important people: Sayyid Bahrayni and his sons. My revered brother was terribly afraid of thunder and lightning, and believed in jinns and peris and all manner of mumbo-jumbo. Of course, this sayyid had to be with him when the weather changed and became cloudy, or when there was thunder and lightning, and chant the Greatest Name or other verses, in order to be a shield against nature, so to speak. Heaven forbid if any injury should befall the blessed and august person of His Imperial Majesty! For this tremendous service that he rendered His Majesty, this man was treated with extraordinary deference and received a disproportionate salary.

And yet, despite such a court and such comportment, I can still say that, behind these tormenting veils of life, my brother was a merciful and sane man. He had a great love of literature and held knowledge and learning in high regard. The first dream he cherished was to send his brothers, his son, and his grandchildren to study in Europe. And he encouraged all the aristocrats to send their children there. We can truly say that he rendered a great service to the cause of learning, even though he himself was not well educated, having finished only a superficial level of study in elementary school.

NUPTIALS AND MARRIED LIFE

Finally, one year after he was seated on the royal throne, my nuptials were formally announced. After my sister, mine was the first wedding in my brother's family to take place in his reign. My mother had made up a very complete trousseau for me, tastefully and beautifully done. My brother had given her five thousand *tuman*s to cover the wedding expenses. The wedding feast began. The celebration, music, and singing continued some four or five days and nights. The celebrants, with all their noise and laughter, were delivering me up to a life burdened with hardship. Nudging me into the great theater called life—the passage of days and nights—they made me an apprentice to affliction and woe. The hatred and anguish that I felt was locked away in a corner of my heart. The enthusiasm for an independent life, however, eased my sorrow-laden heart. Contrary to my usual state, I found myself almost happy and satisfied with the turn of events. The reason for this acquiescence had to do entirely with the fact that after my father, my world had ended and happiness had become a meaningless word. The courtyard in which we were housed was not only run-down and unlivable, but we were virtual prisoners there. Unlike my father's splendid house, which contained every means of comfort and ease, there was no recreation or amusement where we were now. I saw myself being buried alive, and keenly felt the difference between my present and past lives. So, having consented to this marriage and this freedom from captivity, I was no longer unhappy; in fact, I felt a little elated. The aversion I had felt toward my husband while my father was alive was due to my unwillingness to be parted from my father and mother and the pomp and grandeur. Now that nature's resistless hand had robbed me of the object of my worship, I no longer saw any impediments to my being married; instead, I awaited my release impatiently.

The day of the nuptials arrived. They took me to an empty room to dress me in my evening toilette. One of my father's wives began to put on my make-up. All my former happiness flashed before my eyes quick as lightning. I saw my father looking at me and smiling sadly. I remembered my betrothal ceremony, when I had had a father. Without my noticing it, tears began to roll down out of the corner of my eyes. I had been struck by lightning, powerless under the crushing weight of pain and anguish. My head fell back, I gasped for breath. The guests rushed into the room and found me half dead. Reviving me with great effort, they began to offer consolation. My mother's grief was no less than my own. Sadness had left a strange imprint on her mild, beautiful face. In her lovely face her large, tear-filled eyes glowed with pity and love, with the majesty of pain and tender affection. So lovely and pure was her face at that moment that I can still see it when I close my eyes. She touched my head gently, kissed me and said, "My dear! Your father is dead, but there is someone greater than him."

"Who is that?" I asked in surprise.

She raised her head to look at the sky and two tears rolled down her face. She said, "God."

At that moment I saw my weakness and frailty transformed into strength, and a ray of hope shed its light all around me. But alas, the hope was transitory, and I sank back once again into grief. I realized then that the crowd's merrymaking and cheerfulness had been cut short and my misery had infected the others. Summoning all my strength to my aid, I made a supreme effort and disguised my grief.

The make-up was finished and I was taken to the royal palace. Lavish preparations had been made, and I was received with great honor and decorum. After an hour had elapsed and people had been served refreshments, my brother arrived on the scene and showed me a great deal of kindness. Before all else he kissed and caressed me. These expressions of love and tenderness, however, failed to alleviate my emotional distress or chase away the worshipful figure of my father from my mind.

The Shah went to the Almasiyya door and ordered for the fireworks to begin. An hour later, on behalf of the bridegroom's family, the daughter of the selfsame Atabak and the daughters of the Amir Nezam approached the sovereign for permission to take me away. Permission was granted. A white cashmere *chador*, studded with jewels, was thrown over my head, and I was put into a pair of green velvet drawers. Held by my upper arms, I was led into the royal presence. I kissed my brother's feet, bade my mother farewell and took my first step into infelicity. The custodian of the harem and numerous eunuchs accompanied me to the door of the carriage. As was customary, the bridegroom was brought there, too, and he kissed the stirrups before taking his leave. I got in and the carriage began to move. What a scene, what fanfare! Soldiers were lined up on both sides, and with every few steps the horses took, the band would begin to play. With great dignity and pomp I was ushered into the bridegroom's house. When it was time for me to alight, they saw that I was too little to do it by myself. My father-in-law carried me in his arms up to the gate of the courtyard, where he handed me over to my relatives. I had no idea that I must feign modesty and refrain from looking about. Wherever I saw a scene, I would stop to watch. I had lost all sense of what was afoot, failing to understand what it meant.

A few hours passed, and I was anticipating the outcome of this commotion. What were they going to do to me? As I stood there, watching and wondering, I sensed acutely that there was a good deal of murmuring around me. Some faces registered pleasure and approval; others were averted. I heard the word "impossible" a few times. "What are they saying?" I asked.

One of the ladies came up to me and said, "Because of the large number of guests and the presence of dignitaries, the bridegroom has asked permission to eat his supper outside."

Though I considered this a discourtesy to myself, I nodded my head in agreement and said nothing. I was thinking, however, "This husband of mine must be very young indeed to prefer eating with his guests—temporary and ephemeral friends—to eating with his true friend, his constant companion, his mate through good and bad." I swore to myself never to forget this first slight and to treat him with the same wholehearted disrespect.

Dinner was served. I was so flustered that I could not eat, so I diverted myself with play. My shift in mood, however, did not go unnoticed: some of the ladies realized what had happened and immediately informed my father-in-law, lest there should be any ill feelings at the outset. Immediately after dinner, they took the bridegroom's hand and, accompanied by Prince Jahansuz Mirza (Fath 'Ali Shah's son), came to my house. Making the two of us "hold hands," as it were, they stayed briefly and partook of some refreshments. The musicians and guests converged on the scene in large numbers and everyone raised a tremendous ruckus.

An hour or so later people began to rise to their feet. All the guests came one by one to bid us goodbye, offer their good wishes, and leave. The bridegroom and I were the only ones left. We were brought a prayer rug, a pitcher, and a basin. Getting up, we performed our ablutions and offered the prayer of thanksgiving. Then we began to talk. From his very first words I got the sense that my husband was a mere child. Everything he said had to do with childish games. At this time he was very sweet and lovable. Once I became conscious that this was the person chosen for me, that he was mine, I prepared myself to love him. I saw that he was not repugnant to me, but that I was actually quite fond of him. Though not a strong bond of love, this was nevertheless a promising sign of affection. Had I understood things better, perhaps this affection would have bloomed into love and become the means of our mutual felicity. There was no hindrance to my love for him. A young, thirteen-year-old girl with a pure heart and desirable qualities very quickly opens her heart to love and companionship. Unluckily, however, he failed to recognize the way to happiness and rebuffed me, filling me with disgust for him.

The day after the wedding was the "First-Day Feast," the party being held in the garden. I stayed home, and so did my husband. Both of us were so young, still children. Both had spent our obscure lives amid opulence and splendor. Each demanded recognition and respect from the other; each wanted to be obeyed. When two such natures, so similar in their needs, come together, it is inevitable that early on in their permanent life together there will be clashes. Consequently, from the very first day, all our exchanges were hostile. Once when we were playing cards together the bridegroom lost to me. I, too, broke up the game a few times and did other childish things. Being on the losing end was too much for my beloved husband, and he sulked on the very first day. More spoiled and demanding than even him, I also sulked. Each of us sat in a separate corner of the room, lost in our own thoughts.

There was a large mirror in this room in which I could see the whole length of my body. I found myself incredibly pretty, like a queen or a goddess. I wondered in surprise why my husband did not kneel and worship me. Why was he sulking? How could he bear to turn away from me? Was he not human? Did he not have eyes? Good Lord! Was this manner of living not worse than death? Would I have to spend every hour of my life like this?

I brought to mind everything associated with the happiness, the splendor, the dignity of our brief former lives. Then I saw that through one person's insistence, an animal had been made my master, my life partner. My heart pounded heavily and I trembled within. A torrent of tears flowed down my cheeks.

Yes! People called me lucky. I had been given away in marriage amid grandeur and pomp and wealth. A very powerful family had welcomed me in with the greatest alacrity. Supremely beautiful and attractive, and at the very onset of youth, I enjoyed a considerable income and had great prospects for the future. Through all these external shows of happiness and these superficial blessings, however, I was the most wretched, miserable person in all of creation.

Preserving one's happiness is dependent on effort and action. Effort and action follow from unity. And what brings about unity? Love. What engenders love? Understanding. Whereby is understanding made whole? Knowledge.

This dear mate and husband of mine was a headstrong, tiresome child. I saw misery staring me in the face, and I had a strong feeling that it was a disastrous end to which we could look ahead. Thus did the day pass. In the evening I was taken to another party. My beauty shone like a diamond and I drew numerous looks and compliments. I prayed in my heart for these two or three hours of the evening to last as long as Judgment Day itself, so that I would be spared from having to go back home and endure my husband's wild behavior and mocking shows of affection. But man does not get everything he asks for. Nature refuses to transgress her bounds and works her will.

It got late and we returned home. My husband was busy playing. Sitting before a pile of scrap paper, he was making paper demons. He made a throne and set up a king and minister around it. This was no more than a childish game, with no malice behind it. But upon setting eyes on it I stood rooted to the spot as if struck by lightning, then collapsed into a chair. I imagined that he had contrived all of this as an act of hostility toward me—that this paper king made to look like a demon was a sarcastic allusion to my family. Gradually, the thought gained strength in my mind, so much so that speculation was transformed into certainty. With great sadness I called my nanny and said, "Look, nanny, he's insulting my father and my family and taunting me. This is only the first day of our marriage and the first stage in our life. Why is this animal being so horrid to me?"

Bursting into tears, I went into another room. My companions went to my husband's room, rebuked him, and tore up all his paper before throwing it away. Then they brought us together and made peace. But when I turned to kiss him as an act of reconciliation, I felt that I could die.

Two or three days passed, and I had to contend with a fresh difficulty every minute. An instance: this beloved husband of mine never washed his greasy hands and face after eating. Especially when I remonstrated with him, saying, "It isn't nice not to wash your hands," he would become perverse, wiping his soiled hands on the velvet drapes. He never combed his hair or changed his clothes. He was always opposed to my ideas and tastes. If I urged him to be clean, he would be dirty. If I asked him to be calm, he would do something rowdy. Whatever I asked of him, he did exactly the opposite. Immediately and with no reprieve, our lives took separate routes from our very first day together. We never spoke but to squabble with each other. Every move each of us made was thwarted by the other. I had entered a difficult phase of life, far removed from the comforts of my mother and father's house. Sometimes the burden of grief became too oppressive and, helpless, I wept alone in my room. Day or night we were engaged in verbal jousting, or rather, hostility. This is not to say that I was chiefly responsible for this state of affairs. No, I take God as my witness; my only fault was pride. Rather, he was the instigator of everything. Our life consisted of recrimination, tears, and fighting. And when did it begin? The very first hour of the very first night.

The seditious intriguer in all this was the black nanny who had raised my husband after his mother's death. She would make the child get into physical fights with slave girls and then kiss them in jest in my presence. She could see that this made me very unhappy. Or she would keep him confined to the *birun* and not allow him into the *andarun*. If he had to leave the *birun* out of fear of his father, she would take the child into her own room and put him to sleep in her arms. She did not do it out of antagonism toward me. I found out later that it was in this nanny's character to be a trouble-maker and her habit to make mischief.

Some twenty days after my wedding the month of Moharram began. My father-in-law hosted a splendid *rawzakhwani* during the first ten days. I was infinitely grateful to find a diversion from my suffering and an opportunity to weep freely. I never cried in front of relatives because I did not want word to spread of my misery; I was very proud. For Moharram I put on a blue dress and covered myself in jewels from head to foot. All bedecked, I went to the *rawza*. My husband's family and mine were present every day, as was the Atabak's daughter. You could almost say it was a great delight for me to assuage the pain of living indoors with watching the scene outdoors.

I find it necessary to write you an account of the mischievousness of humanity and of the home-wrecking conspiracies of these people. My husband had four sisters. Two of them were the daughters of his maternal aunt, who had been married to his father before she died. Both women lived away from Tehran with their husbands, one in Orumiyya, the other in Maku. Another sister was from the same mother as himself;

she was the daughter-in-law of Eqbal al-Saltana. His fourth sister was still unmarried, living at home. Eqbal al-Saltana's son, entitled Mo'azzam al-Saltana, was well-liked and respected among his wife's family.

When I was engaged to my husband at the age of eight, a picture was taken of me and sent to my husband. The whole family had seen that picture, because I was only eight then, too young to wear the compulsory veil. At that time, this young man had felt certain stirrings of love for me. As I grew, so did the youth's love, until I was married. Now that I had joined his family, the wretch exerted every effort to prevent a bond of love from forming between my husband and me. In this way, he thought that perhaps he could succeed in his goal. My husband, too, was young and gullible. Besides, he was extremely attached to his brother-in-law. The young man had drawn up a careful plan, but realized that implementing it was beyond his power. In this crime, this treachery, he needed an accomplice.

Every day I entertained more than fifty or sixty guests. All my father's wives, sisters, and relations would come in throngs to the *rawza*. At the end of the *rawza*, when they came to my house, my brothers and other near kin would send their greetings from the *birun*. My father's wives would offer to chaperone them into the *andarun* so that we could see them. This young accomplice of my husband's brother-in-law was always with the group. He had warmed up a great deal to my husband and would send him numerous presents, which the poor innocent accepted in childish friendship, never imagining for a moment that they would be the instruments of bringing about his misfortune and darkening his cheerful life.

The young man was about nineteen, very handsome and well-groomed, very courteous and gentle and well-educated.

One of the Atabak's daughters was engaged to be married to him. Whenever this young man came to my house I felt something unnatural and ill-at-ease about his demeanor, in contrast with the others. Every time our eyes met, his sparkled with an unnatural glow, and their nervousness was unmistakable. But I did not understand what this meant, nor was I particularly interested to know. All these comings and goings bore no result. My husband and I were never apart in these meetings; we went everywhere together. Moreover, I never received this young man alone because I was very shy and dared speak to no man other than my husband. And if he chanced to come by when my husband was not home, I excused myself and refused to entertain him.

Little by little, this youth, who had agreed to serve as the means of leading me astray, was thoroughly smitten, conceiving an intense love for me. So far he had been an instrument in the hands of another; now he was working strenuously for himself. His efforts bore no results, however, and brought him nothing but pain and trouble. Finally, exasperated, he complained to his friend and fellow conspirator of the closeness between my husband and me. That gentle friend asked for time to draw up a workable plan. Meanwhile, circumstances came to their aid and provided them with a scheme. A troupe of dancers and acrobats had come to Iran from Russia to open a circus. People rushed in crowds to see the show. In the space of a week, two unsightly, unattractive girls from the troupe had found a score of admirers from the nobility and aristocracy of the land. The two plotters found the presence of one of these girls propitious in advancing their plan and decided to use her. United in their resolve, they were determined to use whatever means necessary to arouse a passion of love for this girl in my husband and to keep him busy with her. At first they would praise the girl, pretending to be in love with her themselves. Then they would interest him in going to the circus to see her.

One evening I was walking about in the yard. My kinsman came in and began to talk to me very gently and quietly. After inquiring about his health, I asked, "But where is my husband?"

"He is outside," was the reply, "and has asked me to intercede with you."

Not understanding his purpose, I looked at him quizzically and asked, "What do you mean 'intercede'? What has he done?"

He replied, "He has done nothing yet that would require forgiveness or intercession. I'm interceding for him to go for some amusement outside."

"I don't understand," I said. "Please speak plainly and tell me what you mean."

He said, "This circus that has opened is a gathering place for all the dignitaries. There is no profligacy there. Please allow him to come and see the circus tonight."

Blushing in embarrassment, I said, "There's no need for permission. My husband is free to choose for himself, so long as you're with him and he goes as your guest."

Evincing great joy, he said, "I'm very obliged to you. I know of no way to express my gratitude other than by kissing your hand."

With great fervor he took my hand to kiss it. Pulling away from him, I said, "No need for gratitude. I have done nothing to deserve your kindness."

Inadvertently dropping his arms to his sides, the youth walked back a couple of steps and fixed his gaze on me for a long time. The blood rushed into his face. Trembling with nervousness, he clasped his hands together and said, "You're fit to be worshiped! Yes, you are! Woe to him who has a beloved other than you!"

Uttering these words, he stumbled his way to the door and ran out like a guilty criminal, leaving me terrified. For a while I felt ill, my head was spinning, and I did not know where I was or what I was doing. Looking around me quickly, I moaned in despair, "Oh, you wretch! You wretch!" Going to my room, I threw myself on the bed and began to twist and writhe like a patient in the throes of death. From that hour on, when I first heard those words, I felt engulfed in wretchedness. At times I would curse my mother in my mind, asking myself why she had complicated my peaceful life and delivered me up to misery with all that fanfare and imposition of demands. I had been married a whole month, during which I had dwelt in a state of constant agitation and tumult. O God! Did everyone live like this, or was I somehow different? Were all husbands like this, or only mine?

My agitation was entirely reasonable. In my father's house, under my mother's upbringing, life had been all simplicity and respect. I had always been obeyed and paid due regard, lacking none of the pleasures of life. This new life was totally unfamiliar. In the ebb and flow of life I had now become helpless, reduced to desperation, especially since my father-in-law had given me full independence, barring the way from my house to his. Instead of making me happy, this free, individualistic life had brought me great sorrow. Alone and guided only by my own actions, I had to navigate in this perilous, tempest-tossed ocean of life. And what was I but a young child, a child who still needed direction, a child who was unfamiliar with and fled from the demands of life, a child who could be taken advantage of?

With my thoughts all in a jumble I fell asleep; the careless abandon of childhood overcame my preoccupations. Suddenly I was awakened and saw that it was dawn and my husband was home. I asked him for a detailed explanation. He answered in a few incoherent words, then pleaded fatigue and went to bed. I fell asleep again. That morning when I awoke, my husband was not with me, which was unusual.

"Where is he?" I asked.

"He left very early this morning," I was told.

I knew quite well what this contravention of custom meant, but attached no importance to it and said nothing. I began to play a new popular tune on the piano which I loved very much.

At about noon my husband came in. He was pale, and I could see the signs of a profound disturbance and worry on his face.

I asked him, "What's the matter?"

"I have a stomachache," he said. "I have come to tell you that I don't want lunch. I'll be out because there's something I need to do."

I looked at him ruefully and said, "Go ahead. Your pain, however, is more like heartsickness. Be very careful. It's dangerous!"

He gave me a confused, inquisitive look and stood still for a while, unsure of what to say. Finally, he lowered his head and went out. Since my husband and I were fighting and quarrelling all the time, I considered his absence a blessing and showed no sign of unhappiness or regret. Actually, I was happy to sleep, play music, or walk when I felt like it and not have anyone arguing with my decisions. I saw quite clearly that I preferred freedom to everything else, including life itself, and that submission and obedience had worn me out.

I had a pretty, little work space where I sat and began to work on embroidery. I embroidered a flower out of my head, without any pattern. Competent at this craft, I considered it my sweetest, most pleasurable endeavor.

The door opened suddenly and the youth walked in. Looking at me wistfully, he asked, "Are you alone?"

"Yes."

"What are you doing?"

"Embroidery."

He asked permission to watch, and I gave my assent. As he bent toward me to watch my work, I felt that he was trembling. Turning my face to him, I gave him a look of surprise. All of a sudden he threw himself at my feet, pleading, "Forgive me, forgive me!"

I asked in amazement, "What are you saying, you wretch? What have you done that you ask for forgiveness?"

He gave no answer. Instead, he reached into his bosom and pulled out a very beautiful letter which he gave me. As though unable to contain himself any longer, he bowed his head and walked away, leaving me indescribably astonished and afraid.

Instantaneously unfolding the letter, I read it from start to finish several times. It was almost ten pages long. Who had beguiled him to come to my house, and to what end; how this poor youth had only been an instrument; how he had subsequently been attracted and fallen in love with me to the point of insanity—all this was contained in the letter. Reading the letter and thinking of its contents, I shut my eyes and briefly reviewed the span of time in which I had known this youth. I saw that everything he had written was true. Every gesture emanating from him which I had chosen to ignore, treating it as of no significance, had actually been quite pregnant with meaning. Suddenly, as if woken from a terrifying nightmare, I began to tremble. I tried to scream, but my breath failed me. I tried to get up, but I fell back on the chair. Was I dying? However, through all this distress, I did not lose control. With a firm resolve I rose to my feet, tore the letter into shreds and destroyed every trace of it. I began to console myself with contemplation, but the trouble that had poured down upon me like rain during this period had completely robbed me of all energy.

That night, unlike his usual practice, my husband did not come home; it was only around dawn that he returned. He woke me up. I saw that his eyes were swollen from crying, that he was in great distress. So simple and pure-hearted was I that I did not realize what the matter was; I could not have imagined that, quick as lightning, he would have fallen in love.

"Why have you been crying?" I asked him.

"I have a stomachache," he said.

"If you have a stomachache, where have you been all this time?"

"I went to see the show with my brother-in-law."

Cutting short the interrogation, I began to feel uneasy. With all my thoughts in disarray, leading nowhere in particular, I feel asleep. Again, when I awoke in the morning I found him missing. No matter how hard I thought about it, I could not come to any conclusion and I had no idea where he was headed. The solitude that had been so pleasant at first was gradually making me anxious. His unexplained absences had filled me with infinite sadness. Wherever I looked for him that day, my husband was nowhere to be found. He was neither in the *birun*, nor in his father's house, nor at his sister's.

Finally, after making several inquiries, I was told, "Early this morning he went out riding with Mazhur, the Count's son." Losing patience, I felt my blood coming to a boil. It was almost evening before my husband returned; his condition was much worse than in previous days. Screaming at him in reproof, I asked, "Where were you?" He did not answer. I insisted vociferously on an answer. He said, "I went where I pleased. You have no right to challenge me."

This rejoinder, so totally unexpected, struck me like a bolt of lightning, fixing me to the spot. Soon I was on my way to my father-in-law's house where I complained about my husband. Receiving me with great kindness and pleasantness, my father-in-law promised to forbid him from leaving the house. When I returned home my husband had disappeared without a trace again.

In a foul mood, unable to concentrate, I received a letter by post. The tone was one of respect and goodwill. It contained the following explanation:

> To Her Exalted and Venerable Highness! An anonymous friend begs your pardon for troubling you with this. Before all else, let me express my sincere and mournful regrets for what has happened. Then I beg your leave to say: O angelic beauty! O spirit of loveliness! What a pity that early in your youth you have become involved with a graceless family of ingrates. This family, raised to such noble rank and the seat of such felicity by your father's generosity, not only pays no heed to your tranquillity and happiness, but treats you with disdain. Do you want to know the reason for your profligate husband's absence? Here it is: he is in love with some "Katy," one of the dancing girls in the circus. His deputy and accomplice is Mazhur, the Count's son, the world's most ferocious wolf. The one who carries his letters and gifts is Hosayn, the private attendant, who has been showered with generosity by yourself. If you wish to

confirm the truth of this matter, look for the English bird-shooting gun number 20 in the box numbered 24 in his private chamber at the corner of the residential hall. Signed: An Anonymous Friend.

My head began spinning. I felt that I was standing at the edge of a bottomless chasm. Tears streamed from my eyes. No longer strong enough to stand, I stumbled around myself once and collapsed unconscious to the floor. A little later I came to and stood up. With my arms lifted in front of me, as though I was trying to drive away a fearsome specter, I cried out, "O God! O God! In all the world is there not one friend or companion to help me?"

An anxious voice behind me said, "Yes, there is. Your friends always watch over you reverently and worshipfully. It is you who ignore your true friends and look down upon them."

Turning around, I saw that it was the same poor young man. I looked at the floor in embarrassment and said, "How long have you been here?"

He said, "I had promised your husband to go to the circus with him tonight as his guest. When I arrived, he had already left. I came to see you and go. That's why you see me standing here. I came at an opportune moment, if you choose to accept me and my friendship."

Weakly, I shook my head in helplessness and said, "Alas, I'm miserable. There's no one I see in this dead end of misery who can be my partner and helpmate. No, no! I can find no friend for myself in this world other than the grave, or any refuge except death."

He let out a fearsome moan, saying, "Oh, oh! Are you going to die? Do you wish to die? No, no, you mustn't. You must find happiness. You must remain alive; you must be free!"

Looking at him in despair, I asked, "By what right do you forbid me from dying? I have no father. My mother doesn't love me. My husband is lost to me. I have to spend the rest of my days alone and friendless. I have no one to love me. The whole world is against me, is my enemy. And have I no right to die, to leave behind this life of woe that I have begun?"

"By what right do I forbid you?" he repeated. "That is a strange question. Look at me closely and see how red and swollen my eyes are from crying. Love and despair over you have ruined my life. I who am giving up my life for you moment by moment, shedding my blood for you drop by drop—do I not have a right to forestall your death for the sake of my ultimate happiness? Why must you die? You are young; you are pretty; you are rich. No, no! Live and avenge all their unkindness to you."

Raising my hand to my brow, I cried, "Death! O Death! Come. Come and free me from this turmoil."

He took a step toward me and took my feverish hand in his ice-cold one. He said, "Say the word and send me to my death. Say you reject my love. Say you want my death. Say that in this impasse that is life you have no need of my love."

He uttered these words so ardently that it sent a chill all over me. I could not reply. I saw that there were two notions forming in my mind: revenge and love. I drew my hand back slowly and said, "I cannot answer you now. Wait a while."

He said, "Then swear by your father's untainted blood that you will not harbor any intention of killing or destroying yourself."

I gave him my word, then collapsed into the chair like a drunkard. He stood there, looking fondly at me several times.

The lovers Ayaz and 'Azra in a mid-nineteenth century court painting. Set in the Qajar period, this unfinished scene, based on a popular Persian lyric, admirably captures the private culture of romance and music behind the walls of the *andarun*. The tall sheepskin cap worn by the man over long hair—in vogue as late as the 1860s among the princely class—and 'Azra's magnificent adornments depict a Persian nobility desirous of enjoying its serene affluence in the context of a sensual tale. The anonymous painter has deliberately substituted Ayaz, the celebrated favorite page of the eleventh-century Sultan Mahmud of Ghazna and a paragon of homosexual love in Persian poetry, for Vameq, the prince of Yemen whose love for the Chinese princess 'Azra is the subject of the famous lyric *Vameq va 'Azra*, rendered by the eighteenth-century Persian poet Mohammad Sadeq Nami.

Then he knelt, kissed my foot with profound devotion and respect, and took his leave.

His departure left me in a confusion of thoughts and feelings. On the one hand, the letter and the revelation of my husband's secret had caused me the deepest hurt; on the other, I wanted to employ this youth and his love as the instrument of my revenge. But I had neither the courage nor the strength to make the first move. I thought, were I to accept this young man's love, how would I answer my mother and father-in-law once the matter came to light? I determined to investigate further and get to the bottom of the affair; then I would voice my complaint to my in-laws. If they interposed to put an end to the affair, then I would tell my husband all about this young man, whom I would then banish from my house. If, by chance, no one came to my aid and my husband continued to violate my rights in the same way, then I would compel myself to fall in love with this youth and get back at my husband. And if, after I was found out, anyone objected to my conduct, I would enumerate all my husband's injustices and his slights of me, thus clearing my conscience.

Armed with this childish resolve, I began to delve into the issue. Chance or misfortune—I am not sure which—came to my aid and my husband left the next morning to spend the day with his beloved. I went into the garden of the *birun* as was my custom when strolling. Following the directions in the letter, I went into the room and opened the box to find a photograph and some letters in French. These I could not read, but I took the photograph and came home. Immediately I walked over to my father-in-law's and began my complaint, showing him the picture. He laughed heartily and said, "This is the work of malicious people. Pay no attention. So what if there was a photograph in his box. How does that affect your freedom?"

I began to weep. I said, "He's never home, whether at night or in the daytime. He's always at the theater or somewhere else with Mazhur."

He laughed again and said, "I don't think my son is so much at fault as to merit your vehemence. One cannot blame young people if they want to have a good time, and men can't be expected to sit at home like women."

Summoning up all my pride, I stood up. In my heart I cursed myself a hundred thousand times for taking my complaint to someone who had absolutely no idea what pain and anguish I suffered. Returning home, I dropped upon the floor, heartbroken, weeping and moaning. I complained to my mother next; she, too, gave me irrelevant answers totally off the mark. Compelled into silence, I held my breath, alone with my agony twenty-four hours a day. In the length of an entire day my husband was home for two hours; and during those two hours he suffered from a stomachache. I felt unimaginable hatred towards him welling up from within. My life was completely worthless and tiresome in my eyes. So I looked for ways to divert myself. During the hours that I was alone, I would bring together all my pretty, expensive dresses, my beautiful shoes, and my smaller jewels which I considered of low value. Then I would draw lots; whatever slave girl's name came up, I gave her my things.

My only solace in this house was my wet nurse, who regaled me with stories. As ill luck would have it, my mother was not particularly enamored of her, imagining that my indifference to herself was prompted by my wet nurse, whereas it should have been attributed to my age and youthful want of understanding. At any rate, goaded from the outside in a thousand different ways, I had no choice but to send her away, and this final joy was also taken away from me. My lifeline severed, I was awash in the ocean of despair and perplexity, and knew nothing better or sweeter than death.

Ultimately, youthful pride combined with childish ignorance and a sense of humiliation for what I had suffered at my husband's hands, and drew me toward that youth. The passage of time also proved helpful and propitious. One day I told him that I loved him. Little by little, my love for him grew and wiped away all my cares and sorrows. My broken, drooping heart had bloomed into a youthful freshness in this new springtime of love, and sorrow had bidden farewell. Merely seeing him and listening to his words of love was enough to immerse me in such ecstasy that I would forget the world and everything in it. When I woke up in the morning, I would wait with eager anticipation for our evening meeting, the time in between passing in great happiness and lightness of heart. In the evenings when we had our customary ten-minute encounters, I was the happiest creature alive. The very memory of his having given me his handkerchief or a letter or a picture was enough to fill me with pride. I never parted with anything he gave me, and would often treat his tokens as if they were living things that I could talk to.

I no longer complained about my husband, nor was I at all unhappy to see him gone. Quite the contrary, if he did happen to come home for an hour, I was very desirous of his leaving as soon as possible. I needed to be alone so that I could think of the man I loved. I wanted nothing of the world but him, and I found no peace except in seeing him. This relationship which goes by the name of love is like a little ball of snow that separates from a mountain peak. As it rolls downward, it grows bigger and bigger. By the time it reaches the bottom, that little speck has grown into a mass that can overrun a settlement.

A love triangle in a watercolor by Mirza Baba Shirazi (d. circa 1240 Sh./1824), the great court artist of Fath 'Ali Shah. The daring depiction of illicit love between a libertine nobleman and his paramour, witnessed on the one hand by the angry wife and her infuriated black nanny and on the other by the gratified procuress, exhibits the enduring preoccupation with amorous affairs among the Qajar nobility. Even in Taj's time, three quarters of a century later, the elements of Mirza Baba's theme were still relevant.

Likewise, initially this disorder grips man every now and then; but later in its course it does so in rapid succession.

Two or three months went by. What had been the means of my happiness—and what I had embraced openly at first—now became a great misfortune. So overpowered and abject had I become in love that I found death easier than the breath of life. I seemed to be ablaze from head to toe. My entire body was overcome by a uniformly nervous quivering. Completely deprived of sleep, I had no recourse but weeping. Finally, after three months, I worked up the courage to write him a letter. In it I explained all that I had been through and gave it to him the next day when he came to see me. Most of these meetings took place in my husband's presence. In these two or three months, not once had we met in private, nor were we desirous of being alone without a third party. As it chanced, I found the opportunity that day to give him the letter. That was when we opened the gates of disaster on ourselves. This unlucky creature, owing to the trust and rapport he enjoyed with his friend, gave him the letter immediately and directly, in the belief that the secret of our love was hidden from him. That miserable wretch gave a complete report to my father-in-law, adding nothing and leaving nothing out, which upset the man greatly. At the same time the fire of a jealous rage was kindled in the recesses of my husband's heart. My father-in-law put his foot down firmly: this dear kinsman was no longer to visit me. Thus were we completely parted.

Two or three days passed and I did not see him. There was no way for me to know what had transpired. Finally we ran into each other one day in the home of one of my sisters. He explained the situation, and we made arrangements to exchange letters and stay in the know about each other.

Amid all this furor, my husband also fell prey to my condition: his sweetheart left for Russia. We went to Shemiran together, both united in heartbreak. Neither he nor I, however, expressed any pain or grief openly, avoiding the subject altogether. Soon I grew accustomed to patience, and learned not to do anything to confirm the gossip. If, perchance, we did run into each other or circumstances brought us together, I would withdraw. Placing my love alongside other incurable agonies in my breast, I kept everything concealed within. But not a moment passed without a thousand sighs or numerous palpitations of the heart. Quite abruptly I became a fugitive from society, preferring corners of solitude to any diversion that life afforded. In love with the pain of love, I took pleasure in anguish and made no effort to alleviate it. It was a worthwhile preoccupation, keeping me far more satisfied than greater things would have.

> In our creed worship of reason sits not well;
> We relish insanity and the rending of clothes.
> Any man can recline on the seat of power;
> We savor discontent and agony.
> Moshtaq! Why suffer and smart any more than this?
> To unmoor oneself from this world of men—how delicious
> that is!

By degrees, I found my youthful excitation and frenzy diminishing, and I was on my way to forgetting him matter-of-factly. The days passed, and with nothing new in my life I spent my time according to a programmed routine. After about a year, nature and God gave me a beautiful, sweet girl to compensate me for my loneliness. I loved her intensely from the moment of her birth, spending every hour of the night with her. The pure and genuine love emanating from the very core of this infant had completely obliterated my sorrow and made me very happy. I loved no one aside from my baby, not even myself. As for my poor husband, after his disappointment with "Katy" he had bought a little rust-colored goat and a little chariot. At any hour of the day he would harness the poor beast to the chariot and, rain or shine, whip it and make it run around the courtyard. Leaving him to his devices, I was occupied with my darling child.

ROYAL EUROPEAN TOURS

There was talk of my brother's impending travels in Europe, and a loan was being negotiated. All the nation's wealth and everything my father had stored up, whether in jewelry or cash, had been spent very quickly by my brother. Over the course of a year, all his attendants and his rabble of hangers-on had come into possession of gardens, villas, and vast sums of money. The miserable man had divided the hapless nation's wealth among some ten or twelve individuals. Eventually, through the Grand Atabak's efforts—so diligent, so selfless, so creative, so sincere—a large sum of money was borrowed from overseas and the European trip arranged. Here it was that this Grand Atabak, this first citizen of the realm, displayed the full measure of his patriotism and honesty: a large portion of the loan lined his own pockets, and the rest was swallowed up by others.

People have narrated strange accounts of this trip. The purchase of twenty hefty trees at high cost, shipped with great difficulty and expense, only to dry up before they ever reached our shores; large quantities of iron piping, big statues, and other useless materials which lie idle and unused in Farahabad; the exorbitant sums of money that went into the activities of Hesam al-Saltana and Sadiq al-Dawla; and the debauchery and free-spending of the royal entourage—these are a few examples of such tales. Finally, after having squandered millions, they returned home sheepishly. The only result and benefit that accrued to the people of Persia from this trip was a huge debt, without any returns in the way of even one rifle or one bullet to defend the independence of this poor nation. Not one factory was set up, not one useful enterprise begun, to promote the progress and facilitation of agriculture or other businesses.

The Grand Atabak was deposed after this trip, and Amin al-Dawla assumed the grand vizierate. A few months later, he arranged for one of my brother's daughters to be married to his one-and-only son. But not long after this, he, too, was deposed and sent into exile in Lasht-Nesha. 'Ayn al-Dawla became Grand Vizier.

During my brother's reign the so-called grand vizierate, or ministership in general, had become like a *ta'ziya:* every few minutes the narrator would leave the scene and come back in different clothes. No one was sure of the premiership, ministerial appointments, or the functioning of government. This venerable brother of mine would depose his premier at the urging of a two-year-old, or dismiss a minister, egged on by a sycophant. Among others, he had the unfortunate Qevam al-Dawla mounted backwards on a donkey and carried from the city to Shemiran. This was because the Grand Atabak had been on bad terms with the man and wanted him removed from the Ministry of Finance. That a minister of finance was mounted backwards on a donkey to be carried from the city to Shemiran is a good indicator of the state of affairs at court and the chaos and lawlessness that prevailed there.

The more ridiculous the man, the more warmly he was received; the more contemptible, the more attention he got.

All the nation's affairs were governed by a bunch of vile, dissolute riffraff. People's property, lives, and honor were in imminent danger of violation. All the great, noble and sensible servants of the realm had chosen to remain at home; every position of great importance was held by a corrupt, illiterate, ignoble man.

Since the part is always subservient to the whole, these odious trends were affecting the general populace as well. People spent their lives in vulgarity and immorality, gambling and indecency. Fraud, thievery, and swindling were the order of the day. Every man of foresight, every patriot, sat at home all day and bemoaned the situation. The Shah had made his sons provincial governors and entrusted the lives and property of the masses to these bloodthirsty tyrants. This sovereign was, in truth, a deep, bottomless chasm for the poor nation. Leave alone all the money in Persia, not all the gold on earth could fill it.

Using this small family as a yardstick, we can well gauge the state of the nation. If the head of a household is wasteful, sanctions his children's and dependents' misappropriation, and spends every hour of his life in debauchery, this lawlessness will gradually come to the attention of his neighbor. He, in turn, will look for an opportunity to lend money on private terms to the reckless man. Soon the creditor will pour the lethal poison of indebtedness drop by drop down the man's throat, and the debtor will eventually have to mortgage his house. Once that happens, the neighbor will start interfering in his household affairs. Then he will exert such control over the derelict that the man will be unable to make a single move without the approval and consent of his neighbor. Finally, the debtor himself will be destroyed and his family will sink into eternal poverty and misery.

Mozaffar al-Din Shah on board the royal yacht, Portsmouth, England, 20 August 1902. On his second European tour the shah was accompanied by his premier, 'Ali Asghar Khan, Amin al-Soltan (standing to the left of the shah). The shah's solemn face probably reflects his frustration at having been denied the Order of the Garter on this occasion. Left to right, seated: Prince of Wales, the shah, Queen Alexandra, King Edward VII, Princess of Wales.

Such was this dear brother of mine. He led Persia and her people into hardship, and summoned up his efforts to wreak an unimaginably swift destruction on the country. He struck at the very root of the unfortunate nation and ushered every kind of suffering into the land through illicit channels. The subject of a loan came up again, and arrangements were made for a second trip to Europe. The loan arranged, he was on the road once more. The only useful thing to come out of this trip was a small number of armaments, purchased at the suggestion of Momtaz al-Saltana, Persia's ambassador in Paris. And there was a travelogue, penned by none other than this imperial brother of mine. Here is an extract:

> Today, Thursday, we arose in the morning to drink water. Then we came back and took a short walk. Since there was still a little water left, we went back and drank some more. Next Razan arrived; we sat in a cafe and drank some tea. After that, we came home on foot. Fakhr al-Molk and the Minister of Court were there. Pulling Fakhr al-Molk's leg for a while, we then teased the Minister of Court. The Minister of Court showed us a telegram which told of Aqa Sadiq al-Dawla's surgery for hemorrhoids. We rejoiced. Eating our lunch, we took a rest. Since it was Friday eve, Aqa Sayyid Hosayn chanted the *rawza;* we wept. We said the prayer for earthquakes and then went to bed.

We may rightfully express gratitude to this discerning, far-sighted person for obtaining the weapons; today we owe our freedom, the security of our roads, and the splendid management of the constabulary to those armaments. But we offer no thanks for this book; it is bound to perpetuate the regrettable memory of those thirteen years that we were in this man's grip—a man whose proof of intelligence was nothing more distinguished than this document.

My relatives are bound to condemn my freedom of language. However, despite the fact that I belong to the same family and dynasty, I will be guided by nothing except my Persianness and my conscience, and will write my family history freely and openly. O my homeland! Is it possible to overlook thy rights out of fear for one man? No, never! Thy love has been etched in my heart as indelibly as the blemishes of thy enemies and destroyers on this page.

> They ask me, "Where dwells that moon goddess?"
> Well, she dwells in my heart, but I know not where my heart is.

Prior to this European trip, my father-in-law was appointed officer of finances to Azarbaijan, where the crown prince lived; as he left for his post, he took me along. Before setting out, however, something farcical happened. Two months after I was married, my father-in-law said to me, "Why not put me in charge of your finances? I will manage them for you and hand them over whenever you ask." I had agreed, thinking that I would thereby have some savings. For two or three years, he had received my income. On the day that we were due to depart for Azarbaijan, Sayyid Ebrahim, the silk merchant who had outfitted me for the past couple of years, came to me and said, "You owe me two thousand eight hundred *tuman*s. Unless you pay, I won't let you go." I sent a message to my father-in-law: "What is this sayyid saying? Have I been responsible for my own expenses all this time?"

He replied, "I took a princess for a daughter-in-law so that she would manage her own expenses."

"Very well," I said. "If you hand over all my money which is in your keeping, totaling nine thousand *tuman*s, I'll pay the sayyid his money."

He replied, "I don't have any money of yours."

I complained to my mother about the situation. Her talking to him, however, proved of no avail, and it became apparent that he intended to keep my money. My mother agreed to pay my debt to the sayyid, and I left her in charge of my income.

In view of this problem and a thousand other family vexations, I was unwilling to go on this trip, but my mother forced me. My grandfather came along, to take over governorship of Orumiyya. The journey was very unpleasant and difficult; everyone was hostile and unfriendly to one another. Poor me! Fallen amidst this band of travelers, friendless, alone, and heartsick, I could hardly draw an easy breath. My one son having died, I now had two daughters, who were the only joy of my life. After traveling for a month, we arrived in Azarbaijan, and I was freed from the hardships of the trip and the sight of insincere faces.

My house was apart and at a great distance from that of my father-in-law, who was now the Amir Nezam. The crown prince and Maleka-ye Jahan were very kind to me; but my inner turmoil kept me from outdoor activity. Grief-stricken and melancholy, I spent most of my time alone. My husband was the commander of the armed forces in Azarbaijan, and should have sought to benefit from his new job. But he had discovered an intense zeal for collecting horses and mules; in a short time, he had amassed ten mules at government expense. All his own income went into the purchase of straw and barley. Another activity that he was inordinately fond of was beating people. Every day he would beat up a few people, then give them new clothes. This was repeated every day. Sometimes this commander of the troops, with all the dignity and stateliness that went with his rank, was reduced to a sergeant's

اسرالامرار معظام شجاع رسلطنه

Mohammad Baqer Khan Sardar Shaja' al-Saltana, Taj's father-in-law, who was the chief of the royal guard in the late-Naseri period and an ally of the premier, Amin al-Soltan.

uniform. When he gave that away as well, he perforce had to stay home for a couple of days until he got his new clothes.

This beloved husband of mine was a devotee of the god of hedonism. He derived enormous pleasure from being with simple youths. There was a dancer named Tayhu, almost twenty years old; my husband was beside himself, enthralled by this dancer, on whom he spent a fortune. I no longer turned to my father-in-law for any favors, having seen how base and niggardly he was. My husband was engrossed in his pleasures and his collection of mules. So I was left with no recourse but to sell my jewelry in order to provide for my expenses. The chief goldsmith bought everything very cheaply. Quietly, I was managing my own finances.

In this land of strangers, my sole companion and friend was an Armenian girl named Anna, and her story follows.

She was eighteen years old, pretty, with beautiful dark eyes, and made her living as a seamstress. A month after we arrived, when I needed to have a new dress made, this girl was sent for. Little by little, I became close to her. She bore an equally sincere love for me and was often in my house. In the corners of her large, dark eyes, there were often teardrops that sparkled like diamonds. With a pleasant voice she would say, "I love you!" Her voice penetrated to the core of my being, and I listened for it with eagerness.

In the beginning, whenever I visited the crown prince's *andarun*, I was received with the greatest warmth. Lately, however, my beauty had caused alarm. The princess's sincere graciousness had given way to a peculiar tension, for no good reason. I was so caught up in despair and under so much pressure from being among strangers that I had forgotten the world and everything in it. Soon my father-in-law's wife became the favorite—a shift in favor that affected me neither

From the beginning of the twentieth century coach service connected centers of population with greater frequency, particularly in northern Iran, as in this photograph of the Rasht–Tehran carriage road. Taj's travels in the provinces were typically undertaken in such vehicles.

physically nor emotionally; I did not give it a moment's thought. A little later, when others were describing and interpreting this relationship to the servants, it made me laugh a great deal. The woman was so unalluring and unlovable that the topic of her love had become the butt of jokes.

News reached us from Tehran of my brother's visit to Europe and my mother's marriage to the royal treasurer. I was terribly disenchanted at first, but then remembered how lonely my mother had been. Though this made me feel a little better, I could not help the profound uneasiness and pain that still lingered in my heart.

My mother wrote me a letter in which she commended her brother, Ahmad Mirza, to me. On making inquiries, I discovered that my uncle was living in Ardabil. Putting together a sum of money for expenses, I charged the captain of our guard with going to Ardabil and bringing the prince back to Tabriz with all due respect and decorum. Here I would ask the crown prince to provide him with honorable employment. The captain of the guard, As'ad al-Soltan, went to Ardabil, but the prince, for personal reasons, did not come back with him, sending word that he would come later. He did send his son and his mother, however. When they arrived, we prepared a house for them and received them with the greatest respect. I committed my uncle's son to my husband's care.

As fate would have it, this prince's son was a beauty of the first order. Nowhere in Tabriz—or Tehran, for that matter—had I seen such a lovely, appealing face. It was not long before my dear husband, so prone to losing his heart, was head-over-heels in love with this youth. Everything he owned, everything he could snatch away from people through force or oppression, went into satisfying the young boy's whims and caprices. I was completely oblivious to all this. After a month or two the news began to spread, and only then did I, wretch that I was, learn of it. It lay within my power to expel the boy from my house, but it was not in my power to purge him from my husband's heart. Over the sixteen-month period of my stay in Tabriz, vast sums of money were spent on this youth every month. My husband loved him ardently, intensely. Had I cherished any real love in my heart for my husband, I would most assuredly have suffered terribly; but I only harbored conjugal respect and affection for him, so I was not particularly concerned with what he did, and left him alone. During my stay in Tabriz I was constantly preoccupied and weary. It was also here that God bestowed a son on me, at which my delight was boundless. I loved my children very much, spending my time on nothing and nobody else.

Some time later we got news of the Shah's return from Europe. It was decided that the Amir Nezam would go to Tehran to receive him and arrange for me to go separately. I was delighted to hear this, for I would be leaving behind my life of loneliness in a strange land and returning home. We set out for the capital. My husband, having quarreled with his father, joined me on the trip, which proved to be very difficult. My dear friend and charming traveling companion, the Amir Nezam's wife, heard of someone's death whom she loved very much. This much-loved friend was one of her servants who tutored her sons. Her husband had sensed her love for the servant, whom he sent on a mission, dispatching another servant to kill him. As a result, the young man was murdered after we had departed. His daughter met us along the way and filled our desert lives with sorrow and regret.

I was overjoyed to arrive in Tehran and see my relatives. This joy, however, proved to be short-lived. My husband went to receive the monarch via Qazvin, and I was left alone in

Tehran. His time away lasted six months because, after passing through Rasht to join the royal reception, he was taken to Azarbaijan by his father. After some time he sent for me, but I refused to go. After my father-in-law's family had left Tehran to join him, he sent my husband back.

I now began a relatively free life under no one's command. This freedom had its price; my disobedience incurred the wrath of my father-in-law, who cut off all my funds for a whole year. Selling the remainder of my jewelry, I bought a horse and carriage and brought some order into my life. My husband had his head in his own concerns: the purchase of horses, the maintenance of mules, the collection of cattle and sheep in flocks, the castration of cocks, the breeding of turkeys. Meanwhile, I was taking care of the children and tending to matters of everyday life. I soon got the urge to study the *tar*. Mirza 'Abdollah, a man so old that he had almost joined the ranks of the departed, was chosen to be my instructor. Before long I was playing the instrument better than my teacher. This proved to be an enjoyable hobby.

The situation at court had undergone numerous changes. After the Shah's return from Europe, matters fell into disarray and financial necessity was leading to desperation. A cabal of courtiers was conspiring to overthrow the Grand Atabak. On the chessboard that Persia had become, these rivals had joined in mighty battle, each charging full force. Lining their pockets and purses with gold, they were squeezing the masses and inflicting irreparable damage upon the nation.

While everyone was thus advancing his personal gains and tearing up the country piece by piece, my brother, the enthroned monarch of the land, was lost in paltry affairs, steeped in a deep slumber of negligence, squandering his time in futility. He had brought back from Europe a certain powder. When spread on someone's body or bedclothes, even to the thickness of a fly's wing, this powder would keep the person awake all night with incessant itching. Having obtained a sufficiently large quantity of it, he would spread some on his servants' beds every day and laugh as they twitched and wriggled comically.

This European tour of my brother's was similar to Peter the Great's, except that the results were vastly different. The souvenirs from the trip included enormous, stocky trees and large quantities of iron piping, for which he paid handsomely. Despite the thousands spent on them, however, the trees dried up, and the piping lay useless in Farahabad. What did result from it was a further deterioration in the state of Persia. Several such purchases were made; the histories relating to this particular sovereign's reign contain complete records.

These exploits of my brother's have brought to mind something similar about my husband, which I now write for you, my teacher. Perhaps you will see what a miserable creature I was and who my contemporaries and companions were, and thereby feel some compassion for me. In fact, I beg you to acknowledge my misery.

My husband was immoderately fond of fine horses and kept a full stable with several packs, each pack containing seven beasts. One day he came in greatly distressed and said, "Madam! I can't go on like this. I must have this horse."

Unaware of what he meant, I asked, "What are you saying? What horse do you mean?"

He said, "'Ala' al-Dawla owns a bay horse with a white forehead which won the pennant in the 1308 [1890–91] horse race in Naser al-Din Shah's time. It's unthinkable for such a horse to be in Tehran and not in my stable."

"Have you looked into the price?" I inquired.

"Yes," he said. "Along with five hundred *tuman*s, I have agreed to part with a gold watch and accompanying chain to be given to his hostler. He will not be content; he says he cannot let me have the animal for less than seven hundred."

Chiding him, I advised, "This horse is ten years old, quite aged. Besides, there's no longer much of a demand for horse-racing. What would you do with it?" I made a point of asking him not to buy it.

For two or three days he complied with my request, but then he went ahead and bought the animal. He rode it two or three times before the horse fell ill. One day, a month after the purchase, I went to Shemiran. Walking in the meadow, I saw a miserable-looking, dirty horse tied amid a verdant patch of alfalfa.

"Whose animal is this wind-broken nag?" I asked.

The caretaker replied, "This is the bay that belonged to 'Ala' al-Dawla." The next day a dervish was given five *tuman*s to take the animal away.

Several juicy stories emerged from the Shah's tour. Among them was that of Amir Bahador, the chief of the royal guard and a member of the retinue. One day in Contrexéville, he mixed henna and dye in a pan he found under his bed and spread it over his beard and mustache. Then he went to bed with the mixture still on his face and smeared all the sheets. In the morning he got up and took a bath in a large pool. As soon as he had finished, the custodial staff immediately drained the pool and filled it with fresh water. This man kept a personal tea-maker, smoked his hookah, took pickled garlic with him and ate it at official dinners. Every time he stayed at an inn, they had to fumigate all the rooms adjoining his, calling it the "niche saleté," the filthy alcove. The other members of the entourage were equally scandalous—perhaps somewhat less

Horse race in Bagh-e Shah, a seasonal event of great significance in the royal calendar, attracting competition from not only the royal stable and the stables of the nobility, but also from nomadic Turkoman horse breeders from northeastern Iran. Taj's husband, Hasan Khan, must have dreamed of winning a trophy in the highly prized Persian sport when he rashly purchased 'Ala' al-Dawla's wind-broken jade.

so. At any rate, the Persians, devoid of decent manners, have always lived in barbarity and uncouthness. These men had made an impression ten times as strong on the Europeans and left a deep, dark memory in their hearts. Sa'di says:

> One may rightly speak ill of three men, as I hear;
> But if you exceed that number to a fourth, that's wrong:
> The first is the king who sanctions the reprehensible—
> He causes his subjects harm.
> It is lawful to spread news of his doings
> To warn people to beware of him.
> As for the second, weave not a veil around the shameless,
> For he will rend his own veil.
> Third is the dishonest vendor of slanted scale;
> Tell all you can of his evil deeds.

THE CHOLERA EPIDEMIC

During these overseas fiascoes, my life followed a quiet course. Summer came and we moved to our summer resort. Before our departure, the death of the Imam Jum'a, my sister's husband, had stirred a minor scare among the people. It was said he had died of cholera. However, not one in hundred paid heed. In order to hearten themselves, people refused to believe it. Two or three others died in a similar fashion. Still, people were not wary enough of the disease. In the summer it assumed major proportions, and it became clear there was an epidemic. Between eighty and a hundred people died every day. Two months into the summer I was still unaware of it, because all references to the subject had been forbidden in the vicinity of the Sahebqaraniyya, lest the Shah should be afraid. Once it intensified, we learned of it. I was terribly anxious and panic-stricken, not for myself—having never feared death from the time I was a child—but for my relatives and children.

Summoning the family physician, I asked him, "Where can we go to get away from this disease?"

He replied, "Stay right here and don't leave the house at all. Be very careful of your health and watch your food and water."

After the physician had left, we, husband and wife, were so terrified we could not remain at home. Unmindful of the fact that heat and travel would increase chances of contamination, we decided to go to Posht-e Kuh. Forming a large caravan with others, we set out from Shemiran. Our traveling companions—men, women, and children—numbered eighty-six. Our first two stops were very pleasant. But for the remainder of the trip we saw sick and dead people everywhere. Most of the contaminated ones had been thrown out of the villages, and these unfortunates were suffering the agonies of death under the hot sun.

The man who had taught me as a child, and who now taught my children, went with us. Despite all this poor man's insistence that we go back, we persisted in moving on. At every stop we made, the disease had ravaged the area like a tongue of fire. One morning I woke up to find that all our fellow travelers had fled. The only ones left were my husband, me, and the women and children. The women, too, were setting off into the desert. On asking, we found out that the bodies of the dead were washed for burial in the very same river on whose bank we had camped. From a very little, ramshackle village nearby ten or twelve dead were carried away that night, which is why our companions had fled in terror.

With infinite care we gathered everyone together and decided to go back. We departed at once. That night, at our next stop, one of our servants who had caught the disease died in a matter of minutes. He died so quickly that the doctor who was with us did not have the time to give the poor youth any medicine. When we awoke the next day, the desert was wrapped in stillness. Not a sound could be heard, except a plaintive, pitiful moaning from the unfortunate youth's mother. The color fled from our faces, and we began to succumb to a ghastly terror and a sense of absolute despair. The poor young victim was laid in a tent near a large stream. I was overcome with horror but realized that, if I betrayed the slightest fear, all my companions would run away and I would be lost in the desert. Quickly I began to talk, threatening some of the travelers and comforting the others, and we set off.

We left behind my teacher and two servants to bury the young victim. No white calico could be found for a shroud in any of the nearby villages. Two horsemen sent to look everywhere returned empty-handed. I had not thought to take along any calico. Being very young, I had not had any experience of death. Others had forborne from causing me alarm by suggesting that I take some with me. At any rate, the poor youth was laid to rest with much trouble and the others returned.

Traveling with speed, we returned to our residential garden. There also we found that two of the people left behind had died: a very handsome, strapping young Caucasian who had been my husband's coachman, and a poor, unknown Turkish soldier. All the people had resigned themselves to their fate, living in imminent expectation of death. The shah lived in the Sahebqaraniyya, terribly rattled. All traffic around the royal mansion, even in the village, was forbidden. No one could see the royal person, except a few servants and Sayyid Bahrayni who was constantly reciting from the Holy Book and chanting prayers for protection. The functioning of the state had been suspended totally. Persia was an unremitting graveyard and her people the dead. In fact, they lived in far greater fear and silence than ever before. High or low, the people had turned to repentance. Temporarily renouncing the deeds and actions that they knew were wrong, they spent all their time in prayer.

My teacher! You are well accustomed to the Persian character. You know when their lives become impossibly difficult how kind, honest, true to their word and fawning they can be, and in times of prosperity how pernicious, malevolent, and vile.

Among the papers of the late Amir Nezam one day a letter was discovered in the handwriting of 'Abbas Mirza, our forbear, addressed to Fath 'Ali Khan. It read: "In times of need, we princes become so kind and obsequious that one better than us cannot be imagined. After our needs are met, however, we no longer recognize our helper. In fact, we forget everything." I laughed a great deal at this confession on our noble forbear's part because I saw that he was being truthful. After this episode, however, I saw that Persians in general are afflicted with this disease, and that this distinction did not pertain exclusively to the royal household. But since royals are in the public eye, their manners and character are more closely scrutinized than those of others.

In any case, that sweltering summer was ushered out, leaving several thousand dead in its wake. In a month or two, everyone returned to his former condition and resumed his prior activities. It is a noteworthy aspect of the Persian character to suddenly take up a pursuit for a while and follow it to its extremity. But by the same token, as quickly as they erupt, Persians are liable to simmer down and forget. Everything about them is superficial, impromptu, and lacking a sound foundation. I swear to you that between morning and bedtime, every Persian spins dreams of prominent services to his country—the endeavors he will undertake to promote the common weal, the profitable business ventures he will launch, the fallow, despoiled lands he will make fertile and prosperous, the beautiful aqueducts he will construct. But these are all dreams with no basis in reality. Europeans say, "There are two people who are never capable of accomplishing any work: he who thinks too much and he who thinks not at all." When our ideas prove futile, we comfort ourselves with the thought that God is great, that the Lord of the Age himself will come to our aid.

Having been assured that the epidemic had ended, we came into the city, which we found ravaged and its people utterly transformed. Though this epidemic was a sign of divine wrath and chastisement, we can still say that it was engendered by an inattention to hygiene and the contamination of the water. Every government's first duty is to see to the cleanliness of the streets and the water, as well as the tranquillity of the people. There was a municipality in name, but, like other arms of the government, none in actual fact—and yet the employees felt entitled to their undeserved salaries. Throughout the year in Persia, and particularly in Tehran, several fatal, infectious diseases rage because of unhygienic conditions. The streets are all filthy—in winter covered in mud and sludge, and in the summer dusty and dirt-encrusted. The watercourses are open and the filth from the houses is washed away into them. This water circulates through the town and people drink it and fall prey to all manner of maladies.

Oh, for all my deep-seated, heart-felt anguish! Believe me, my teacher! In writing down each of these words, I am overwhelmed by sorrow and regret and tears flow freely from my eyes. How is it possible for man to add a misery by choice to his catalog of miseries of compulsion? If we choose to, can we not free ourselves from our abasement? Yes, we can, but we choose not to.

If every resident of Tehran kept only the doorway to his house clean and saw to the cleanliness of his own street, undoubtedly the number of fatalities would be reduced by half every year. Or the watercourses could be covered and plumbing brought in. Each person would need to pay a small amount which would ensure his safety all year round. Despite the fact that individuals who form corporations and take money from the people for public works—such as Haji Malek and other companies—give nothing back to the people but loss and regret, one deception must not make us withdraw from the arena. We must continue to look until we find a trustworthy person with whom to cooperate, and thereby save ourselves from the wretchedness of squalor. We, the people of Persia, unfortunately desire not one good thing, not one hundred, but thousands upon thousands for ourselves; hopefulness flows through our veins. But we do not recognize the lawful way of doing things. We seek progress and material acquisitions through unlawful channels, and that is why we never succeed or attain our goal.

LIBERATING WOMEN

My teacher! If the women in this country were free as in other countries, enjoyed comparable rights, could enter the realm of government and politics, and could advance their lives, then without a doubt I would not seek the path to my progress through a ministerial position, through trampling on the people's rights and usurping the property of fellow Muslims and selling away my beloved homeland. I would choose a legitimate way and a determined plan for my advancement. Never would I spend the people's wealth to buy myself a mansion, a garden, household furniture, carriages and automobiles. These I would obtain through hard work and service.

I am sure you smiled as you read this and chuckled at my opinions and said: the men of our land have found no path to progress but this; you, an uninformed woman—how have you found a lawful way toward advancement?

My dear teacher! Do we not enjoy freedom of thought?

Yes, we do.

Then peruse carefully what I write next. Then, if you have any objections, you may speak up. I would adhere to a conservative position, not for my personal good but for the commonweal. I would make every effort to promote trade within Persia. I would build factories, not like the Rabi'ov soap-making plant, but ones that would make us independent of foreign trade. I would tap the mines, which God has liberally bestowed on Persia. I would seize the rights to the Bakhtiyari oil fields which generate tremendous annual profits, not leave them to the British. I would find the means to facilitate agriculture and provide its necessities. I would build the Mazandaran highway and regulate the transportation of essential commodities. As they do in California, I would hand over barren land to the people and ask them to make it productive. I would dig numerous irrigation wells and create artificial forests. I would divert the Karaj River toward the city and thereby rescue the people from the misery of filthy water. Not neglecting my own overall welfare, I would live in comfort without committing thievery and treason. The people, too, would benefit from my service and efforts, and live in peace.

Alas! Persian women have been set aside from humankind and placed together with cattle and beasts. They live their entire lives of desperation in prison, crushed under the weight of bitter ordeals. At the same time, they see and hear from afar and read in the newspapers about the way in which suffragettes in Europe arise with determination to demand their rights: universal franchise, the right to vote in parliament, the right to be included in the affairs of government. They are winning successes. In America their rights are fully established and they are striving with serious determination. The same is true in London and Paris.

My teacher! How I wish I could travel to Europe and meet these freedom-seeking ladies! I would say to them, "As you fight for your rights happily and honorably, and emerge victorious in your aims, do cast a look at the continent of Asia. Look into the houses, where the walls are three or five meters high and the only entryway is a door guarded by a doorman. Beneath the chains of captivity and the resistless weight of subjugation you will see a mass of oppressed cripples, some sallow and pale-faced, others bare and hungry, yet others endlessly expectant and mournful." I would add, "These are women, too; these are human, too. These are also worthy of due respect and merit. See how life treats them."

Again I would say, "The lives of Persian women consist of two things: the black and the white. When they step outdoors to take a walk, they are frightful images of mourning in black. When they die, they are shrouded in white. I am one of these ill-starred women, and I much prefer the whiteness of the shroud to that hideous figure of mourning; I have always demurred from putting on that garb. The counterpart to this life of darkness is our day of white. In a corner of my house of sorrow, I comfort myself with the thought of that day, yearning for its advent with incalculable joy, as though it were an eagerly-awaited lover."

During the Minor Tyranny a Caucasian Armenian named Bakianov, a militant and freedom fighter for Persia, sent a questionnaire to several Persian ladies of birth and a few aristocrats, including me. I will share the gist of it with you:

I request the venerable Persian princess to answer the following questions:

1. What is the meaning of constitutionalism?
2. Which is better: despotism or constitutionalism?
3. What is the path to progress for Persia?
4. What duty do the women of Persia have?

In response I wrote the following:

1. Constitutionalism means acting under conditions of national freedom and advancement, without self-interest or treachery.

2. The restitution of its people's rights is the duty of every progressive nation. When can it have its rights restored? When the country functions under constitutionalism and a proper system. What brings forth progress? The rule of law. And when are laws implemented? When despotism is overthrown. Therefore, we see from this that constitutionalism is preferable to despotism.

3. Once individual self-interest, destructive intrigues, and the pursuit of profit are overcome, advancement lies in the building of factories and roads, the facilitating of agriculture, the sinking of mines, the balancing of the country's budget, the regulation of its financial affairs, the suspension of salaries to idle, undeserving people, the freedom of women to lay aside the veil and to support and cooperate with men as equals.

4. The duties of Persian women consist of: insisting on their rights, like their European counterparts; educating

Women's outdoor outfit around the turn of the century. The full cover *(chador qalebi)* and full trousers *(chaqchur)* concealed a woman's figure, while a long facial veil *(ruband)* did the same for her face. The depersonalizing features of the women's outfit reduced social distinctions, unlike male clothing which had subtle variations in fabric and style. In the post-Constitutional period the facial *ruband* was modified to a lighter *picha* and a less cumbersome *chador*, before they were abolished altogether under Reza Shah in 1935.

their children; helping the men, as do women in Europe; remaining chaste and unblemished; being patriotic; serving their kind; eradicating laziness and a sedentary lifestyle; removing the veil.

He asked me to explain, "What does the unveiling of women have to do with the country's progress?"

I wrote in reply:

A Persian wage-earner makes two *qeran*s a day. He has to support his mother, his sister, his niece, his wife, and his daughter. If we divide two *qeran*s by five, we get seven *sha-hi*s a day. With these seven *shahi*s, how can one person provide for clothing and food as well as have a savings? Thus it is that necessity corrupts people. In order to gain comfort and ease, they will submit to any gross indignity, prepared to perform any wicked deed. Now if these five women and children were not forced into a veil, they would have to be educated. After education, each of these five could take a job in a store, a tea-house, a shop, a school, or an office. Then every person would have an income of two *qeran*s a day. Six people making twelve *qeran*s a day could feed and clothe themselves comfortably, without the need to degrade themselves or change their life-style. And they could preserve their conscience, their honor, their chastity, and their family and national pride. In addition, there would be a spiritual unity within this group, and many great benefits accrue from unity.

The same is true for the aristocracy. This nobleman, this prince or that minister, even on a very generous salary, will earn no more than three hundred *tuman*s per month. The earnings from his properties and commissions, however great, cannot total more than seven hundred *tuman*s in such a poor country as this. That adds up to one thousand *tuman*s a month.

Let us suppose that such and such a nobleman marries a woman whom he does not know at all. The lady is now married to an aristocrat or a minister. The gentleman wants a harem, a chief overseer, a doorman, a pantry, a but-lery, a treasure house, a coach house, a stable, a page boy, a servant, a coachman. The lady wants a maidservant, a household menial, a singer, a musician, a chief attendant, a satin gown made in Europe. She has a spouse and every-thing she needs. She hosts parties, receptions, social baths. She wants a wet nurse.

As for the poor gentleman, who has not been affectionate or on good terms with his wife from the first day, owing to the lovelessness between them, he has married the daugh-ter of such and such military commander or shah in exchange for fifty thousand *tuman*s from his inheritance or ten thousand *tuman*s in dowry. In order to get away from this distasteful life he wants a garden outside; he wants a mistress, a confidant, a private servant, cratefuls of wine and food in his private retreat.

Meanwhile, the poor lady, scorned by her husband, wants five or six women of humble means to talk to, so she will not be lonely. And sometimes, on the advice of these afore-mentioned busybodies, she will want a large sum of money to spend in the Jewish quarter on casting a spell over the gentleman so that she can win his affection.

When the gentleman comes home late, the lady loses patience and smashes some of the dishes and household furniture. In this way she vents her anger, as well as hears a sound other than the voices of her gaggle of busybodies in her confinement. Such being the case, will a thousand *tuman*s a month suffice this lord or this so-and-so-Saltana, so-and-so-Dawla, so-and-so-Molk? No, it will not. He has no choice but to steal, despoil, sell his country and wreak its ruin, receive bundles of cash from a certain source in a midnight tryst. Ultimately his life will amount to nothing.

His shame brought to light, he will be left with an inward blemish on his soul, bewildered, with nowhere to go.

Now, if the women were unveiled and, as in all civilized societies on the planet, husband and wife saw each other and tied the knot of eternal union before their Lord with love, thereby living their lives in spiritual tranquillity, would that not be better? If they lived like the aristocrats and nobility in Europe—without harems and armies of menservants and maidservants and excessive, unnecessary expenses—would that not be nobler? This husband and wife who have chosen one another out of love, these two companions whose hearts are the surest guarantee of their fidelity and chastity and union—are they not worthy of commendation and praise? Yes, they are!

The source of the ruination of the country, the cause of its moral laxity, the obstacle to its advancement in all areas, is the veiling of women. Owing to fatalities, the number of men in Persia is always smaller than that of women. In a country where two-thirds of its population has to remain idle at home, the remaining third has to exert itself to the utmost to provide the comforts, sustenance and clothing for the others. So they cannot attend to the affairs of the nation and its progress. Now if these two-thirds were employed in meaningful work, the nation would make two-fold progress, and everyone would be wealthy.

Traveling along the Tabriz road, I saw men and women everywhere working side by side in the villages, the women unveiled. In no village could a single idle person be found. When I tried to hire one of the peasants as an attendant, none of them was willing to give up his or her life in the wilderness. All these peasants and farmers are honorable, proud people. There are no prostitutes in any of the villages, because so long as a man and woman are not equal in wealth neither will marry the other. Besides, since the women do not cover their

A Jewish Fortune-Teller and His Female Clients, by Mohammad Ghaffari, Kamal al-Molk, the royal painter (*naqqash bashi*) of the late-Naseri court. An early example of the Persian realist school produced in the late-nineteenth century, the picture vividly shows women resorting to charms, described by Taj as a costly recourse for reclaiming a husband's lost favor. The cheerful women in Kamal al-Molk's painting seem pleased by good tidings—perhaps a sign of the artist's mildly disapproving attitude toward women's susceptibility to fortune-telling.

faces, mates are able to choose one another for themselves. After they are married, they always work together as partners in their farming and herding.

The husband is the guardian and keeper of his wife; she is his mate and companion. Never will these two noble souls neglect one another, or turn their attention elsewhere. They will observe all the love, sincerity and unaffectedness of life toward one another, and always live in happiness and good fortune, leaving to posterity honorable and proud descendants. The character of rural folk and desert dwellers is a hundred thousand times better than that of city people. This is for no reason other than their freedom from want, their lack of pretension, their genuine spiritual unity, all of which arise from their living as social beings free from corrupt and unlawful thoughts. The veiling of women in this country has spawned and spread thousands upon thousands of corrupt and immoral tendencies.

Oh, my teacher! You who are an educated man and recognize the evils of the veil, why do you not take the women of your house, your larger family, your tribe by the hand and lead them outside? How long must you continue to be these poor women's servant, or, to put it more grandiosely, their "lord and master"? Oh, will I have a receptive ear? Undoubtedly, with all the thousands of logical proofs I have used to establish the harmfulness of the veil to you, nonetheless, since you are Persian and perversely rigid in your ideas, and since your mind has always turned to superficial things without any true thinking, you will say: "She is good-looking and weary of sitting at home, or she wishes to move about freely; therefore she pens these opinions which are contrary to general attitudes." You might even curse me in your heart and say, "What illicit proposals she puts forth to the women!"

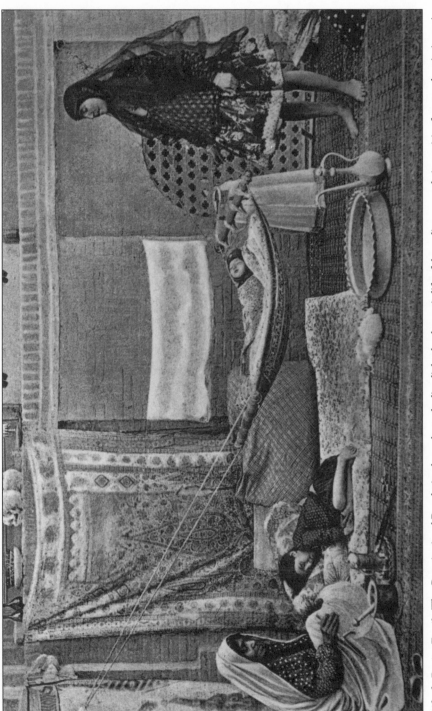

Life of a Persian Family. The Constitutional Revolution brought to the limelight the domestic life of the ordinary people in a spirit of postcard curiosity, as in this specimen from the 1910s. Though an urban household, this *"famille persanne,"* is close to Taj's idea of the simplicity of Persian pastoral life. In a symbolic absence of the husband from the family scene, the children are the focus of motherly care that is shared by the inevitable presence of a mother-in-law.

But I swear to you, my teacher! When the day comes that I see my sex emancipated and my country on the path to progress, I will sacrifice myself in the battlefield of liberty, and freely shed my blood under the feet of my freedom-loving cohorts seeking their rights.

But for now let us return to our history. Let me not keep you waiting any longer or tire you with my futile cries and complaints.

> O thou misinformed of the state of my heart,
> I cannot tell thee of my sorrow—thou knowest not my pain.

PILGRIMAGE TO QOM

Two or three months after his return from Shemiran, the Shah departed on a pilgrimage to the shrine of Ma'suma. In thanksgiving for our health and deliverance during that frightful year, we accompanied him. We hired an omnibus for twelve, formed a little caravan, and set out. My husband, a doctor, and a renowned musician traveled with us in a separate carriage. A wagon carried the servants and supplies, another brought our baggage and belongings. We rode in the omnibus. Although traveling in Persia is never without its fair share of hardship and terror, we enjoyed ourselves on the road. We stayed at the shrine of Ma'suma for ten days before going back. Nothing new happened on this trip for me to report, other than pilgrimage and sightseeing. I tended to participate very little in either of these activities, because I had to walk through a graveyard. Inevitably, every time I stepped outside, I saw many corpses being buried—corpses with ghastly faces and hideous figures.

The gradual removal of the veil in the early decades of the twentieth century brought women into public life (including the stage, as in the above portrait of the first Muslim ingenue by an American artist in the 1930s). Taj's expressed wishes to see women unveiled anticipated the reformist spirit of the Reza Shah era as the influence of traditional Islam waned.

This trip was a very humbling experience. Seeing the corpses—the way all of us would end up—was a great lesson for me and held in check my youthful pride, my vivacity and self-centeredness. Although like the rest of humanity I am forgetful and the vivid impressions from this trip did not leave any lasting results, yet now that several years have passed I shudder as I write this, as if I can see our end with my eyes. Let me write something of what I saw that terrified me so.

These corpses were laid in coffins, wrapped in felt, brought there by mule from faraway places. At every stop, when the mules were to be rested or fed, the ropes were untied and the two coffins came crashing down to the ground, mangling the corpses. By the time they reached the shrine of Ma'suma, the coffins were in pieces, the shrouds ripped to shreds, and the corpses' heads and limbs broken. Then the corpses were carried around the shrine in circumambulation and brought to the graveyard. There were so many corpses piled atop one another in the graves that there was no room for others. So they had to open other graves and lay the new corpse on the others and cover them all with a little dirt. When graves were reopened the corpses appeared in varying degrees of decay: on some the flesh had rotted away and turned black, on others a part of it had separated from the bones while the rest hung loosely. Such eerie shapes, such horrid faces! May God preserve us all from such sights! Severed hands, severed legs, wild and disordered hair that had fallen, rotting shrouds.

Oh, my teacher! Oblivious to such an end, what lofty hopes we cherish, what unbearable suffering we inflict on our own kind, what corrupt deeds and intrigues we devise to destroy the good fortune of someone we consider happy! What agonies of greed and avarice we suffer night and day! Oh, alas!

A view of the public cemetery adjacent to the shrine of Ma'suma in Qom in 1880. A quarter of a century later, when Taj visited the shrine, the cemetery was far more crowded, thanks to frequent epidemics of cholera. Extensive rebuilding and beautification of the shrine during Amin al-Soltan's premiership only attracted more dying believers wishing to be buried in the vicinity of the tomb of the Shi'ite woman-saint. The morbid practice, witnessed by Taj, of corpses being hurriedly squeezed atop one another in packed graves was only acceptable in the eyes of the believers because their proximity to the shrine facilitated the saint's intercession on their behalf in the Final Judgment.

Negligence, man's greatest enemy, is closer to him than any friend. Sa'di says:

> The world has turned much, and more will it turn—
> The wise man sets not his heart upon it.
> You, strong of hand, put forth your power now
> Before you are forever rendered helpless.
>
> The epics tell of Rostam and the invulnerable Esfandiar.
> Why? So that today's rulers might know
> That the world retains a memory of innumerable souls.
> They all departed, and we, frivolous and impudent,
> Learned no lesson from them.
>
> You, once a germ in the womb
> And a suckling babe soon after,
> Grew to maturity
> And gained the stature of a silver-cheeked cypress,
> Until you became a man with a name
> As a horseman of the arena and a warrior—
> All that you saw had no permanence;
> Neither will endure what you see now.
>
> Sooner or later, this man of delicate frame
> Will turn to earth, and the earth to dust.
> The gardener will undoubtedly pick the flower;
> And if he does not, it will fall of its own weight.
>
> All this is nothing, in that it passes away—
> Fortune, throne, allegiance, abasement, strife.
> It is better that a man should leave behind a fair name
> Than a gilded palace.
>
> What do we know about life next year
> Or whither has gone our companion?
> The sleepers lie helpless in the dust of the grave
> While serpents and ants nestle in their heads.
>
> A pretty face means nothing;
> My brother, beautify your inner self.

Do you know which is better: sense or conscience?
I'll tell you the truth—cherish my words.

Man's mind must nurture good sense within itself,
Else it will nurture an ass.
If he gives in to overreaching ambition,
The world's turning will snatch away the reins of his life.

If you seek treasure, strive for it;
If you want a harvest, sow the seed.

Since God saw fit to grant you power,
Refrain from nibbling on the poor man's meat.
Since heaven has endowed you with skill,
Treat well those lower than yourself.
Forgive the transgressions of the contrite;
Shelter the fugitive under your wing.

Make good deeds your gratitude for Heaven's generosity;
God loves the grateful among his servants.
His bounty is a bounty beyond measure;
His grace is a grace incalculable.
If you had a tongue on every one of your hairs,
You could not thank him for one of his thousand favors.

Pay heed to the longings of the dervishes and the poor,
That fate may grant you all your desires.
Cast no aspersions on the good names of the departed,
That your own good name may endure.

Is it fitting to find rulers, day or night,
Lost in intoxication, or concealed behind a guise?

Be profusely kind to strangers,
That you may enjoy good repute among men.
You will thus have a strong arm and a piercing sword;
And if the world is overrun by hostile parties, do not fear.

Give thought to the feelings of the weary
And to the prayers of the pious.

At dawn the sighs of the oppressed, hurled like missiles,
Will encircle the tyrants in violent hold.

Return evil with evil, and good with good;
Be a rose to the rose, a thorn to the thorn.
Have no fear: devils mingle little with mortals;
Rather beware of diabolical men.

He who nurtures evil, associating with the wicked—
Sooner or later they will bring him to his knees.
Should you respond with kindness to the vile,
Remember the snake-charmer who dies from the bite.

You, who have eyes, mind, ears and sense!
Hang this advice upon your lobe like an earring.

As much as I had enjoyed the trip out, I had a miserable time going back, haunted by thoughts of despair. Not a day passed without my sighing fifty times and my eyes tearing up, as I thought of man's helpless plight. From then on, I renounced my haughtiness and ostentation, and my aristocratic pride abated. Although I nursed an extreme fear of death, there never passed a day but that I longed for it. In order to win a measure of release from my various tiresome, oppressive preoccupations, I hung my head down in thought most of the time. It was not long before my health was adversely affected and I fell prey to a dreary sleeplessness. Despite taking several doses of sedative every night, I lay awake until the morning.

At about the same time my husband fell ill with a chronic case of gonorrhea. The truth of the matter was kept from me by the doctor. I was told that he had a fever. Nursing the patient while suffering inside proved a great strain. I was three months pregnant when I heard news of my niece's death; Ehteram al-Saltana, Mozaffar al-Din Shah's daughter, had died in childbirth. This caused me great anxiety, and I was terrified at the prospect of my own delivery. Turning to a highly-regarded doctor, whom I will not name here, I gave him a large diamond ring in exchange for medication to induce a miscarriage.

Unbeknownst to anyone in my house, I took the drug. Six hours later, I was seized by a frightful convulsive fit. Leaping about two meters into the air, I crashed to the floor. It was the poison in the drug that caused my convulsions—a fact of which I was unaware. I told no one that I had taken any medication. The doctors gathered together over me could find no way to relieve the fit. I was constantly agitated, trembling, and felt a burning sensation as though I had bruises in the region of my heart. The doctors were nonplused in their attempts to diagnose my ailment and could find no explanation. Finally I told them what I had done. But despite their insistent questions, I refused to divulge the doctor's name. I was given an antidote, and through a difficult process the fetus was aborted. My nervous condition, however, stayed with me.

For three years I was unwell and nervous. The illness had changed me completely; my attitudes and behavior were different. I was capricious, quick-tempered and irascible. No longer able to cope with the slightest annoyance, I would quickly lose my composure and become indisposed and bedridden in misery. Doctors prescribed going outdoors for airings. Every afternoon the carriage would be prepared and, willy-nilly, I would be taken for a ride and let off at shops where I would be kept busy. For a while, by virtue of the malady of "hysteria," I obtained some relief from confinement to the house. But there were numerous spies who accompanied me and had to make a full report of the excursion to my husband.

BREAKDOWN OF THE MARRIAGE

My husband was no longer a callow child. He was now a young man of eighteen or nineteen and kept a firm lock on his treasury of happiness. My beauty and freshness had occasioned jealousy and given him trouble. He would often say, "How I wish something unexpected would happen, like smallpox or facial scars, to make you ugly and rid me of having to keep watch over you."

Among all the women of Persia there was none so pretty as I. Whenever I attended large gatherings—weddings, feasts, royal audiences, and other formal occasions—at which there were almost a thousand princesses and women of high birth, I was always the most beautiful. All eyes were turned on me. The ladies would often ask, "What tailor has sewn your dress?" even though my dress was very simple. I would respond plainly and guilelessly, "Such and such a tailor." The poor ladies would have the very same dress copied for themselves, but wearing it would not make them pretty. Then they would turn my enemies and curse me.

Or they would ask, "Where did you buy the powder you have on your face?" I would say, "Such and such a shop." They would buy it for themselves, but it would not help their complexions. Again, there would be hostility.

All the women of Persia, whether high or low, related to me or not, were my enemies because of my good looks. Their enmity was heightened when they saw that my looks were complemented by a pleasant disposition, kindness, and good nature. I had a great desire for learning and took every opportunity I could to improve my understanding. On this front, too, I was ahead of the other ladies in conversation, demeanor, and general knowledge, and this was one more reason for their jealousy. They saw that I was accomplished in all respects. All my life I have had to put up with a general envy. These people made my life so difficult, and inflicted such harm, that no human has suffered as I have. But I never lost my composure. God was always with me and protected me from the mischief and venom of all that hostility.

Believe me, my dear teacher, I have never consented to hurt an ant or kill a fly, even though in enmity's name I was entitled to vengeance in a hundred ways. But guided by a placid disposition and a sound mind, I refrained from returning evil for evil. This was not because I was weak, but because I had a high sense of purpose and valued the things of this world lightly. So I never did anything but good, and was rewarded by nothing but evil. Despite all this, I never strayed from my path, nor did I ever complain.

Know this, too, my teacher: the passage of time and grief and suffering leave their mark on the body, but the immortal soul of man is left untouched by them. In nature, man remains as he has always been, though the world never stays the same. So it seems that we are tied to the strings of fate, which continually drags us behind and makes us taste the changes and chances of life. Sometimes we step into majesty and greatness; and sometimes, humble and abased as slaves, we wander in the valley of forgottenness and forgetfulness and inconstancy. Sometimes we are ravished by ease and wealth and friendship; and sometimes we have to avert our faces from anger and enmity and ill-wishers. Sometimes we are steeped in plenty and the delight of the mind and spirit; and sometimes befriended by suffering and eternal damnation. And through all this ebb and flow, we remain exactly where we were, and outwardly there is no turmoil. This in itself is one of the marvels of almighty God.

At this time I had a fair number of flattering admirers, because both of us, husband and wife, were young and wealthy. My husband was sole commander of a body of troops, earning close to thirty thousand *tuman*s a year from managing these ten regiments. In addition, he enjoyed good credit in all the trading establishments and banks; if he suddenly asked for a large sum of money, he got it on the spot.

Our home was always open and ready to entertain friends, relatives, and ladies of status. We spared no expense, and our house, which displayed all the signs of happiness and good fortune, could provide every means of comfort. It was unheard of for someone who entered our doors to leave without a warm reception or a gift. We two youngsters spent all we had, always imagining that life would continue in the same fashion. We had never tasted the hardship of poverty. Having always been surrounded with wealth and respect, we could not conceive of the springs of our riches and dignity ever running dry, or the river of gold and eternal happiness ceasing to flow. We had not reckoned that a rock untimely loosened, or a tangle of underbrush carelessly tossed in the water, could impede the flow and afflict us with a deathly thirst.

The flatterers and sycophants continued to urge us on to greater lunacy and recklessness and fed us the fatal poison of negligence drop by drop. With dizzying speed we were hurtling toward our doom, never peering into the vortex of the whirlpool of misery and destruction prepared for us, for the veil of ignorance stood between us and reality. Our heartless flatterers deepened the eddy and muddied the waters further. Innocent and childlike, we considered all these people to be angelic, affectionate and kind, and saw them to be as pure-hearted and unself-interested as ourselves. Our two young hearts were like the unrippled and spotless surface of a lake.

Hasan Khan Shaja' al-Saltana, Taj's husband, in the military uniform of the late-Qajar period, wearing a ceremonial sword and a cap in the style of Mohammad 'Ali Shah. Heir to a military family, he apparently lost his post after the defeat of the royalists in the civil war of 1908–1909.

We had not been exposed to any of the trickery that humans are capable of. Indeed, in the terrain that is life and amid human deceit we were still strangers. By contrast, our remorseless flatterers had the venom of vipers for saliva and their sting was incurable. The path on which they directed us with the utmost kindness led to the nethermost regions of hell and to brackish, perilous ocean depths.

Among all these friendly-seeming foes, among all these hawkers who sold us barley for wheat, there was not one sensible, conscientious person to rescue us from the abyss—to turn us back from this dangerous path—as a gesture of humanity. All were busy emptying our pockets and filling their own.

The incendiary thoughts of these "genuine" friends transcended even this, and they sought ways to improve on their gains and consolidate their fortune. Not only did they want to destroy us and reduce us to dust, but they also wanted to lay hands on all we had. They began to sow discord between my husband and me. Every day they carried lewd and indecent tales about him to me and about me to him. They tossed our happy, free lives into a fresh perplexity and turmoil. This boundless sea in which I had to navigate only by the light of the star of my fortune—that is, our joint life—was strewn with enormous reefs that were impossible to avoid. Though I was calm and quiet for the most part, there were times when I was swayed by their words and brought unhappiness on myself and my husband.

Owing to constant interaction with my husband and me, these people had learned our characters quite well. They knew that nothing really troubled us—neither the depletion of wealth, nor the loss of jewelry, nor the intrigues of family and servants. So, ignoring this line of attack, they hit upon a plan of softening me up. They said to me, "Look at you, how beautiful and lovely you are! The daughter of a king, a real lady, the first among Persia's women in nobility and dignity. And your husband is chasing some other woman!"

"But who? Tell me, please!"

"No, we can't tell you. You'll talk to him about it, and he'll become our enemy."

After I swore I would not give them away, they would tell me, "Such and such a European hussy who is the washerwoman for the French embassy."

Such a report was enough to bring me grief and dejection and provoke ill humor for a whole month. After having embittered my life and happiness for quite awhile, I would only then ask him about the truth of the matter and the identity of the tattletale. After my questions, it would become evident that, whether true or false, it was never as they had represented it.

These flatterers, who had surrounded me from childhood and who during every crisis in my life changed their facades but retained their inward natures, had fostered in me two base, obnoxious traits of character: pride and ostentation. These twin vices had made me rabidly jealous of my husband. He was equally proud, even a little on the mad side—not truly mad in the brain, but spiritually unhinged. He had been raised in such opulence and luxury that he could not have conceived of life being difficult as well.

One day, as we were talking, I said, "If I don't have that pair of diamond earrings which cost three thousand *tuman*s, I will be very unhappy."

He replied, "By my life! Tell me truly what the taste of unhappiness is and what it's composed of."

Do not imagine, my teacher, that I jest. As God is my witness, he said it most nonchalantly. After he had laughed his way through my analysis of unhappiness, he gave me the earrings. Had it not been for these flatterers, these inciters of human caprice, there is no doubt that no two people could have been as happy as we. But alas! Our social intercourse resulted in wretchedness for us and even greater wretchedness for our children. Oh, woe! Why could I not have died then and been spared the taste of strife and turmoil and the sight of so many harsh, unexpected things in the brief span of my life?

My teacher! Though I poisoned myself three times, I am still alive to write my memoirs for you. So, the plan of nature and the will of God must have decreed this. In the face of such power, I felt feeble and was unable to remove myself from the arena of life's struggles.

They had made my husband deeply suspicious of me. The poor man had no sleep or comfort or a peaceful meal—and all for nothing. I was in no way at fault, leading a carefree life but also a God-fearing one. I had a dread of hell and eternal damnation; I was terrified of death. Whenever I prayed, I humbled myself at God's threshold and begged for a good end, forgiveness, and a painless death. I took diligent care to ensure that I always protected myself with firmness of resolve against the torments of the life hereafter.

The flatterers saw that my religiosity and keen interest in divine things were not conducive to their corrupt designs. They wanted to pull me apart completely from religion and then, with perfect ease, separate me from my husband. One of my close relatives who was very learned and accomplished, and who loved me beyond measure—rather, entertained a fervid, intense affection for me—agreed to be the instrument to this end. He advised me, "Come and learn something.

Study French. An illiterate person is hardly a human being."
Keenly inclined to do so, I agreed. This noble youth taught
me three days a week. Whenever we had a recess or an
interval of rest, he brought up the topic of religion and spoke
of the "naturalists." Initially, I took issue with him and argued.
Little by little, I began to listen more. After a while, I was won
over. My first act was to change my mode of dress. I began to
dress in the European style, my head bare, while women in
Persia still dressed according to the old style. After this
change, the next was that I abandoned praying and acts of
piety; performing ablutions and praying was difficult in a
corset and the tight sleeves of a close-fitting dress. After for-
saking prayers, I repudiated all religions and beliefs as invalid,
arguing, "Thunder is thunder and lightning is lightning. The
tree is exactly as it appears, and so is a human."

Right up to my eighteenth year, I had held the beliefs
taught me by my nanny that the heavens were pulled by a
chain in an angel's hand, or that when God's wrath was
incurred, the sound of thunder came. This esteemed teacher
of mine, however, told me, "This is all absurd. Thunder and
lightning are generated through collision of clouds," and gave
me the scientific proofs. Or he said, "You claim the earth rests
on a yellow bull's horn. That's false. The earth is spherical and
rests on nothing."

As I progressed in my studies day by day, my irreligiosity
grew, until I was a complete naturalist myself. Since these
ideas were all new to me, I was eager to impart them to my
mother, my relatives, and my children. As I would begin to
talk, however, my mother would curse at me, "You have
turned Babi!" My relatives would invoke God's forgiveness
and keep their distance, refusing to listen. The only ones who

were happy about it were the mischievous flatterers and enemies, goading me on, "Yes! This is the path to progress."

The whole person benefits from knowledge, like most
people; I suffered a loss for having knowledge. Bereft of any
basic understanding of the world, of life and of humanity, I
consequently adhered to no set of beliefs, and neither
depended on anyone nor feared anyone. Lacking fear of anything and freed from any particular beliefs, there was nothing
with an individual's life are themselves incapable of understanding the pleasures of life. They are jealous. Or they're
simple and stupid and don't understand."

And all the while, I was oblivious to the fact that it was I
who had turned simple and stupid, with help from a certain
group. And what did they want? Profit. Everyone expected
something: one looked for advancement, another wanted
money, another sought gratification. And so I became adept at
anything that was harmful to me.

Now I was inundated with new ideas, casting out all the old.
Formerly I had believed that if I did not obey my husband or
disregarded my mother's wishes, I would burn in hell. Therefore, out of fear, I accepted it as an article of faith. Now things
were different. I would say, "Man has been created free and
invested with free will. Man has been created to eat, sleep,
enjoy himself, partake of pleasure, and live free." Thus, little
by little, the idea of freedom gained strength in my mind. All
the European histories and novels that my teacher had read to
me, all his descriptions of the world's beautiful cities (accompanied by the reminder, "The world is not confined to
Tehran!") made me long desperately for Europe. This desire
ultimately, grew to a point at which it became the cause of my
separation from my husband.

Taj al-Saltana in European-style clothes at the dawn of women's emancipation in the early Reza Shah era. Her demeanor conveys a sense of modern self-confidence unknown to the women of the harem.

POSTSCRIPT

Even as this book was in the final stages of preparation, some new information came to light about Taj al-Saltana's later life (thanks to the editor of the Persian edition of Taj's memoirs, Dr. Mansureh Nezam Mafi [Ettehadieh]).

After her divorce from Hasan Khan Shaja 'al-Saltana, Taj lived a life of unrestrained pleasure before remarrying some years later; her second husband was a commoner rather than a member of the nobility, probably a sign of the changing times and of Taj's declining fortunes. Her public image as a libertine made her a symbol of bashful sensuality, providing popular art in the early Pahlavi period with a subject for ornamental trays and pictorial rugs. Taj saw herself, however, as a liberated socialite whose life mirrored her commitment to women's emancipation. The comparison she reportedly made between herself and the famous nineteenth-century French novelist, George Sand, was not far-fetched.

Taj's later years must have been fraught with hardship. She died in Tehran in February, 1936, an obese and impoverished woman.

HISTORICAL BIOGRAPHIES

"Afghani" (Asadabadi), Sayyid Jamal al-Din (1838–1897). A celebrated political activist and advocate of Pan-Islamism, he was born a Shi'ite in northwestern Iran but adopted the sobriquet "Afghani," presumably after being expelled from Kabul in 1869. The presumed Sunni identity brought him wider acceptance among Muslim rulers, dignitaries, and disciples as he traveled from India to the Ottoman Empire and to Egypt. Chastised by the conservative ulama in Istanbul for his outspoken views on philosophy and prophecy, and expelled in 1879 by the British who feared his agitational activities in Egypt, Afghani was held under surveillance in India until 1882 when he traveled to Europe. There both his political and religious messages were modified to fit the diverse audiences he addressed. Nonetheless, he was consistent in his opposition to the British, in his Pan-Islamic call to regenerate Islam as a political force to combat imperialism, and in his semi-mystical self-portrayal as the "Oriental Philosopher" (*filsof-e sharq*) and the Martin Luther of the Islamic world.

In 1889 Afghani was invited, presumably by Amin al-Soltan, to come to Iran for the second time primarily, so he claimed, to aid Iran in her negotiations with Russia. However, wary of Afghani's criticism of the growing corruption and indolence in the government, Naser al-Din Shah gave him a cold reception. Afghani took shelter in the shrine of 'Abd al-'Azim but was soon evicted and expelled to Ottoman Iraq.

The humiliating experience hurt Afghani deeply, and from Iraq he began an intense campaign against the shah. He called upon the celebrated Shi'ite leader, Mirza Hasan Shirazi, to denounce Naser al-Din for granting a damaging tobacco concession to foreigners. His open letter to Shirazi, which circulated widely in Iran during the Régie protest (1891–1892), called for the overthrow of the Qajar ruler while exalting the Shi'ite leader to the position of a Supreme Exemplar. He continued his campaign from London, where he joined forces with Mirza Malkom Khan, the veteran diplomat turned dissident.

On the invitation of the Ottoman Sultan 'Abd al-Hamid, Afghani returned to Istanbul in 1892 primarily to advocate the sultan's claim to the Islamic caliphate. There Afghani continued to attract dissident Persian intellectuals in exile, among them the celebrated political thinker, Mirza Aqa Khan Kermani. His highly publicized role in inciting another Kermani, Mirza Reza, to assassinate Naser al-Din was a source of concern to 'Abd al-Hamid, who kept him under virtual house arrest to the end of his life.

Amin al-Soltan (1858–1907), Mirza 'Ali Asghar Khan, later Atabak, was the last premier of Naser al-Din Shah who also served under Mozaffar al-Din Shah and, briefly, under Mohammad 'Ali Shah. A master of political maneuvering, he was brought up in the Qajar inner court under the direction of his father, Ebrahim Khan Amin al-Soltan, who himself was the shah's trusted butler and had risen to become the minister of court. Appointed to his father's post after his death in 1883, his monopoly on lucrative administrative posts—particularly the royal mint and the customs—concentrated in his hands enormous powers, with the shah's blessings. As a confidant to

Naser al-Din, he was able to mediate for the exhausted monarch in domestic matters and in foreign policy. His periodic vacillations between pro-British and pro-Russian positions were motivated by the dictates of a pragmatic and expedient foreign policy as well as a concern for his own political survival. Though Amin al-Soltan deserves credit for resisting imperial pressure to acquire diplomatic, strategic, and economic concessions, his career was often marred by petty compromises, intrigues, and vindictive behavior toward his political opponents.

In spite of implicit allegations in Taj al-Saltana's memoirs, there is no serious evidence to implicate Amin al-Soltan in the assassination of Naser al-Din Shah. Defying political odds, he survived under Mozaffar al-Din for six months. He was dismissed by the monarch, but restored to office less than two years later to start a second turbulent tenure which continued up to 1903. In many ways his term of office was the continuation of the Naseri high politics, except that a weaker and more impressionable ruler sat on the throne. Contrary to Naser al-Din's era, the growing economic problems facing the new monarch led to explicit expressions of popular discontent, often targeted at Amin al-Soltan and his allies. When he was finally dismissed from the prime ministership for the second time, the immediate reason given was his failure to secure a third loan from foreign financiers, but the underlying theme was the growing social unrest in the provinces.

His world travels between 1903 and 1907, which included trips to Europe, China, Japan, the United States, Egypt, and North Africa, were prolonged by an informal political exile for which his rivals were responsible. Having been kept away from the political arena during the early stages of the Constitutional Revolution, he was appointed on his return by

Mohammad 'Ali Shah as the chief minister and acquired a vote of confidence from the Majles with some difficulty. His stay in Europe and visit to Japan no doubt reformed Amin al-Soltan's conservative views, but not extensively enough for him to change his old political habits, particularly when faced with a revolutionary parliament and an increasingly reactionary monarch. His attempts to employ the old instruments of machination and control turned the Constitutionalists against him at a time when revolutionary fervor, a deteriorating economy, and growing foreign intervention conspired against political stability. His assassination in front of the Parliament in August 1907 by a certain 'Abbas Aqa, a revolutionary with possible links to the nascent Persian socialists, gave rise to much speculation.

Amina Aqdas, Zobayda (c. 1840–1893). A favorite wife of Naser al-Din Shah, she was the daughter of a poor Kurdish shepherd brought to the royal harem in the early 1850s. She accompanied the shah as a female attendant in his nocturnal visits to the private quarters of Jayran Forugh al-Saltana. Over the years, despite having her face deformed by fire in her childhood, Zobayda rose to the status of a "temporary" wife and secured the shah's trust to become his private maid, having been trained under another wife for that purpose. A rival of Anis al-Dawla, she offered loyalty and dedication to the shah, thereby compensating for the absence of other royal qualities. Playing on the shah's weaknesses and indulging his many emotional cravings, Amina Aqdas allied herself with the shah's influential confidant and court minister, Mirza Ebrahim Amin al-Soltan, and later with his son, 'Ali Asghar Amin al-Soltan, the future premier. She took charge of Babri Khan, the shah's favorite cat, and subsequently Malijak I and Malijak II, in order to reinforce her ties with the monarch; in return he placed the supervision of royal treasures and gifts in her custody, bestowed upon her the title of Amina Aqdas (trustee of the blessed sovereign), allocated to her private quarters with servants, eunuchs and a secretary, set up for her a hefty pension, and gave her much private property. Though not of the same status as Anis al-Dawla, she was highly influential in the politics of the court and instrumental in the rise of 'Ali Asghar Khan Amin al-Soltan.

Suffering from cataracts, she lost one eye before she was able to visit Vienna for treatment in 1891, an unsuccessful trip much criticized by the ulama during the Régie protest as a dishonor to Islam. Shortly after her return she died of a stroke.

Anis al-Dawla (c. 1842–1897), Fatema Soltan, a favorite wife of Naser al-Din Shah and head of his harem after 1873. A peasant girl from a village in the vicinity of the capital, she was spotted by the shah while on a hunting excursion and was brought to the harem where she first served as a maid to the shah's favorite, Jayran Forugh al-Saltana. Married to the shah as a temporary wife, she became his new favorite even before Jayran's premature death in 1859. She rose to become the shah's most distinguished wife and, after the death of Mahd 'Olya, the shah's mother, the head of his harem. In spite of occasional challenges to her authority by Amina Aqdas and her ally Amin al-Soltan, Anis al-Dawla held her position of seniority up to the end of her husband's reign. Though she never wished to be promoted to the status of a permanent wife, her position as the shah's chief wife was acknowledged by contemporary sources, who occasionally referred to her as the "queen of Iran" (*malaka-ye Iran*).

Anis al-Dawla's great influence on the shah should be seen as one example of the royal women's involvement in the affairs of the court and the government. She has often been credited for reflecting the view of the ordinary people and for criticizing the monarch for his personal excesses and for the corruption in his court and government. Though her collaboration in 1873 with the conservative princes to oust Mirza Hosayn Khan Moshir al-Dawla was motivated by a personal grudge, her support for the ban on tobacco during the Régie protest in 1892 reflected some political commitment. Anis al-Dawla also rebuked the shah for his infatuation with the Malijaks, first the father and then the son. She died childless soon after the assassination of Naser al-Din Shah.

Kamran Mirza (1855–1927). The third surviving son of Naser al-Din Shah, he was favored by his father who bestowed on him the grand title of Na'eb al-Saltana (vice regent), in deliberate contrast to the title heir apparent (*vali-'ahd*). A commoner on the maternal side of his family—his mother was the daughter of the architect to the crown—he had virtually no chance for succession, even though his father wished to overrule Mozaffar al-Din's right to succession in his favor. Contrary to his brothers who were sent to the provinces, Kamran remained in "royal attendance" to become the governor of Tehran as early as 1861 when he was six years of age. Soon after, he was appointed commander-in-chief of the army in 1868 and war minister in 1871. Though all appointments were nominal, he was also given the title of Amir Kabir (grand commander), the highest rank in the Qajar military which was abandoned after the dismissal of Mirza Taqi Khan Amir Kabir in 1851. Kamran competed for royal favor with his powerful brother Zell al-Soltan, while counterbalancing at the same time the growing power of the young premier 'Ali Asghar Khan Amin al-Soltan. The two men's rivalry for greater revenue and control over the government and the court from the late 1880s led to frequent petty clashes. Kamran's role in quelling the anti-tobacco concession protest of 1891 proved inglorious, insofar as the defense of the royal citadel was concerned, and repressive when he tried, as chief of his father's military police, to compensate for his cowardice with cruelty toward those arrested.

The star of Kamran's fortunes plummeted after the assassination of his father, but it was not entirely eclipsed. His daughter, who was married to Kamran's nephew, Mohammad 'Ali Mirza (later Mohammad 'Ali Shah), retained crucial access to the throne. His hopes for a return to power were revived briefly during the Constitutional Revolution (1906–1911) when, in collaboration with like-minded nobility, he established the pro-court society (*anjoman*), based on the model of the political societies of the time but with the aim of defending the royalist cause. After the Minor Tyranny (1908–1909) and the subsequent defeat of the royalists at the hand of the Constitutionalists and the forced abdication of his son-in-law, he tried in vain to remain in the political limelight, but was completely overtaken by the pace of events. He died in obscurity in 1927.

Kermani, Mirza Reza (c. 1847–1896), Naser al-Din Shah's assassin and a disciple of Sayyid Jamal al-Din Asadabadi (Afghani). Born to a minor land-owning family in Kerman province, he spent some years as a novice in the religious colleges in Yazd before moving to Tehran. There he was engaged as a petty dealer in luxury clothes, working for the well-known merchant and financier Hajji Mohammad Hasan

Amin al-Zarb. In this profession he visited the houses of the nobility and at times was mistreated by powerful men offended by his repeated requests to settle their arrears. It was probably through Amin al-Zarb that he first met Afghani in Tehran in 1890 and was captivated by Afghani's charisma and message of dissent. Soon after Afghani's expulsion, Kermani was arrested on charges of public agitation and carrying fire-arms with the intention of assassinating the shah and his premier, Amin al-Soltan. The fact that, as an agent of Afghani, he delivered a threatening note to the shah (presumably through his wife's sister, a secretary [*mirza baji*] to the shah's favorite, Amina Aqdas) added to the gravity of the charges against him. On the eve of the Régie protest he was tortured by Kamran Mirza and jailed for four years. Under pressure he revealed the names of a number of collaborators, including the famous traveler Hajji Ebrahim Sayyah.

After his release in 1895 he resided briefly in Istanbul, where he became acquainted with Persian dissidents such as Shaykh Ahmad Ruhi. Reportedly moved by Afghani's call to "reciprocate tyranny with tyranny," Kermani returned to Iran and stayed in the shrine of Shah 'Abd al-'Azim near the capital. His intention to assassinate the shah was certainly known to a few other dissenters with ties to him. Amin al-Soltan, too, was reportedly warned of the threat, but the secret note sent to him by an informant was apparently never opened. During the shah's visit to the shrine on the eve of his jubilee celebration (1 May 1896), Kermani shot the monarch at point-blank range, having moved close to him on the pretext of handing him a petition.

To give his trial a semblance of fairness, a thorough interrogation was carried out in which Kermani confessed to his sole involvement in the crime. The records of this interrogation were widely publicized, conceivably to remove any suspicion that may have surrounded Amin al-Soltan. Kermani was executed publicly shortly thereafter, but his memory endured. During the Constitutional Revolution he was elevated to the status of a popular hero.

Mohammad 'Ali Shah (1872–1925). Son of Mozaffar al-Din Shah and the sixth ruler of the Qajar dynasty, he spent his early years in Tabriz, first in his father's household and later as the crown prince and the governor of Azarbaijan. His explicit pro-Russian proclivities owed as much to his early education under a conservative Russian tutor as they did to his efforts to secure Russian support for his succession, since he was under the impression that the British were supporters of the Constitutional cause. His exposure to the Tabriz revolutionaries must have reaffirmed his anti-democratic disposition. He saw the revival of the waning Qajar house not in parliamentary Constitutionalism but in an absolutist monarchy on the model of Russia, particularly after the suppression of the 1905 Russian revolution.

After he succeeded his father in early 1907, in spite of his oath of allegiance and later his signing of the Supplement to the Constitution, he remained unenthusiastic toward the Majles and suspicious of the radical revolutionary societies. His suspicion turned into open hostility when, in early 1908, an assassination attempt was made against him. The coup of July 1908 and the bombardment of the Majles, carried out by Cossack forces under Russian command and resulting in the deaths of several revolutionary leaders, gave Mohammad 'Ali an ephemeral illusion of victory, but these events never enabled him to consolidate his power and bring the civil war to an end. The era of Minor Tyranny ended in July 1909 when a coalition of Constitutionalists occupied the capital and deposed Mohammad 'Ali. He was sent into exile in Russia with a hefty pension, and his minor son, Ahmad Shah, was placed on the throne.

Backed by the tsarist regime, Mohammad 'Ali quickly launched an anti-revolutionary campaign from exile, culminating in the 1911 expedition in northeastern Iran at the head of a tribal army. His advance toward the capital was eventually halted by a revolutionary army. Another lukewarm Russian attempt in 1915 to restore him to the throne failed, and soon after the Bolshevik revolution he left for Europe where he died in Italy in 1925.

Mozaffar al-Din Shah (1853–1906), fifth ruler of the Qajar dynasty (1785–1925) who ruled over Iran between 1896 and 1906. After a difficult childhood, marked by illness and an intense dislike for his father, Naser al-Din Shah, he was nominated in 1862 as the heir apparent and sent to Tabriz, the provincial capital of Azarbaijan. There, in true Qajar tradition, he spent the next forty-four years of his life as the governor, away from his father's court and government. In sharp contrast to his father's facade of grandeur and authority, Mozaffar al-Din seemed administratively docile and possessed of an impressionable mind, reinforced by the presence of an omnipotent "guardian" and later "supervisor" overlooking all his public and private affairs. In competition with his brothers, Zell al-Soltan and Kamran Mirza, he was often the loser. The shah's unceasing quest for political symmetry only fostered the princely rivalry, leaving the succession a matter with potential for volatility.

After the assassination of Naser al-Din Shah, however, Mozaffar al-Din's accession to the Qajar throne took place with little turmoil, thanks in part to the political astuteness of Mirza 'Ali Asghar Khan Amin al-Soltan and the Anglo-Russian endorsement of the new ruler. Much to the dislike of the old guard in the Tehran court and government, Mozaffar al-Din brought with him a new Azarbaijani entourage hungry for position, profit, and power. The excesses of the new elite soon brought the government to the verge of bankruptcy. Imitating his father's European ventures, from which he was deliberately barred, he visited Europe three times between 1900 and 1905 for pleasure and medical treatment, thus incurring massive public debts which were to be paid by the sale of concessions and mortgaging customs and other revenues.

The most positive aspect of Mozaffar al-Din's reign was a receptivity to modern ideas and institutions that stands in marked contrast to his father's attitude. The growth of modern education and the press, the establishment of modern schools, the publication of Western works in Persian translation, greater freedom for religious minorities, and above all a greater access to Europe's educational institutions were made possible partially by Mozaffar al-Din's benevolence and urge for modernization. The brief but important term of Amin al-Dawla's premiership (1896–1898), though a political failure at implementing major reforms, was instrumental in bringing about social change. Even under the heavy-handed government of prince 'Ayn al-Dawla, Mozaffar al-Din's attitude toward reforms did not change substantially. His hands-off approach toward government anticipated somewhat the nature of the monarchy called for in the Constitutional Revolution. When he signed the so-called Constitutional Decree on his deathbed, he could not have envisioned the magnitude of the unfolding revolution, but at least he recognized the need for some degree of popular participation.

Naser al-Din Shah (1831–1896), the fourth king of the
Qajar dynasty (1785–1925) whose rule over Iran for close to
half a century (1848–1896) was a mixed record. The insecurity
of his early life was exacerbated by dislike of his father,
Mohammad Shah (r. 1835–1848), and a struggle for succession which made him aware of the influence of the European
powers. The early years of his reign were dominated by the
premiership of the celebrated Mirza Taqi Khan Amir Kabir, a
fatherly figure for the shah, whose authoritarian reform program to create a centralized and efficient administration and
army and to introduce Western-style education, press and
industry ran against the vested interests of the Qajar nobility
and the conservative religious establishment. Though Amir
Kabir succeeded in consolidating Naser al-Din's throne by
putting down internecine revolts within the royal house and
crushing the revolutionary Babi movement, he lost favor with
the shah. In 1851, under the influence of his mother, a matriarch with a powerful personality and an intriguing mind, the
monarch dismissed the premier and soon after secretly put
him to death. The low-intensity struggles between the shah
and his paternalistic prime ministers remained a hallmark of
his reign in the following years. They led to numerous dis-
missals and humiliations in the ensuing decades, and to
intermittent intervals that witnessed the abolition of the office
of the prime minister.

Though from the late 1850s the shah periodically toyed
with reformist ideas, his measures, when actually put into
practice, never extended beyond the bureaucracy and material
improvements into the realm of social or political change. His
deep fears of social upheaval, abetted by a capricious
temperament and sheer greed, offset much of his goodwill,
administrative competence, and intellectual aptitude, and
turned him, increasingly by the end of his reign, into a

reactionary ruler with some traits of modern absolutism. Recurring persecutions of dissidents—the most severe of all carried out against the Babis, who once tried to assassinate him in 1852—and a reluctance to incorporate any meaningful political and judicial reforms or to rationalize the government had long-term consequences, leading to the Constitutional Revolution.

In his much-publicized European tours of 1873, 1878, and 1889 (during all of which he kept diaries), the shah's attention was largely directed toward royal opulence, entertainment, and nature. Treated as an exotic ruler of a land of faded glory, he nevertheless was persuaded by his entourage and his hosts to grant sweeping economic concessions with far-reaching consequences. The ill-fated Reuter concession of 1873, which granted major economic, commercial, and financial rights to a private financier, became a pretext for a conservative revolt within the ruling elite and for the temporary ousting of the shah's reformist prime minister, Mirza Hosayn Khan Moshir al-Dawla. The famous Régie concession in 1891–1892 led to a popular protest of revolutionary proportions, mobilizing the bazaar and the secular dissidents under the aegis of the religious establishment. The shah's success in avoiding a full-scale revolt lay largely in his political savvy and ability to compromise whenever necessary.

The shah's tenuous record of domestic reforms, however, was counterbalanced by his steadfast resistance to territorial intrusions and his efforts to preserve Iran's political integrity in the age of high imperialism. This hard-earned advantage secured Iran's relative independence, but at the cost of material development and the reforming of tattered institutions. The shah perceived his own survival as the ransom in a complex game of diplomacy and intrigue to maintain a precarious balance on all grounds, a game at which he was a master and which became a hallmark of his reign.

A man of complex character, the shah had much of the veneer of a modern monarch while retaining some earmarks of the Qajar tribal culture. In private he was a consummate admirer of the good life and leisurely pursuits, which he seldom allowed to be spoiled by the pressing demands of government. A great hunter and a true lover of camp life and the countryside, his endless days in the saddle, wandering about in the picturesque resorts in the vicinity of his capital, bore discrete signs of a melancholic solitude. Escaping the pressures of government and the irritations of the harem, he became increasingly haunted by memories of his tormented past, for which he found consolation in the company of his favorite page boy, Malijak.

The shah's relations with the women of his harem were often dominated by the presence of a matriarch—first his own mother, Malek Jahan Mahd 'Olya, and later his influential wife, Anis al-Dawla. But it was his amorous love for his attractive favorite, Jayran Forugh al-Saltana, to whom he was married in his late twenties, that left a deep impression on him. Years after her early death the shah sought traces of Jayran among his wives. Though generally kept in strict isolation, some of the powerful wives of the shah exerted much political influence on him as well as on the high-ranking officials of his government. The shah's long period of infertility, perhaps a psychosomatic trauma, came to an end when he reached his mid-fifties. A host of princes and princesses born to him in the 1880s, with the exception of Taj, did not enjoy the shah's affection. The shah's relations with his two senior sons, Zell al-Soltan and Mozaffar al-Din, were not free from emotional trouble.

Naser al-Din's artistic taste and intellectual pursuits were comparatively modern. An amateur sketcher of some originality himself, he was the royal patron to an efflorescence of Persian painting, culminating in the works of the proto-impressionist Mahmud Khan Saba and the realist-romanticist Kamal al-Molk. The remarkable development of Persian calligraphy, music, religious performing art (*ta'ziya*), and Perso-European architecture (and to a lesser extent poetry and historiography) also benefited from his patronage, though he often actively barred his people from exposure to liberal ideas and tried hard to eradicate political and doctrinal dissent through coercion.

Naser al-Din Shah was assassinated by Mirza Reza Kermani on the eve of his royal jubilee while visiting the shrine of Shah 'Abd al-'Azim on 1 May 1896. The epithet of the "Martyr King" gained currency posthumously when the relative tranquility of his time was contrasted nostalgically to the chaos and revolutionary upheavals of the later decades.

Zell al-Soltan (shadow of the sovereign) (1850–1918), Mas'ud Mirza, Naser al-Din Shah's senior son and long-time, powerful governor of Isfahan. He was born to a commoner mother and thus denied the status of heir apparent, according to the Qajar rule of succession. A man of strong character and commanding capabilities, he soon demonstrated his potential for running a harsh but efficient provincial government when, at the age of thirteen, he was appointed to the governorship of Fars province. Playing on his father's weaknesses and sense of guilt he soon managed to monopolize not only the government of the central and prosperous province of Isfahan in 1874—a tenure he kept for the rest of his active career and up to the time of the Constitutional Revolution—but extended his control to neighboring provinces to include, in 1886, fourteen governorships in southern and western Iran. His virtual autonomy over the domestic affairs of a large chunk of southern Iran was accompanied by ambitions for independent rule over the southern part of a partitioned Iran under the aegis of the British, with whom he developed intimate relations. His ambitions were nipped in the bud in 1886 when he was forced by his frightened father to resign from all offices except the governorship of Isfahan. Though in the following years he tried in vain to cancel off the growing influence of the shah's premier, Amin al-Soltan, he never regained the omnipotence and military capability of the earlier years. His ruthless, and at times highly intriguing, control over Isfahan was challenged by influential ulama, the Bakhtiyari tribal chiefs and the notables of the city. It resulted in endless power struggles, repeated persecutions of the Babis, and recurring mob violence.

Zell al-Soltan's downfall came not in 1896 with the accession of Mozaffar al-Din Shah—to whom the prince declared his unconditional loyalty in spite of their former bitter rivalries—but in 1907. Facing popular opposition in Isfahan and pressure from Constitutionalists who criticized him for cruelty and despotism, he resigned from his post and soon after the coup of 1908 left Iran for a tour of Europe. On his return the next year he faced increasing pressure from the Constitutionalist militia in Rasht and was forced to return to Europe. The virtual absence of Zell al-Soltan from Taj al-Saltana's memoirs may be explained by his political eclipse in the post-Constitutional period. In 1917 he returned to Iran and spent his remaining years as a recluse in Isfahan.

A NOTE ON THE TEXT

A selection of the memoirs of Taj al-Saltana was first published in a series of articles by Abolfazl Qasemi entitled "Sargozasht-e por majara-ye Taj al-Saltana dokhtar-e Naser al-Din Shah be qalam-e khodash," *Vahid* 13 (1354 Sh./1975): 757–62, 850–52, 935–7, 1065–7; and 14 (1355 Sh./1976): 75–6, 314–17. A summary of the memoirs also appeared in F. Adamiyat and H. Nateq, *Afkar-e ejtema'i va siyasi va eqtesadi dar asar-e montasher nashoda-ye dawran-e Qajar* (Tehran, 1356 Sh./1977), 155–164. Later it was published in full as *Khaterat-e Taj al-Saltana* (M. Ettehadiyeh [Nezam Mafi] and S. Sa'dvandiyan, eds., Nashr-e Tarikh Iran, No. 8 [Tehran, 1361 Sh./1982]). An incomplete manuscript of Taj's memoirs in the Tehran University Central Library (No. 5741) was the basis for these publications. (For the manuscript see *Noskhaha-ye khatti, nashriyya-ye ketabkhaneh-ye markazi-ye daneshgah-e Tehran* vi [1348 Sh./1969], 79). This copy is entitled *"Tarikh-e halat-e zendegani-ye Khanom-e Taj al-Saltana"* (A history of the stages of Mrs. Taj al-Saltana's life) and is dated 19 Rabi'a II 1343 Q./25 'Aqrab 1303 Sh. [1924], ten years after the actual date of the memoirs. The original manuscript from which this copy is made was in Taj al-Saltana's own hand and, according to the copyist, was incomplete.

The copyist, Rahmatollah Da'i Taleqani, an employee of the Afghanistan embassy in Tehran, who was commissioned by the ambassador, Mir Mohammad 'Ali Khan Azad Kaboli, to make a copy of the manuscript, has indicated that "the rest of this manuscript has not yet been recovered." No other manuscript or any trace of the missing part has yet been found.

The absence of other manuscripts has caused some textual handicaps. The editors' reading in the published version is at times inaccurate. The apparent omission of passages in the memoirs has further impaired the wholeness of the text. This is even more limiting, given that our knowledge of Taj is largely based on her memoirs. There is no doubt, however, about the authenticity of the work, even in the incomplete version available.

Some objections have been made to the authenticity of the memoirs, but with little evidence to back them. Ebrahim Safa'i, a Persian historian with conservative views, claims that the memoirs were a fabrication to defame his historical hero, Amin al-Soltan ("Khaterat-e Taj al-Saltana," *Rahnama-ye ketab* 12, nos. 11–12 [1348 Sh./1970]: 682–4). He does not provide any convincing evidence.

In his 1923 notes to *Divan-e 'Aref-e Qazvini* ('A. Sayf Azad, ed. [Berlin, 1923], 356), Rezazada Shafaq pointed out: "Mrs. Taj al-Saltana has written a book about the condition of her father's court in which she has discussed the circumstances and causes of her own misfortune. If the book's content matches its fame, from the historical viewpoint it would be highly valuable and one hopes that it will be published in future." One may speculate that the reason for the fame as well as for the unavailability of Taj's memoirs was the uninhibited language with which Taj had divulged her liaisons in the years following her divorce—confessions that would have proven difficult for the society of the time to digest.

There is a wealth of contemporary sources in European languages dealing with the time span of Taj al-Saltana's memoirs; there are also a number of studies that investigate the period.

FURTHER READINGS

For a general history of Qajar Iran one may consult the *Cambridge History of Iran*, vol. 6, P. Avery and G. Hambly, eds. (Cambridge [England], 1991). The collection of articles in E. Bosworth and C. Hillenbrand, eds., *Qajar Iran* (Edinburgh, 1983) and A. K. S. Lambton, *Qajar Persia* (London and Austin, 1987) are also useful. Studies on Naser al-Din Shah's period include H. Algar, *Religion and State in Iran, 1785–1906* (Berkeley and Los Angeles, 1969); A. Amanat, *The Pivot of the Universe: Monarchy under Nasir al-Din Shah Qajar of Iran, 1848–1871* (Berkeley and Los Angeles, forthcoming in 1994); S. Bakhash, *Iran: Monarchy, Bureaucracy, and Reform under the Qajars, 1858–1896* (London, 1978); F. Kazemzadeh, *Russia and Britain in Persia, 1864–1914* (New Haven, 1968); N. R. Keddie, *Religion and Rebellion in Iran* (London, 1966); and idem., *Sayyid Jamal al-Din "al-Afghani"* (Berkeley and Los Angeles, 1972). On the Constitutional period E. G. Browne, *The Persian Revolution of 1905–1909* (Cambridge [England], 1910) and W. Morgan Shuster, *The Strangling of Persia* (New York, 1912 [Washington, 1987]) remain valuable primary accounts. Recent studies in English include M. Bayat, *Iran's First Revolution* (New York, 1991); A. B. Hairi, *Shi'ism and Constitutionalism in Iran* (Leiden, 1977); and V. Martin, *Islam and Modernism* (London, 1989). There are numerous entries in *Encyclopaedia Iranica* on the personalities and events of the Qajar period, including articles on the Constitutional

Revolution. For the post-Constitutional period see E. Abrahamian, *Iran between Two Revolutions* (Princeton, 1982) and S. A. Arjomand, *The Turban for the Crown* (New York, 1988).

On women in the Qajar era see Mary Sheil, *Glimpses of Life and Manners in Persia* (London, 1856); Carla Serena, *Hommes et choses en Perse* (Paris, 1883), Clara Rice, *Persian Women and their Ways* (London, 1923) and Badr al-Moluk Bamdad, *From Darkness into Light: Women's Emancipation in Iran* (Hicksville, New York, 1977). Recent articles on Taj al-Saltana and her time include J. Afari, "On the Origins of Feminism in Early 20th-Century Iran," *Journal of Women's History 1*, no. 2 (1990): 65-87; S. Mahdavi, "Taj al-Saltaneh, an Emancipated Qajar Princess," *Middle Eastern Studies* 23, No. 2 (April 1987): 188–93; F. Milani, *The Veils and the Words* (Syracuse, 1992); A. Najmabadi, "A Different Voice: Taj os-Saltaneh," *Women's Autobiographies in Contemporary Iran*, A. Najmabadi, ed. (Cambridge, Mass., 1990).

GLOSSARY OF PERSIAN TERMS AND NAMES

Amir(-e) Nezam (literally, commander-in-chief): military office in the Qajar period, first instituted in the 1820s for the commander of the European-style New Army *(nezam-e jadid)* of Azarbaijan. Several prominent military leaders and statesmen bore the title, most notably Mirza Taqi Khan Amir Kabir, Naser al-Din Shah's first grand vizier, and later Hasan 'Ali Khan Garrusi, the diplomat. As with many other military offices, the post of Amir Nezam had diminished considerably in importance by the time of the Constitutional Revolution.

andarun or *andaruni* (literally, interior): women's and children's inner residential quarters, physically separated from the exterior quarters of dwellings (see *birun*). In the houses of the nobility and the wealthy—who had a larger number of wives—the *andarun* was practically synonymous with "harem." Unlawful *(na-mahram)* male visitors were forbidden entry into the *andarun*, or they could enter only under the watchful eye of a chaperone.

Babi: follower of Sayyid 'Ali Mohammad Shirazi (1819–1850), more commonly known as the Bab (the gate to the Hidden Imam). Claiming that he was the Imam expected by the Shi'ites, the Bab launched a revolutionary messianic movement, Babism, and proclaimed that his advent marked the beginning of a new prophetic cycle. His followers challenged the entrenched authority of the Shi'ite clerical establishment and later the Qajar government, leading to a series of bloody confrontations with Qajar forces in the late 1840s and early 1850s and the Bab's execution in 1850. Their unsuccessful attempt to assassinate Naser al-Din Shah in 1852 intensified the persecution of the Babis and laid them open to charges of anarchism and heresy. In the ensuing decades Babism served as the medium for the emergence of two rival factions, of which the present-day Baha'i faith is one.

birun or ***biruni*** (literally, exterior): public residential quarters (as opposed to its counterpart, the *andarun*). The *birun* was physically located close to the entrance of houses, and it was here that male visitors were received.

chador: traditional one-piece, full-length covering worn by women in Iranian cities. Occasionally in colorful and ornate patterns, the *chador* goes over the head, extends all the way to the ankles, and is held in front by the hands. It affords the complete covering of a woman's body required by orthodox Islam.

Imam Jum'a: Friday prayer leader of a large city appointed by the government, often by virtue of hereditary rights. While different in rank from the jurists (*mujtahids*), the Imam Jum'as enjoyed a fair degree of respect and authority and were influential figures in the urban politics of the Qajar period.

mirza (contraction of *amirzada*): common honorific for men in the Qajar period. Appearing after a man's name, it indicated royal descent. (For example, before he ascended the throne, Mohammad 'Ali Shah was referred to as Mohammad 'Ali Mirza.) Appearing before the bearer's name, it marked one as a clerk or simply a literate man of consequence.

qeran: silver coin denomination used in Qajar and early Pahlavi times, equivalent in value to one-tenth of one *tuman.* (See also *shahi* and *tuman.*)

qoroq: designation of certain areas (such as the royal harem, hunting grounds, and resorts) as off-limits to anyone but the person of the king. An officer, called *qoroqchi*, oversaw the preservation of the sovereign's exclusive access to such areas.

rawzakhwani (literally, *rawza* recitation): a gathering in which the sufferings of the Shi'ite imams (more particularly, Imam Husayn) are lamented in the form of a threnody by a professional mourner (*rawzakhwan*). Aside from their primary purpose, *rawzakhwani*s also served as social gatherings, especially for women. (See also *ta'ziya.*)

shahi: one-twentieth of a *qeran.*

Shemiran: lush village in the foothills of northern Tehran with extensive hamlets dotted with gardens and villas. In Qajar times these were owned by the nobility and in subsequent years by wealthy residents of the capital.

ta'ziya (literally, mourning): performance of the traditional passion plays that commemorated the martyrdom of Imam Husayn at Karbala (7th century) during the first ten days of the lunar month of Moharram, as well as other events of religious significance. Highly stylized, the performances were often accompanied by mournful music.

tar: long-necked, double-bodied, six-stringed Persian lute played with a plectrum. With the evolution of complex playing techniques in the nineteenth century, the *tar* became one of the most widely played of the Persian classical instruments.

tuman (Turkish, literally, ten thousand): unit of Persian currency equal in value to ten thousand *dinar*s or ten *qeran*s. (See also *qeran* and *shahi*.)

INDEX

SOURCES AND CREDITS

Jacket illustration: "Women Around a Samovar," Esma'il Jalayer, ca. 1885, courtesy of the Board of Trustees of the Victoria & Albert Museum.

Backjacket illustration: A modern rendering of Taj al-Saltana by Ghassem Hajizadeh, from the collection of M. & N. Batmanglij, Washington, D.C.

Fronticepiece: Oil painting of Taj al-Saltana in European clothes from the late-Qajar period (artist unknown), from the collection of M. & N. Batmanglij, Washington, D.C.

15. Dust 'Ali Khan Mo'ayyer al-Mamalek, *Yad-dashtha-'i az zendagi-ye khosusi-e Naser al-Din Shah*, 2d ed. (Tehran, 1362 Sh./1983), 129.

19. G. Curzon, *Persia and the Persian Question* (London, 1892), vol. I, 309.

20. S. G. W. Benjamin, *Persia and the Persians* (London, 1887), 157.

21. Curzon, *Persia and the Persian Question*, I:304.

22. Benjamin, *Persia and the Persians*, 171.

23. Benjamin, *Persia and the Persians*, 79.

24. Curzon, *Persia and the Persian Question*, I:341.

25. Mo'ayyer al-Mamalek, *Yad-dashtha*, 155.

27. Mo'ayyer al-Mamalek, *Yad-dashtha*, 134.

29. Mo'ayyer al-Mamalek, *Yad-dashtha*, 128.

31. J. Dieulafoy, "La Perse, las Chaldee et la Susiane," *Le Tour du Monde*, XLV (XLVI: 1881–1882), 151.

43. Mo'ayyer al-Mamalek, *Yad-dashtha*, 185.

53. Revolutionary postcard from the 1910s, A. Amanat collection, courtesy of M. Sinanian.

55. A. H. Savage Landor, *Across Coveted Lands* (New York, 1903), vol. I, 134.

57. E. G. Browne, *The Press and Poetry of Modern Persia* (Cambridge, 1914), illus. 28.

67. Savage Landor, *Across Coveted Lands*, I:224.

68. N. Najmi, *Dar al-khelafa-ye Tehran*, 4th ed. (Tehran, 1356 Sh./1977), 246.

69. C. Singer and C. LeRoy Baldridge, *Half the World is Isfahan* (New York, 1936), 27.

75. Dieulafoy, *Le Tour du Monde* XVIII (XLVII: 1881–1882), 159.

79. E. G. Browne, *The Persian Revolution of 1905–1909* (Cambridge, 1910), 140.

81. Savage Landor, *Across Coveted Lands*, vol. I, frontispiece.

87. Browne, *The Persian Revolution of 1905–1909*, 132.

105. Taj at fifteen, 1899, by Mirza Abol-Hasan Khan, court painter. Watercolor from the collection of Massoud Nader.

111. A. Arnold, *The Graphic Persia Illustrated* (June 6, 1885), 577.

123. Benjamin, *Persia and the Persians*, 203.

131. Mo'ayyer al-Mamalek, *Yad-dashtha*, 153.

133. D. Fraser, *Persia and Turkey in Revolt* (London, 1910), 158.

139. Fraser, *Persia and Turkey in Revolt*, 174.

145. Mo'ayyer al-Mamalek, *Yad-dashtha*, 186.

149. "A Persian wedding," P. M. Sykes, *The Glory of the Shi'a World* (London, 1910), 73 (from the collection of H. F. B. Lynch).

151. Golestan Palace museum, reproduced in E. Pakravan, *Teheran de Jadis* (Geneve, 1971), 30.

155. Courtesy of H. Khoromi, from his private collection.

165. Postcard from the 1910s, courtesy of R. Kenna.

167. Postcard from the 1910s, courtesy of R. Kenna.

181. Mo'ayyer al-Mamalek, *Yad-dashtha*, 130.

185. Curzon, *Persia and the Persian Question*, I:421.

187. Savage Landor, *Across Coveted Lands*, I:224.

189. Benjamin, *Persia and the Persians*, 140.

197. Postcard from the 1910s, courtesy of R. Kenna; also Sharaf, no. 65 (1306 Sh. /1888).

205. P. M. Sykes, *A History of Persia*, vol. II (London, 1915), 476.

211. Benjamin, *Persia and the Persians*, 121.

213. Curzon, *Persia and the Persian Question*, I:346.

217. Benjamin, *Persia and the Persians*, 61.

219. Revolutionary postcard from the 1910s, A. Amanat collection, courtesy of R. Kenna.

225. Savage Landor, *Across Coveted Lands*, I:240.

227. Moʻayyer al-Mamalek, *Yad-dashtha*, 126.

255. Qajar Paintings (Tehran, 1971), pl. 63.

259. Courtesy of M. Karimzadeh Tabrizi, private collection, reproduced in M. Karimzadeh Tabrizi, *The Lives and Art of Old Painters of Iran*, vol. III (London, 1991), 1489.

265. *Illustrated London News*, 30 August 1902, reproduced in D. Wright, *The Persians Amongst the English* (London, 1985), pl. 15.

269. M. Bamdad, *Rejal-e tarikh-e Iran*, vol. III (Tehran, 1347 Sh./1966), 303.

271. Savage Landor, *Across Coveted Lands*, I:50.

277. Moʻayyer al-Mamalek, *Yad-dashtha*, 178.

287. Dieulafoy, *Le Tour du Monde* VIII (XLV: 1881–1882), 55.

291. Golestan Palace Collection, reproduced in A. Sohayli Khonsari, *Kamal-e honar* (Tehran, 1368 Sh./1989), 292.

293. A. Amanat collection, courtesy of M. Sinanian.

295. Singer and Baldridge, *Half the World is Isfahan*, 30.

297. Dieulafoy, *Le Tour du Monde* VIII (XLV: 1881–1882), 93.

305. Bamdad, Rejal, III:304.

311. A. Qasemi, "Sargozasht-e por majara-ye Taj al-Saltana," *Vahid* 13 (1354 Sh./1975): 757.

NOTE ON THE AUTHORS

ABBAS AMANAT IS A PROFESSOR OF HISTORY AT YALE UNIVERSITY. HE IS THE AUTHOR OF *RESURRECTION AND RENEWAL: THE MAKING OF THE BABI MOVEMENT IN IRAN, 1844–1850*. HIS FORTHCOMING BOOK, *THE PIVOT OF THE UNIVERSE: MONARCHY UNDER NASIR AL-DIN SHAH QAJAR*, WILL BE PUBLISHED IN 1994 BY THE UNIVERSITY OF CALIFORNIA PRESS. HE IS CURRENTLY WORKING ON A DOCUMENTARY HISTORY OF MODERN IRAN.

ANNA VANZAN WAS BORN AND LIVES IN VENICE, ITALY. SHE RECEIVED HER PH.D. IN NEAR EASTERN STUDIES FROM NEW YORK UNIVERSITY. HER INTEREST FOCUSES ON THE HISTORY AND LITERATURE OF QAJAR IRAN AND ON THE RELATIONS BETWEEN IRAN AND THE WEST.

AMIN NESHATI RECEIVED HIS MASTER OF ARTS IN ENGLISH FROM BOSTON COLLEGE. HE LIVES IN NEW HAVEN, CONNECTICUT, WHERE HE IS FOLLOWING A CAREER IN TRANSLATION AND EDITING WITH A SPECIAL INTEREST IN LITERARY AND HISTORICAL TEXTS.

COLOPHON

THE JACKET ILLUSTRATION IS THE WORK OF A REMARKABLE PAINTER OF THE MID-NASSERI PERIOD, ESMA'IL JALAYER. SET IN THE COZY MILIEU OF A NINETEENTH-CENTURY PERSIAN ROYAL HAREM, THE STORY OF JOSEPH AND ZOLAYKHA (THE BIBLICAL POTIPHAR'S WIFE) HAS BEEN GIVEN A DELICATE FEMININE FLAVOR BY THE ARTIST'S RENDERING OF THIS POPULAR AMOROUS THEME FROM THE KORAN REFLECTING A ROMANTIC DIMENSION ECHOED IN TAJ'S MEMOIRS. ZOLAYKHA'S CENTRALITY IN THIS SELF-CONTAINED FEMININE ENVIRONMENT AND THE PROMINENCE OF THE REST OF THE WOMEN LOOKING STRAIGHT AT THE VIEWER RELEGATE JOSEPH, RECEIVING A CUP OF WINE FROM HIS BELOVED, ALMOST TO THE PERIPHERY. IN THE ENCLOSED SENSUALITY OF THE PERSIAN GARDEN, WHOSE FRUITS ARE LAID OUT IN THE FOREGROUND, THERE IS A SUBTEXT OF SERENE OPULENCE PRESENT IN THE MUSIC OF THE *SETAR*, THE BUBBLING OF THE WATER-PIPE, THE AROMA OF THE TEA SERVED FROM THE SAMOVAR, AND THE ELEGANCE OF THE WOMEN'S DRESS.

THE PHOTOGRAPHS WERE SELECTED BY ABBAS AMANAT, WHO ALSO WROTE THE LEGENDS.

THE TEXT WAS COPY-EDITED AND PROOFED BY PAUL SPRACHMAN AND SET IN A DIGITIZED VERSION OF JANSON BY MARK BOWERMAN.

THE BOOK AND JACKET WERE DESIGNED BY MOHAMMAD AND NAJMIEH BATMANGLIJ.

THIS FIRST EDITION WAS PRINTED BY THE MAPLE-VAIL PRESS IN YORK, PENNSYLVANIA.